Toward

a

More

Livable World:

Social Dimensions of Sustainability

Edited
by

Dr. Jerry Williams
Dr. William Forbes

Toward
a
More
Livable World:

Social Dimensions of Sustainability

Edited
by

Dr. Jerry Williams
Dr. William Forbes

STEPHEN F. AUSTIN STATE UNIVERSITY PRESS
2012

Permissions
Stephen F. Austin State University Press,
1936 North Street, LAN 203,
Nacogdoches, Texas, 75962.
sfapress@sfasu.edu

Book design: Kristi Warren, Brittany O'Sullivan
Copy Editors: Tracey Leigh Hunt, Kristi Warren

LIBRARY OF CONGRESS CATALOGING-IN-PUBLICATION DATA

Forbes, William and Jerry Williams
Toward a More Livable World
/ William Forbes, Jerry Williams 1st ed.
p. cm.
ISBN-13: 978-1-936205-60-8

First Edition: April 2012

Foreword

Dan Shilling
— Institute for Humanities Research, Arizona State University

The theme of *Toward a More Livable World* is close to my heart. I have worked on incorporating humanities and social sciences into sustainability studies for the past decade. Since the concept of sustainable development became prominent with the book *Our Common Future* in 1987, engineering and technology have dominated the solutions discussion. This direction is understandable, given the need to redesign many basic tools and processes. Treating wastewater with constructed wetlands, conserving energy with LEED buildings, and commuting with alternative transportation are largely technological challenges.

Yet the sustainability movement was, from its start, not intended to focus solely on environmental conservation from a purely technological perspective. Cultural heritage was also recognized as a prominent resource to be sustained. Therefore, anthropology, geography, and history, all of which deal with "cultural landscapes" and "sense of place," play an important role in sustainability research. Profit, poverty, and the dollar value of ecosystem services are also key factors, given the recent attention to sustainability's "triple bottom line," which ties economic development to social and natural resources. Also, three "P's" — philosophy, psychology, and political science — help us appreciate how values, ethics, motivation, and public policy fit into the search for a sustainable world. Finally, faculty in English, modern languages, and communications help us understand stories that shed new light on the sustainability discussion.

One important step is taking place in my state, where the Global Institute of Sustainability at Arizona State University, one of the leading sustainability initiatives on any U.S. campus, has infused the humanities and social sciences into the classroom and research. It is heartening to see parallel efforts at other universities, such as Stephen F. Austin State University. The dean of their College of Liberal and Applied Arts, Brian Murphy, deserves accolades for engaging his faculty in an interdisciplinary focus on sustainability. A new focal point for sustainability research, their Center for a Livable World complements new undergraduate and graduate degree programs in sustainable community development. Numerous campus sustainability initiatives around the nation are highlighted in the regular bulletin of the Association for the Advancement of Sustainability in Higher Education (AASHE). Yet a focus on the humanities and social science aspects, naturally coming out of colleges of liberal arts, provides a unique perspective. This book highlights the value of such an approach.

Contributions to this anthology come from a range of disciplines. Co-editors Jerry Williams (sociology) and William Forbes (geography) are formally based in the social sciences. However, both have additional backgrounds in philosophy, which is reflected in their contributions referencing John Dewey's pragmatism and Aldo Leopold's environmental ethics. Formal philosophers also contribute, including Ben Dixon's "green" update of the golden rule and Kelly Salsberry's look at moderation as a possible core value of sustainability.

In some ways, the humanities and social sciences can act as the "heart" of sustainability by examining its central values. The first section on "cultural change" also includes essays that challenge assumptions in education (Frye, Williams and Williams), U.S. superiority (Stoehr), and positive predictions (Lauter).

These foundational pieces help set the context for the next, more applied section on sustainable communities. Alex Garvin is a leading urban planner whose emphasis on private-public partnerships complements the global emphasis of sociologist Scott Frey - both are prominent external contributors (i.e., not from Stephen F. Austin State University). Internal faculty contributions address the important roles of multiculturalism, religion, and social capital in assessing sustainable communities. The third section, on economics, also contains leading outside contributors. Henrik Harjula, former environment minister for the Organization for Economic Cooperation and Development (OECD), highlights the increasing importance of incorporating measures of quality of life and "happiness" to complement more traditional standards of development, such as gross domestic product or median income. Tom Mote, vice-president of Hines Corporation and a global leader in mixed use development, also weighs in on broader measures of wealth and development. Internal contributions include healthy countering perspectives on regulatory versus free market approaches to environmental policy.

My essay attempts to relate sense of place to sustainability's "triple bottom line." These wider measures of well-being form a central theme for working with communities in applied settings, a theme re-emphasized in the conclusion to which dean Brian Murphy contributes. The plan is for the Center for a Livable World to act as a facilitator in private-public partnerships that broaden the discussion of economic development in Texas and beyond. As one who has worked with communities on heritage-based development, I believe the Center is off to a good start with this anthology. Communities would be wise to capture the expertise of this effort and use it for their benefit. Sustainability and livability are not tangential issues in economic development – they get to the "heart" of the matter in more ways than one.

Preface

This book represents the culmination of efforts begun in 2008 when the College of Liberal and Applied Arts at Stephen F. Austin State University brainstormed about interdisciplinary collaboration. An ad hoc committee suggested a new program in sustainable development, even though this topic was typically the realm of more technically oriented programs. For that reason, we decided to carve a niche that was under-served: the human (or social) dimensions of sustainability. This approach was selected because we became convinced that movement toward sustainability required a shift in cultural values. More specifically, sustainable development cannot occur without human development.

In 2010, the Center for a Livable World was launched with a three-fold mission:

1. To educate the citizenry through a new bachelor's degree, certificates in sustainable community development, and a vocational training program;
2. To influence public policy through recommendations that build consensus on how to accomplish sustainable development. Toward that end, a workshop was conducted in the Texas capitol building in June, 2010 that assembled leaders from diverse corporate, governmental, and non-governmental sectors of the sustainability movement. The recommendations from this workshop (Appendix A) constitute the framework of the current book;
3. To assist communities in transitioning to a livable lifestyle based on principles of sustainability. It is through applied projects where sustainable living becomes a reality.

I wish to thank not only our faculty for their enthusiastic participation, but especially our prominent outside contributors in both the workshop and book. These include former OECD environment   minister Henrik Harjula; leading public space planner Alex Garvin; environmental sociologist Scott Frey; Hines Corporation vice-president Tom Mote; Adams Engineering planner Eric Davis; Arizona State University humanities and sustainability researcher Dan Shilling; IHS consultants Marilyn Johnson and Melissa Manning; and many others.

The last chapter offers a look at how we propose to help municipalities apply our theoretical approach to real-life communities. The concept of sustainable development began in 1987 with the Brundtland Report, Our Common Future, reinforced at the 1992 United Nations Conference on Environment and Development, with the summary moral maxim "Sustainable development is development that meets the needs of the present without compromising the ability of future generations to meet their own needs." By focusing on its human (social) rather than technical dimensions two decades later, we hope this effort helps advance the important work of sustainable community development.

Dr. Brian Murphy,
December 14, 2011

CONTENTS

CHAPTER IV
ECONOMICS

CHAPTER V
CONCLUSION

CHAPTER 1

The Problem and Promise of Sustainability

Introduction

Jerry Williams, William Forbes, and Ben Dixon

Over the last 100 years, humans on average have lived well. At no time in our past have more human beings been able to meet their basic needs. The past century has seen unprecedented growth in human population and economic well-being. Yet surveys indicate that, once a household reaches a certain low to middle class income level, happiness does not necessarily increase in direct response to rising income. This century of growth has been fed by equally unprecedented material resource consumption and associated negative environmental impacts. There have also been periodic setbacks in our well-being. World Wars, economic troubles, and natural disasters such as earthquakes and hurricanes have occasionally made us pause to think about our collective past and future. Writing in 1920, John Dewey (1920, p. 3) comments about the impact of one of these setbacks, the First World War:

> The First World War was a decided shock to the earlier period of optimism, in which there prevailed widespread belief in continued progress toward mutual understanding of all peoples and classes, and hence a sure movement toward harmony and peace. Today the shock is almost incredibly greater. Insecurity and strife are so general that the prevailing attitude is one of an anxious and pessimistic uncertainty. Uncertainty as to what the future has in store casts its heavy and black shadow over all aspects of the present.

Our modern world is presented with a new worry about the future. Can our present standard of living, or anything like it, be realized by future generations? Disturbing evidence that this may not be possible is all around us. We see emerging nations surpass long-established ones in industry, science, education, and access to resources. We see continental ice sheets melt and severe weather increase as a result of global warming. When we buy gasoline for our automobiles, we see ever increasing prices, but that is not all. Even our health is threatened, as evidenced by increasing cancer rates from exposure to toxic chemicals and repeated outbreaks of contaminated food. Confronted with these upsetting indicators, we worry about the future, concerned that we must do something. To use Dewey's terms, these economic and environmental problems have become a "decided shock."

It is the purpose of this book to offer both a vision and a path to a sustainable future while maintaining a livable world. We contend that sustainability is a human concern. As far as we know, no other species thinks about the prospects of future generations. Sustainability is also a human problem, because the environmental problems faced by us are themselves caused by us and might one day be solved by us. For these reasons, conversations about sustainability must always be cast in the context of human realities.

To date, however, most approaches to sustainability have not properly addressed the human world and its values, cares, and concerns - aspects that cannot be managed and overcome through use of better technology and reduced consumption. As a result, most sustainability conversations have become quite dehumanizing. It is as if all that really counts about human beings is that we damage the environment and that science is our only hope for a sustainable future.

Little attention is paid to how the well-being of our communities, our appreciation of history, our love of the outdoors, and our concern for our health and happiness can enable conversations about sustainability that are more than just condemnations of present conditions. By treating the principle cares of everyday life such as love, beauty, faith, compassion, accomplishment, fear, and family as irrational inconveniences not worthy of consideration, current discussions about sustainability become exercises in scientific hubris.

We contend that if progress is to be made toward a sustainable future, human considerations must be brought into the scientific conversation, not simply as inconvenient problems to conquer, but as real and in the fullness with which they are experienced and embraced by people living their everyday lives.

Science and the Human World

Science has always had an uneasy place in society. This is certainly true of the relationship between science and faith. Early scientific thinkers such as Copernicus often faced conflict with organized religion for contradicting established teachings. These early battles, however, were about more than power. The scientific movement threatened our deeply held notions about what it means to be human and the nature of truth itself.

Our resistance to apply and embrace science in everyday life is quite understandable. For example, the feeling of love we feel for our children is "real." It provides a motivation for us to earn an income, to protect them, and to teach them what they must know to be successful in life. To learn that this impulse can be scientifically explained as somehow related to evolutionary outcomes and brain chemicals seems in a way to make our actual experience of love for our children less real. Similarly, if scientists explain the beauty of wilderness as a response to socially learned and culturally linked patterns of aesthetics, it seems to diminish our experience.

Science was also threatening for another reason. Prior to science, truth obtained a status thought to be independent of human activities. That is, to know the "truth" about the "real" world we had only to reconcile our minds to the way things "really" are. Of course, what was "true" and deemed a matter for acceptance was most often derived from *Middle Ages* doctrine, as established by authority and tradition. Personal observation and experience were of little consequence, if contradictory to the "truth," as defined by monarchies and theocratic states. Support for this worldview is often categorized in philosophy as the "ontological argument." Alternative worldviews could too easily be dismissed in an officially sanctioned system that explained away annoying observations. The dominance of these institutions was nearly unassailable. It offered a powerful way to make sense of the world, even in the face of quite chaotic circumstances.

Science provided a new means to understand the world that made truth a moving target. Science both told us about the world, but also provided the means by which it could be changed. The steam engine, for example, became the foundation for the industrial revolution, but it also gave us new realities such as urbanization, pollution, and cheaply manufactured goods.

In response to the successes of science, history shows us that the tension between the old and new ways of knowing could be reconciled in an ingenious fashion. Our ancestors simply determined that science operated only in the natural world, not in the ideal or spiritual worlds; in short, science was to treat the human world in a "hands-off" fashion. From the earliest days of the scientific revolution, the world was carved into two discrete and irreconcilable spheres. John Dewey (1920, p. 3) puts it this way:

> The adjustment which finally moderated, without completely exorcising, the earlier split between science and received institutional customs was a truce, rather than anything remotely approaching integration. It consisted, in fact, of a device that was the exact opposite of integration. It operated on the basis of a hard and fast division of the interests, concerns, and purposes of human activity into two realms, or, by a curious use of language, into two spheres - not hemispheres. One was taken to be high and hence to possess supreme jurisdiction over the other as inherently low. That which is high was given the name

spiritual, ideal, and was identified with the moral. The other was the physical as determined by the procedures of the new science of nature.

The importance of the split between the human and natural worlds is hard to overestimate. Looking back at the First World War, Dewey and his contemporaries saw the horror of mechanized war as directly related to it. Science is capable of transforming reality in ways that even today seem astonishing.

However, the inhumanity expressed by the war, Dewey believed, was not to be blamed upon science, but rather upon the failure to apply the scientific method in the human (social) world as well. The social institutions of the human world had not kept pace with the natural world as modified by science. The solution, according to Dewey, was to include the human world in the scientific calculus.

The current state of the global environment is not unlike the problems of the early 20th century. The environmental crisis is real and threatens the future of our children and grandchildren. This conclusion was reached by the United Nations' *Millennium Ecosystem Assessment* (2001, p. 2), which found that problems like resource depletion, global warming, and unprecedented levels of species extinction are evidence of the human strain upon the natural world. The report states:

> Over the last 50 years, humans have changed ecosystems more rapidly and extensively than in any comparable period of time in human history, largely to meet rapidly growing demands for food, fresh water, timber, fiber, and fuel. This has resulted in a substantial and largely irreversible loss in the diversity of life on earth.

It goes on to suggest that modern social institutions are not up to the job of managing these problems, especially common resources shared among nations (United Nations 2001, p. 02).

Just as pragmatists like Dewey argued in the early 20th century, the current environmental crisis presents us with problems driven by science and a human institutional system incapable of solutions. Without a means to reconcile these spheres, hope for a sustainable future is not a good bet.

A Path Forward

The Brundtland Commission report (World Commission on Environment and Development 1987) defines sustainable development as "development that meets the needs of the present without compromising the ability of future generations to meet their own needs." We agree, but argue that economic concerns, on which the Brundtland report centers, are only part of the picture. For sure, humans have a primary concern with meeting their basic human needs, but these needs must always be understood in the context of the totality of human experience. Both poverty and affluence are not simple matters of the surplus or scarcity of environmental resources; both are experienced and understood by real people with histories, diverse cultures, and sometimes conflicting beliefs. To treat sustainability as only a matter of economic distribution or as a scientific concern is to over rationalize both the problem and the solution. Rather, we must embed the Bruntland definition in the realities of everyday life. We suggest that human factors such as culture and religion can at times be an impediment to sustainability but, if properly understood and marshaled accordingly, they can also provide a means to make sustainability a realistic possibility.

At present, the identification, management, and solutions of environmental problems have typically fallen in the hands of biologists, physicists, climate scientists, and other natural scientists. This is probably true because features of the human dimension just mentioned, while of critical importance in everyday life, are often less amenable to scientific investigation. Without doubt, science has had an important role in pointing out both environmental dangers and potential solutions. Policy makers have relied upon these scientists to lead the debate about sustainability. Scientists who offer technology to increase energy efficiency and to provide alternative energy sources, for example, will play an important part in our collective futures. But as we have learned from experience, this approach alone is not enough. Rather, the science of sustainability must also include serious consideration of the human world, complete with its emotions, values, notions of happiness, and its prejudices. Such factors should not be considered as external to the scientific debate but rather as legitimate variables to be factored into what can and should be done.

In the essays that follow, we introduce the human dimension into the sustainability debate by applying what we call the golden rule of sustainability: "Do unto future generations as you would have had previous ones do unto yours." Guided by this ethical imperative and by harnessing the power of science in both the physical and human worlds, we can remake national and global institutions in ways that offer real hope for future generations.

Roles for Disciplines

This book frames our project in three key areas related to the human side of sustainable communities: cultural change, economics, and community development. An interdisciplinary approach grounded in the humanities and social science is taken (and needed) in each topical area to build upon what science has begun.

For example, the section on cultural change examines the process of how both individuals and communities change their cultural practices to move towards (or away from) sustainability. This necessitates looking at attitudes, values, and public and social systems among individuals or communities of individuals. Broad definitions of community may include not just a local village, but a scientific community, corporate business community, or other communities of interest.

An interdisciplinary examination of economics is essential, as the subject underpins our global society and its goals. Critical subtopics include corporate sustainability initiatives that also reduce operating cost, and the interrelationship of human happiness, income, and consumption rates. Community development is a key focus because communities are a tangible area in which to work out more of the practical, pragmatic solutions in sustainability. We must understand diverse community values in order to make progress on sustainability. A new approach to sustainability depends upon including the contributions of various disciplines.

Philosophers are adept at helping individuals and communities think critically about values, moving us towards knowledge of which values are separate and which overlap among communities. Psychologists study what motivates individuals and communities--such as consumers, corporations and their employees, or farmers--in order to help us identify more easily implementable conservation practices. Political scientists and public administrators study what governance systems work best in institutional reform, whether they are voluntary, regulatory, or incentive-based systems.

Historians are key consultants if we want to gain perspective on the scale of community change over time and learn from past mistakes or successes. Sociologists help us identify social groups and their conflicts and interactions. Geographers help us understand *where* communities and issues exist, their migration patterns, and international perspective on issues.

Social work enables us to understand the lack of choices among the underprivileged that may trap them in lifestyles in conflict with sustainability. Communications experts illuminate the role of media in framing common public perceptions of issues.

Finally, those adept at languages (including but not restricted to English) can synthesize cultural values by adding the human touch so often missing from institutional and scientific reports on sustainability.

Jerry Williams, PH. D., Sociology, Stephen F. Austin State University
William Forbes, Ph. D., Geography, Stephen F. Austin State University
Ben Dixon, Ph. D., Philosophy, Stephen F. Austin State University

References

Dewey, J. (1920). *Reconstruction in Philosophy*. Boston: Beacon Press.

United Nations (2001). "Millennium Ecosystem Assessment Summary Report."

World Commission on Environment and Development. (1987). *Our Common Future*. New York: Oxford University Press.

CHAPTER II

Cultural Change

Culture and Sustainability

Jerry Williams

Introduction

When Americans think about the long term future of the human species they quite naturally think about what life will be like for those who will be alive then. Will they drive cars? In what sort of houses will they live? How will they entertain themselves? It is impossible to know the answers to these questions for sure. What the future will look like is dependent upon at least two unknown factors. The first is the availability of resources - will there be enough? Human life requires natural resources either in the form of energy or raw materials. All the money in the world is useless unless it has resources to transform into the things we need and care about. The second unknown factor about the future is a matter of culture – what will people think, value, and create? Today Americans consume at an unprecedented rate. We live in large single family homes, drive single occupant cars to and from work, and entertain ourselves with sophisticated electronic gadgets. Fifty years from now will we still value the same things? Will still be able to produce them? We just can't say.

In this section we entertain the cultural side of sustainability. We argue that sustainability is a human concern. No other species, as far as we know, thinks about how their activities shape the future. In the following essays, we address the role education, ethics, moderation, a sense of place, and a sense of history can play to transform culture towards a more sustainable future. Such change will not be easy. Culture is very resistant to change because it serves an order making function in human societies. To understand why this is so, first we examine what culture is, but more importantly how it functions. It is argued that culture is not only produced by humans, but also something that produces or creates us. To put it another way, culture is a paradox, a chicken and egg kind of question.

Culture as Pattern

It is common to think of culture as product, as something created by people who make choices, work together, and participate in a shared life. For example, we build governments to meet our needs, we share ideas about beauty, and we invent electronic devices to entertain us. From this perspective culture is rather passive. Made by humans and changed by humans, culture is a product, a thing. This notion of culture, however, misses something important. Once established, culture provides its creators a pattern for thought and for action. Along these lines, Alfred Schutz (Schutz and Luckmann 1973, 3-4) suggests that culture provides a "pattern for group life." Not only do humans shape culture, culture also shapes humans. For example, many of us were born in America and we think like Americans, eat what Americans eat, and believe what Americans believe. If we are to bring about cultural change, it is evident that we must address culture not only as a product but also as a producer of ideas; ideas that promote unsustainability, but also might include concern for the future.

In the 1970s much of Idaho faced a crisis. Over the preceding one hundred years, predators such as wolves and coyotes were systematically hunted out of existence. As a result, much of Idaho was covered with jackrabbits. In my youth, I recall driving with my family on the Oregon / Idaho border and seeing hundreds of these rabbits cross the road in front of our headlights. Without the population control offered by predators, rabbits simply did what rabbits do. This phrase "what rabbits do" refers to an important feature of being an animal, what they "do" is patterned by instinct, not by choice or will. For them, fecundity is inevitable because "reproducing like a rabbit" is an inherent characteristic of being a rabbit. Just to be clear, this phrase implies that rabbits most certainly did not make choices to multiply in the numbers seen in Idaho in the 1970s. If they did, they did not anticipate the mass poisoning, rabbit roundups, and starvation that resulted. To this day, I cannot forget the rabbit drives covered on the nightly news that ended with townspeople wielding clubs against a mass of captured rabbits. Fortunately humans are not rabbits.

In theory, human behavior is not so much governed by instinct as it is a product of our will and choices. At least, this is the common way we think about what it means to be human. The explosion of human population over the last 1,000 or so years, however, suggests that we too have not been terribly successful at limiting our population growth. Why is this case? Why do humans not patterned by instinct often act as if they are?

Extending the work of Arnold Gehlen (1988), Berger and Luckmann (1966) argue that humans inherently exist in a state of "world openness." That is, they are born with little instinct and are therefore presented with a world that is not predefined. "Lower animals" on the other hand, live in a world largely without choices; they do what they do because they follow a pattern set down for them in their genes. For this reason the human world is one of possibility compared to that of the so-called "lower animals." This possibility, however, is not without cost.

World openness also exposes humans to insecurity on a grand scale. A world without instinct is a world of potential chaos. Life as we know it would not be possible without some way to limit or restrict world openness. Berger and Luckmann suggest that, in order to do this, we collaboratively construct culture and social institutions. They argue that culture and its social institutions are created in three stages or moments: habit, mutual typification, and institutionalization.

Habit

The first step in constructing social institutions is habit. Confronted with a bewildering number of choices, humans form habits that allow us to take an unthinking approach to daily life. For example, in the morning we get up, drink coffee, shower, and go to work. The following day we do it all over again. Berger and Luckmann (1966) characterize the mindset associated with habit as "here I go again." That is, habit is repetition that allows us to not think; we simply do what we have always done. In fact, most of our daily affairs are simply strings of habits. In this first step of institution building, world openness is certainly limited. Habit is not completely effective in reducing chaos, however. World openness and chaos remain possible because habits are products of our choices. Therefore, just as we created habits we can destroy or change them. The world, if we think about it long enough, is still precariously full of anomic possibilities. The next stage of institutionalization occurs when our individual habits are carried out in relation to others. We call this mutual typification.

Mutual Typification
     Mutual typification occurs when our habits are pursued in the presence of others who pursue their own. For example, let us say that it is your habit to make coffee in the morning and it is your spouse's habit to let the dog outside. If one day you fail to remember to make coffee, you will likely remember as you observe your spouse let the dog out. This is to say that habits are mutually reinforcing. Berger and Luckmann characterize the mindset associated with mutual typification as "here we go again."
     Mutual typification is important because it is a better remedy for the chaos of world openness than is habit. Alone I can change my habits; in the presence of others it becomes much more difficult; most of the time we just do what we are expected to do. However, mutual typification is not a perfect answer for world openness. Even while performing our mutually typified habits we nevertheless, upon introspection, can recall that our habits were once choices and that as such other choices are (were) possible. It is not until the next step of the institutional process that the chaos of world openness finds its most effective remedy. This stage is institutionalization.

Institutionalization

In this final stage or moment we find the most important and effective antidote to the precarious position of world openness. Following habit and mutual typification, institutionalization occurs only when people are born into an already existing social pattern. Once mutual typification occurs - you make coffee and your spouse lets the dog out, institutionalization happens when your children are socialized in context with your mutually typified behavior. Because our child knows no other reality, this state of affairs becomes taken for granted as "just the way it is." Berger and Luckmann characterize this mindset with the statement "that's just the way those things are done."

It is important to point out that this last step is substantially more able to limit world openness than the first two because subsequent generations do not have direct knowledge that the existing social order was constructed, that is, "cooked up" by those who have come before. Culture and social institutions, then, become nomic instrumentalities, the instruments of social order. To put it another way, for social order to be obtained, the social habits of others must be transferred to those who follow, without the knowledge that these habits were social constructions.

Sustainability and Cultural Change

As we have just seen, culture together with the institutions of which it is comprised serves an order making function in society. Unsustainable cultural practices common in the world today, practices such as suburban commuting and prepackaged food, therefore, represent not only the choices of individuals, but also a statement about what is taken for granted as proper, expected, and "just the way it is." Such practices are resistant to change because to consider them threatens our collective sense of social order. The implications of this are important. A move toward sustainability will not be easy; the cultural order is inherently conservative and generally only changes when confronted with a crisis. John Dewey (1920, 30) puts it this way:

> In what is distinctly human, invention rarely oc-
> curs, and then only in the stress of an emergency.
> In human affairs and in its relations that range
> extensively and penetrate deeply the mere idea
> of invention awakens fear and horror, being re-
> garded as dangerous and destructive.

How then is cultural change possible under normal, non-crisis circumstances? After all, waiting for a global environmental catastrophe is risky when the future of the global ecosystem is at stake. We suggest that any change in non-crisis circumstances to a more sustainable future must be embedded in deep, already existing cultural themes. In the United States these themes include faith, ethics, concern for human health, aesthetics, democracy, and a sense of the common good.

American history is replete with examples of how social change happens by utilizing existing cultural themes. Faith, for example, was variously used as a theme to bring about cultural changes such as the abolition of slavery and the civil rights movement. Might faith also be martialed to bring about sustainability? To cite an additional example, a sense of common good and social responsibility in the United States following the depression helped to bring about the social security system, aid to the poor, unemployment insurance, and health insurance. Can sustainability also be fostered with help of this cultural theme? In the essays that follow, we attempt to place sustainability in this established cultural terrain. By doing so, we hope that conversations about sustainability will less likely to be perceived as a threat to collectively order, but perhaps rather as a means to perpetuate the order and wellbeing of human societies for generations to come.

References

Berger, P. L. and T. Luckmann (1966). *The Social Construction of Reality; a Treatise in the Sociology of Knowledge*. New York, Doubleday.

Dewey, J. (1920). *Reconstruction in Philosophy*. Boston, Beacon Press.

Gehlen, A. (1988). *Man, His Nature and Place in the World*. New York, Columbia University Press.

Schutz, A. and T. Luckmann (1973). *The Structures of the Life-World*. Evanston Ill., Northwestern University Press.

Sustainability's Golden Rule

Ben Dixon

A hundred times every day I remind myself that my inner and outer life are based on the labors of other men, living and dead, and that I must exert myself in order to give in the same measure as I have received and am still receiving...

-Albert Einstein, 1931[1]

Introduction

This essay formulates a moral principle I call *sustainability's golden rule*. This principle, I will argue, goes a long way in providing correct moral guidance for sustainable development. In laying out these ideas, the essay proceeds as follows: first, a very basic, oft-privileged definition of sustainable development is put forward; second, I make clear how sustainability's golden rule is formulable from basic moral considerations that explain why sustainable development should be pursued at all; and lastly, I deduce some of the general implications sustainability's golden rule has for sustainable development.

The Idea of Sustainable Development

Alan Holland traces the idea of sustainability or "sustainable development" back to a report issued in 1980 by the International Union for the Conservation of Nature. But it was in 1987 that the World Commission on Environment and Development put forward what is widely considered the seminal text on sustainability: *Our Common Future*, also called *The Brundtland Report*. The sustainability principle argued for in the *Brundtland Report* is that pursuing development represents good policy, so long as such development is consistent with maintaining environmental capacity (Holland, 2003, pp. 390-391). In short, *Bruntdtland* recommends that we ought to embrace "development that meets the needs of the present without compromising the ability of future generations to meet their own needs" (as cited in Holland, 2003, p. 391). This will also serve as this essay's operative definition of sustainability.

Consider that we share the Earth and its resources with a human population quickly approaching seven billion. There will be an estimated nine billion of us by 2050. Currently, it is within developing countries that eighty-two percent of the world's inhabitants live, and such countries are also home to the fastest growing populations (Engelman, 2010).

In these nations, development for the world's poorest ideally means more persons meeting more of their own basic needs over time, deriving, in turn, increased dignity. Development can also create a middle class from which some may even launch themselves into the stratospheres of great wealth. Indeed, with the latter two types of development in China and India, for example, more persons are behaving like the hyper-consumers of North America and Europe. We humans are expecting Earth both to provide for all the differing kinds of development and to maintain the industrialized world's quality of life *if* it can. And it is no exaggeration that this may be one of the biggest *ifs* human history has faced. Yet despite risks, such as resource despoilment and resource exhaustion, we proceed. Should we?

Toward Sustainability's Golden Rule
The idea of sustainable development captures a kind of fair treatment owed to both present and future humans. Indeed, its prima facie reasonableness is demonstrable by appeal to our own considered preferences. If you are reading this paper, chances are you either live in an industrialized nation or you are among the more affluent members of a developing country. The benefits of development, then, are something with which you are familiar and give you a standard of living you likely value. It is a short

rational step from admitting such valuing to the idea that it is only fair others have the opportunity to live similarly, at least when they so choose or when governments badly need development to meet citizens' basic needs. Such fairness is the stuff of moral thinking, and it flows from the impartiality requisite of any ethical worldview thought reasonable.

It is understandable, then, that humans move forward with development of some kind. Also reasonable is the idea that such development must be sustainable: it must occur in ways that allow future generations, temporally near and far, to provide for their needs too. That development should also be sustainable is arguably an additional product of the aforementioned way of moral thinking. Impartiality and fairness, that is, coupled with valuing development's benefits, also entail leaving an Earth that provides for future generations. In sum, because we have an Earth that continues satisfying many of our needs and wants (and which increasingly provides more resources for persons in developing countries), it is only fair we leave an Earth for future generations that similarly provides. This is despite our not knowing *exactly who* will be included among the Earth's population in the more distant future. It is simply a reasonable assumption that the future, comprised by whomever, will need resources in perpetuity.

If the key constraint to sustainable development imposes upon how we act, then current production and consumption must allow future generations to meet their needs also. This constraint is morally explainable, as the above demonstrates, by coupling self-referential valuing with a basic idea of fairness. Notice that morally deliberating in this manner is seemingly the stuff of golden rule thinking. That is, the logic of "Do to others as you want others to do to you"[2] is apparently present here, and future reasoning about ways to sustainably develop, then, is justifiable insofar as it is consistent with this logic.

Unfortunately, using the golden rule to make sense of and further guide sustainable development appears problematic. Consider a straightforward, first-person singular recasting of the rule as applied to whether development should be sustainable: *I* (a current human) *should do* (support or reject some form of sustainable development) *to others* (future generations) *what I want others to do to me* (I want future generations to foster my well-being).

One glaring oddity is that almost all future generations are so far removed from me in space and time, no member of it can ever act toward me in any way whatsoever, let alone contribute to my well-being. There is no possibility of reciprocity.[3] Distant posterity, that is, will be consciously present on Earth when I am not. Thus, how can I base my current actions (i.e., what I should do to future generations) on how I want their future actions to affect me? One possible response is to conceive of future generations' actions toward me as solely consisting in remembering me either well or poorly, and this can be the basis of my deciding how to act. Applying this to the above recasting, what I want future generations to do to me (i.e., how I am remembered) will depend upon how I consumed and what kind of development I supported. If I want the future remembering me well, then I should support sustainable development, as it will leave resources for them. Isn't this workable? After all, it is quite common for persons to speak positively of leaving legacies behind and of otherwise wanting to be remembered fondly.

Of course, given whatever actions I take in supporting sustainable development, the likelihood of future generations remembering *me*, specifically, is infinitesimally small; all I can reasonably hope for is my generation and those overlapping and acting in concert with mine being remembered well and not poorly. Indeed, unless I am something like a noteworthy leader of a sustainable development movement (and even then, such a status is earned largely because others were willing to be led or influenced), my being lumped-in with a much larger group is only appropriate, given the kind of collective actions sustainable development ultimately involves if it is to be truly efficacious. Still, in this case of past generations being lauded by distant future ones, such appreciation is never really experienced when those doing the lauding are living in the remote future and the lauded are long gone. This response does not get us away from the lack of intergenerational reciprocity that seemingly prevents us from figuring how to act appropriately using a certain understanding of the golden rule. It does, however, direct our attention to the fact that moral thinking about sustainability involves not only the well-being of whole generations on the receiving end, but that moral action on the giving end must involve large groups of right-acting persons.

Another response to the lack of interaction between certain generations is simply to argue that direct interaction, through reciprocity, is unnecessary. Instead, when figuring how to act, we need simply to imagine ourselves being in the position of future generations, where our imaginings make them the contemporaries and ourselves the members of future generations. The question becomes how we would want these future generations to act toward us if roles were reversed. If while vacationing abroad, I happen across a stranger who has just fallen and hurt herself, the golden rule need not stifle me because of the improbability of my ever benefiting from any of the woman's future actions. I can easily put myself in her position and do to her as I want her to do to me *if I were in her position*—thus, golden rule thinking could (and would) instruct me to find her first-aid. The improbability of reciprocity is actually a regular feature for many of us in our day-to-day interactions with others, and it is no surprise that some interpretations of golden rule thinking do not hinge on actual reciprocity. Instead, the emphasis is putting oneself, as they say, in the shoes of another. Thus, justifying actions that benefit future persons, even though future persons cannot directly reciprocate, is possible using golden rule thinking. Admittedly, there is an awkwardness in wording when referring to future generations as "others that can do to us." And I believe improving upon this phrasing is possible with sustainability's golden rule, but a further point needs making first.

Rejecting a golden rule aiming at reciprocity and instead embracing one urging role-reversal appears to improve golden rule thinking generally, and it helps us with intergenerational applications specifically. This switch, however, brings to the foreground an additional problem of whether present persons can adequately predict the needs of future persons. Putting myself in the place of a contemporary is one thing; placing myself in the position of someone five generations into the future is quite another.

Picture yourself as an ancestor. With only their knowledge to work with, could you, say, two hundred years ago have adequately predicted the needs and wants of persons today? Were their resources our resources? Their needs our needs? Certainly some were, among them being clean water, clean air, nutritive soil to grow food, and a hospitable environment to sustain life. So much of what we do today would be unrecognizable to them: our modes of travel, our communication technologies, how we manufacture goods, and much of the resources that make these activities possible. The changes are mind-boggling to be sure.

The above forces the following questions. What are tomorrow's resources that will satisfy their particular needs and wants? And are their needs and wants predictable to begin with? Actually, listing items such as clean water, clean air, nutritive soil to grow food, and a hospitable climate, among others, is an exceptionally good beginning to answering these questions. Zeal in listing differences between past and present generations may unreasonably de-emphasize what is still so common intergenerationally and what in all likelihood will remain so. The basics are the basics. Our doing to the future what we want them to do to us cannot ignore such basics and all that makes them possible. Still, prudence is a virtue when speculating about the future. Real differences between generations need factoring in when deciding the nature and scope of what must be set aside.

Ideal, then, is encapsulating, into a single decision procedure, the merits of all these observations about golden rule thinking as applied to sustainability. This means formulating a version of the golden rule that features: the fairness and impartiality that is typical of golden rule thinking; actual reciprocity being a nonassumption; an emphasis on the collective benefits and burdens the rule's correct use entails (although, in practice, individuals will often need to act in isolation, though, hopefully, with institutional support); a phrasing that mitigates the awkwardness of implying future generations are actors capable of benefiting previous generations; and lastly, accommodating the fact that there will likely continue to be some intergenerational changes in what is valued. With these constraints in mind, I propose the following modifications to golden rule thinking as applied to sustainability: *We should do unto future generations what we would have had previous generations do unto ours.* This is sustainability's golden rule (hereafter abbreviated as SGR).

General Implications of Sustainability's Golden Rule

First and foremost, SGR anticipates future generations to be comprised of valuing beings with all that makes that possible, and so the fairness and impartiality owed to such individuals motivate the rule. It does not presuppose any reciprocity by future generations (its wording makes that clear); instead SGR urges present persons to develop in ways we would have had previous generations do for us (the use of "would have" does not mean that past generations got everything wrong, much of what they did is precisely what we *would have had them do*).

Cast in the first person plural, SGR's proper use will quickly lead to collective action. For example, it will have us organize human behavior to leave both sufficient raw materials to sustain future organic life and enhanced technologies to make this easier, but also leave institutions respectful of these goals and intellectual materials that justify these changes and situate them historically. Generally speaking, these are amongst the best of what previous generations gave us. SGR also reminds us that we are inheritors of previous generations' mistakes, ones that we should not replicate. Indeed, such successes or lack thereof help us keep in mind the limits of our predictive powers; thus, the aforementioned caution against overconfidence in knowing all the goods of future generations is strongly implied.

Various golden rule formulations are found in different philosophies and religions throughout the world. Sustainability's golden rule has a family resemblance to many of these formulations is certainly a plus. Sustainable development is a global endeavor, and norms that guide it need cross-cultural currency. The hope here is that sustainability's golden rule can resonate with the consciences of many.

References

Einstein, A. (1931) *The world as I see it*. Retrieved from http://www.aip.org/history/einstein/essay.htm

Engelman, R. (Dec. 17, 2010) *World population growth slows modestly, still on track for 7 Billion in late 2011*. Retrieved from http://vitalsigns.worldwatch.org/vs-trend/world-population-growth-slows- modestly-still-track-7-billion-late-2011

Holland, A. (2003) Sustainability. In Dale Jamieson (Ed.), *A companion to environmental philosophy* (pp. 390-401). Malden, MA: Blackwell
Wattles, J. (1996) *The golden rule*. Oxford: Oxford University Press.

Endnotes

[1] I am indebted to Josiah Thompkins for suggesting this quotation from Einstein.

[2] This is Jeffrey Wattles (1996, p. v) approximate definition of the golden rule. His work is an excellent source for the cross-cultural use of the rule, its various formulations, and a defense of an ethic based upon it.

[3] The moral and political philosophy of Thomas Hobbes seemingly necessitates actual reciprocity being part of golden rule thinking. This is because Hobbes argues that human psychology is inescapably egoistic, yet he fits the golden rule within his theories accommodating such egoism.

The Virtue of Sustainability

Kelly J. Salsbery

This essay draws its inspiration from some of the ethical views of Aristotle. Aristotle characterizes a virtue as a mean between two extremes (which, in turn, are vices of excess or deficiency). Thus, virtue is found in moderation rather than in extremes. This notion of moderation is also evident in the *Analects* of the ancient Chinese thinker, Confucius. In this essay, I will examine how this notion of moderation may be applied to the issue of sustainability both in the context of individuals and within societies (and drawing from both traditional and modern views).

Moreover, I will examine how expanding this notion of moderation can help us avoid the polarization generated by the controversies associated with environmental issues. It seems that we are ultimately seeking a notion of sustainability that comes from a kind of moderation or balance between growth and stasis, between the local and global, between the individual and the community, between the traditional and the revolutionary, and perhaps even between the simple and the complex.

Aristotle, Confucius, and Virtue Ethics

Virtue Ethics differs from an ethics based on the morality of our actions and instead focuses on issues of personal character. Thus, the focus of virtue ethics is not so much on what one should do, but rather on what sort of person one should be. Morality is then not about following rules or evaluating whether or not a given action is morally right or wrong. It is instead about being the sort of person who is disposed to do what is right.

Contemporary virtue ethics finds its origin in the moral thought of the philosopher Aristotle[1]. Aristotle claims that overall human happiness or flourishing (what he calls *eudaimonia*) results from conforming oneself to the dictates of reason. This, in turn, requires a person to cultivate certain sorts of character traits, known as virtues or human excellences (**areté**), within one's own character. Typically, one might think that we ought to maximize any sort of good character trait, but Aristotle would disagree. In what is known as "The Golden Mean," Aristotle characterizes a virtue as a mean (a sort of midpoint) between two extremes or vices of excess and deficiency. Deficiency or lack of some specific good character trait or quality is a vice, but an excess or surplus of that very same trait or quality is also a vice. The mean or midpoint where there is neither too much nor too little of the given trait is the virtue. Thus, virtue is found in moderation rather than in extremes.

Perhaps the best way to understand this concept is through a specific example. One of the best known of Aristotle's examples of virtues is the case of courage. According to Aristotle, courage is a virtue because it is a mean between two extremes (two vices), one of deficiency or lack, and one of excess or surplus. A deficiency or lack of courage is the vice of cowardice while an excess or surplus of courage is the vice of foolhardiness or recklessness. For instance, in the context of a battle, cowering in one's tent away from the fight displays cowardice while bravely, but thoughtlessly dashing into enemy fire clearly displays foolhardiness or recklessness.

During the course of his discussion of virtue, Aristotle addresses many examples of virtues. Moreover, he distinguishes between so-called intellectual virtues and moral virtues. He claims that the former are "teachable" whereas the latter are not. How then does one cultivate a moral virtue? One does so by acting as though one has the virtue already. This practice eventually leads to a habit of behavior which, in turn, instills the specific virtue within one's own character. If you lack courage, then the way to instill courage into your character is to act in a courageous way. Eventually, this will result in you actually having the virtue of courage. Various approaches to virtue ethics are open to the possibility of cultivating virtues in the individual through the examples of role models, moral exemplars, or wise persons in the community or the society. This sort of approach to ethics differs markedly from the typical conception of ethics as based on evaluating specific actions as right or wrong. Some might claim that a virtue ethics approach to sustainability based on the ideas of Aristotle is much too grounded in the western intellectual and philosophical tradition to be of much relevance or use to people in the developing world. This need not be the case, however. For instance, there is a striking similarity between the notion of virtue as portrayed by Aristotle and that of the ancient Chinese thinker, Confucius. In his *Analects*,[2] Confucius relates a number of aphorisms which describe what it is to be a "superior person" or "wise person." In doing so, he focuses on the development of the character of this wise person with an emphasis on finding a balance between extremes. A harmonious society is one that fosters these virtues in the society at large, in families, and in individuals.

Sustainability as a Virtue

How do we apply the ideas of virtue ethics to the issue of sustainability and the overall notion of a livable world?   One thing that we need to do is to get some idea of the specific sorts of virtues associated with sustainability. Such virtues would be the sorts of traits that would dispose someone to act in a way consistent with a sustainable lifestyle. It is important to note here, however, that we need not be monolithic or absolutist in answering this question. Indeed, in applying virtue ethics, it seems clear that the discovery of virtues must be relative to the social and community context in question. Likewise, attempting to impose some sort of *a priori* conception of specific virtues seems implausible and impractical. Thus, in applying a virtue ethics approach we must be open to various practical and pragmatic considerations. The general idea then would be for communities and societies to develop a notion of virtue and moderation (with respect to sustainability) relative to their own social context. Thus, the general notion of sustainability would be applied within the context of a certain specific type of lifestyle and the associated use of limited resources.

For instance, in many western societies, individuals flagrantly waste energy through carelessness and inefficiency. Vital resources that could be reused and recycled are instead trapped in landfills while at the same time whole ecosystems are damaged or destabilized by pollution. Such a lifestyle and the attitudes associated with it clearly exhibits a kind of vice of environmental excess. On the other hand, living a lifestyle of extreme asceticism or deprivation in order to avoid wasting resources or generating pollution seems to exhibit a vice of deficit. The virtue of sustainability with respect to such a society (and for the individuals within that society) lies in people being disposed to act in way that is a mean between these two extremes. What exactly this would involve or entail is not something that we can spell out in advance. Individuals in a given society or community must explore this question and come to some sort of consensus. Ultimately, this virtue of sustainability might well be fostered by families, or through educational institutions, governments, or corporations.

Expanding the Notion of Moderation

These notions of virtue, moderation, and balance also bring to mind the attitudes of various indigenous and traditional peoples around the world. Central to many of these conceptions is the notion of harmony and balance both within our own lives and in how we interact with the natural world. This is especially the case with respect to the western conception of the relationship between humans and the natural world. First of all, such cultures view humans as part of the natural world rather than separate from it. Moreover, they think of humans merely as co-inhabitants of the natural world along with other living creatures rather than as something superior to or above other aspects of the natural world. Second, cultures of this sort view their own connection to the natural world in terms of having a personal relationship with the natural world and with other living creatures. They recognize that they must rely on other living things in order to live, but that in order for this process to continue, their use of resources must be limited and their relationship to other living things must be reciprocal.

Thus, these indigenous and traditional peoples insist that we focus on the idea that various human activities (especially over the last several centuries) have caused the order of the natural world to become out of balance. These traditions urge us to do what we can to restore this balance, to recognize the long-term significance of our actions, and to again connect with the natural world.

When considering very extreme views with respect to environmental issues, we might also take a lesson from the life the Buddha. During his life he had initially pursued a life of comfort and pleasure and then went on to live a life of extreme asceticism. After undergoing his enlightenment experience he went on to preach about a "middle path" between these two ways of living one's life. Indeed, it seems clear that one of the most serious obstacles to the notion of sustainability is excessive polarization with respect to the morality of various environmental views. What seems to be needed is a middle path of moderation between various extreme positions. Philosopher Anthony Weston suggests that we can overcome extreme polarization with respect to moral issues (at least to some extent) by modifying the assumptions of our moral debates.[3] Instead of asking **"In what way or ways am I right and my opponent wrong?"** we can instead "reframe" the question as **"In what way or ways is my opponent right?"** At such a point there is a common basis for discussing and addressing the relevant moral issue as well as for finding points of agreement.[4]

Concluding Remarks
Over the last 25 to 30 years, there has been a great resurgence of interest in the ethical ideas of Aristotle. A number of philosophers

have attempted to apply the ideas of virtue ethics to the various moral problems that we face including moral issues specifically connected with environmental ethics.[5] In this essay I have discussed in a general way how one might apply virtue ethics to the issue of sustainability and how an expanded notion of moderation and balance can help us address a broader context of environmental concerns.

References

Aristotle. (2000). *Aristotle: Nicomachean Ethics.* (R. Crisp, Ed., & R. Crisp, Trans.) Cambridge, UK: Cambridge University Press.

Confucius. (1999). *The Analects of Confucius: A Philosophical Translation.* (Roger T. Ames, Trans. & Henry Rosemont Jr., Trans.) New York: Ballantine Books.

Sandler, R. & Cafaro, P. (2005). *Environmental Virtue Ethics* . Lanham, Maryland: Rowman & Littlefield Publishers, Inc.

Weston, A. (2002). *A Practical Companion to Ethics* (2nd Edition ed.). New York: Oxford University Press.

Endnotes

[1] For instance, see Aristotle (2000).

[2] For instance, see Ames and Rosemont (1999).

[3] Weston (2002), Chapter 4.

[4] Ibid.

[5] For instance, see Sandler and Cafaro (2005).

Sustainability and American Education

Jerry K. Frye

This chapter maintains there are many alternative paths toward a sustainable world and public education is one path that should be included among the options. As used in this chapter, the "public education path" refers to all types and levels in the American educational system. And, although there are many ways private educational facilities can contribute, the focus here is public educational institutions, for two reasons. The primary reason is that governmental funding, agencies, and policies are targets for the required cultural shift. Secondly, on a personal level, most of my formal education has occurred in public education; it is the arena I know best based on more than forty years of university teaching experiences.

An inherent factor of the classic chicken--egg scenario is involved with this research. On the one hand, based on years of research evidence, it would be foolish to suggest education, as the solution as we strive toward our goal of a sustainable world. (In this chapter, education is intended as generally synonymous with information, facts, beliefs, awareness, attitudes, and knowledge.) In fact, communication research and other social sciences have provided convincing evidence that there is frequently a disconnecting gap between education and human behavior (Littlejohn and Foss, 2011; Williams and Parkman, 2003; Zimbardo and Leppe, 1991; Canary and Seibold, 1984). And, other researchers have addressed the fact that pro-environmental attitudes seem poor predictors of pro- environmental behaviors (Kollmus & Agyeman, 2002; Hines, Hungerford, & Tomera, 1986).

On the other hand, it would also be foolish to ignore the opportunities of America's existing extensive public education infrastructure that could be used for the common good toward sustainability. The American population includes 48,888,000 of public school ages. And, according to the United Nations Educational, Scientific, and Cultural Organization (UNESCO), the US has the highest number of higher education students in the world. These students are taught in traditional classrooms, conferences, seminars, internships, field-trips, and other education related activities (U.S. Census Bureau, 2011). That means almost 49 million opportunities to instruct, direct, teach, and persuade toward sustainable practices. Some researchers ask: "What will move people to act to save their beloved worlds? Clearly, information is not enough. What is missing is the moral imperative, the conviction that assuring our own comfort at terrible cost to the future is not worthy of us as moral beings" (Moore and Nelson, 2010, xvi).

The public education path and the pro-environmental behavior path might be bridged via "direct learning," hands-on, personalized, experience. Our government is in the best position to enact, implement, and support a positive cultural shift in American education through the existing infrastructure. The shift in American public education requires fundamental, philosophical change "toward a global consensus for ethical action" (Moore and Nelson, 2010). But, the public education path is not straight and is not without potholes and barriers. Kollmuss and Agyeman indicate "the question of what shapes pro-environmental behavior is such a complex one that it cannot be visualized in one single framework or diagram" (Kollmuss and Agyeman, 2002).

Of course, it is expected that healthy skepticism accompanies the cultural shifts in the American educational system toward increased applications of sustainability in the curriculum and related educational activities with government involvement in public education. As the Dalai Lama states: "We need knowledge to care for ourselves, every part of the Earth and the life upon it, and all of the future generations as well. This means that education about the environment is of great importance to everyone" (Dalai

Lama and Piburn, 1997). Consider the following story: "An old man was walking down the beach just before dawn. In the distance he saw a young man picking up stranded starfish and throwing them back into the sea. As the old man approached the young man, he asked; "Why do you spend so much energy doing what seems to be a waste of time?" The young man explained that the stranded starfish would die if left in the morning sun. "But there must be thousands of beaches and millions of starfish, exclaimed the old man. "How can your efforts make any difference?" The young man looked down at the small starfish in his hand and as he threw it to safety in the sea, he said: "It makes a difference to this one" (Eiseley, 1979). Commenting on a similar analogy of one drop of water in an ocean of despair, Maiteny adds that community based involvement can be ". . . morale-boosting. It gives a sense of not being the only drop in the ocean but one of many which, added together, could well make a difference" (Maiteny, 2002). "For although there is a limit to what we as individuals can do, there is no limit to what a universal response might achieve. It is up to us as individuals to do what we can, however little that may be" (Dalai Lama and Sidney Piburn, 1997). The Dalai Lama provides a moral framework: "The key thing is the sense of universal responsibility; that is the real source of strength, the real source of happiness. If our generation exploits everything available-- the trees, the water, and the minerals--without any care for the coming generations or the future, then we are at fault, aren't we" (Moore and Nelson, 2010)?

A recent personal experience emphasizes that global solutions often begin locally. My wife and I had the opportunity to tour the manufacturing facilities of the Celestial Seasoning Tea Company's home in Denver, Colorado. A member of our group asked the tour guide, "Why don't your tea bags have strings or tags? The answer: "Our unique pillow–style tea bag is the result of our commitment to doing what's best for the environment. Because these natural fiber tea bags don't need strings, tags, staples or individual wrappers, we're able to save more than

3.5 million pounds of waste from entering landfills every year!" (Celestial Seasoning Tea tour, November, 2010). The benefit of this local manufacturing plant's focus on the environmental impact of such tiny elements -- tea bag strings, tags, staples, and wrappers provides evidence that small, incremental steps become significant when these small steps are added together. The vast environmental mountain is climbed ("conquered") one step at a time; or, consider the famous space exploration perspective, "one step for man, one giant step for mankind." This same philosophy is the connection with the exponential impact of the linchpin of education and sustainability.

No singular solution toward sustainability seems probable; rather, multiple paths toward sustainability appear to be needed. Public education is a viable alternative path or approach. It can be argued that work toward sustainability can be achieved with sustained, long-term governmental economic support of public education. Advances in public education are the most efficient, effective, and economical means to empower people to become individual change agents in solving problems that, in turn, ultimately change the world. This "one to many" view suggests that teachers and professors can teach others the necessary strategies and techniques involved in sustainability issues. Teachers and professors can train students to employ market-based solutions with a minimal of government involvement. Students can become those who take leadership positions and create sustainable change. Initial and early exposure in primary grades can have profound influences on individual's personalities. These early experiences help to determine brain structure and shapes the way people think, learn, and behave for the rest of their lives (Louv, 2008; Bloom, Nelson, & Lazerson, 2001). Consider the idiom "As the twig is bent so is the tree inclined" or "Train a child in the way he should go; and when he is old, he will not depart from it" (Proverbs 22:6). Additionally, balancing is necessary for connections and convergence of (1) social, (2) economic, (3) cultural, and (4) environmental objectives. These pillars of sustainability contain inherent conflicts between individual and societal objectives requiring a balancing act perceived simultaneously as fair and progressive. Always, it is critical to first recognize, and then combat, the inevitable bi-polar nature of progress and prosperity amid contexts of hopelessness and poverty. The famous Yale series of attitude and communication defined "persuasion" as the attempt of one person to change (reinforce, modify) another person's beliefs, attitudes, values, and behavior through symbolic means, usually language (Larson, 2010; Rosenberg, 1966).

Several philosophical assumptions (foundations) support an education pathway toward a sustainable, livable world. One is similar to the teaching--learning philosophic notion that learning through education leads to life changing behavior that promotes independence. The familiar idea is that if you give a person a fish, you feed him for today, but teach him to fish and you feed him for a lifetime (Chinese Proverb). The second is the mathematics of geometric progression involved in an AIDS poster. If you have sexual contact with a stranger, you are also (in effect) having sex with whoever that person was with and with whoever those persons were with, and on and on for the past 15 years (the estimated life of the AIDS virus) so that you end up with very poor odds of staying healthy when engaging in risky behavior (avoiding the use of protection). This same math works for the disregard of sustainability factors (clean air, clean water, etc.) in that you can only ignore paying proper attention so long, and the odds work against you, negatively. Interestingly, educational principles work the same way mathematically, but in a positive way. If I learn to conserve water, and teach several others to conserve water and they in turn teach yet others -- and so on -- in other words, I'm suggesting a cultural change through education which, in turn, helps to promote positive progress and thus helps us advance, along the road toward sustainability.

Another philosophic perspective visualizes the public sector as a wheel with many spokes suggesting the large variety of publics affiliated with educational agendas, including public schools (K-12, colleges, universities), libraries, museums, governmental agencies, and commissions. Learning theory posits that all humans have increased positive educational experiences accompanied by increased learning when activities are perceived as enjoyable. Using one example -- our nation's museums (from small town, regional, to the largest and best Smithsonian Institution museums) can provide positive activities that reinforce learning. Of special importance are those activities that involve the "hands-on learning" of personal engagement. As Albert Einstein stated, "all learning is experience; everything else is just information."

Finally, the digitized philosophic perspective: the singular experience many millions of people share is the internet. A public educational approach toward sustainability with the focus on social, economic, cultural, and environmental objectives for a more livable world is a perfect internet task. Because of the diversity of cultures involved in a global perspective, the public educational approach should incorporate all the technological advances into the mix such as today's most popular social network platforms YouTube, Facebook, and Twitter. *Time Magazine* reports: "Groupon, the sizzling social-network-powered discount shopping site, recently told Google to shove its $6 billion buyout offer" (Saporito, 2011). Many have never heard of "Groupon," but it exemplifies how fast information flows in our digitized world. To be effective change agents, we must figure out some ways to attach our sustainability vehicle to travel the information highway too.

The public educational path gives hope for a future with a healthy environment, a strong economy, and a just society. Young people need to be taught to understand the important roles they play in creating a sustainable future. Not through public education alone, but public education coupled with energized, enthusiastic, competent, knowledgeable teachers, can help persuade young people to become leaders who, in turn, work directly with their entire community – educators, government officials, community members, and the businesses for sustainability issues.

Varied strategies through the public educational path permits individuals, family, school groups, communities, and corporations to work cooperatively toward sustainability. And, the public educational path encourages diversity, <u>balancing</u> connections and convergence of the (1) social, (2) economic, (3) cultural, and (4) environmental objectives which can be achieved, in part, and in concert with other approaches. Sustainability activities can be integrated into student learning across disciplines. Active student involvement in sustainability education increases student interests, knowledge, and skills for positive behavior in environmental values as well as increased use of service learning and various school-community connections. And, public funding for environmental problem-solving activities that make a difference and pave the way for a more environmentally conscious generation can be supplemented with grants to reinforce the multi-disciplinary nature of sustainability education in public schools. Those areas of sustainability with inherent conflicts between individual and societal objectives also require a balancing act through the public education path to sustainability that is perceived simultaneously as both fair and progressive.

And finally, it is clear that the public educational path is just one path, and <u>no one approach will suffice</u>; it will, in fact, take several -- probably all the approaches discussed in this book, working in concert, and although there are multiple paths, the goal remains the same--a sustainable, livable world.

References

Bloom, Floyd E., C. A. Nelson, A. Lazerson. (2001) *Brain, mind, and behavior.*

Canary, Daniel J. and David R. Seibold. (1984) *Attitudes and Behavior: An Annotated Bibliography.* New York: Praeger.

Dalai Lama and Sidney Piburn, (compiler--editor). (1997) "An ethical Approach to environmental protection," in *The Dalai Lama: A policy of kindness.* Snow Lion Publications, 1997), p.17, 107, 19.

Eiseley, Loren C. (1979) *The Star Thrower.* New York: Houghton Mifflin Harcourt.

Hines, J. M., Hungerford, H. R., & Tomera, A. N. (1986). Analysis and syn thesis of research on responsible environmental behavior: A meta-analysis. *Journal of Environmental Education*, 18, 1-8.

Kollmuss, Anja and Agyeman, Julian (2002) "Mind the Gap: Why do people act environmentally and what are the barriers to pro-environmental behavior?" *Environmental Education Research*, 8: 3, 239-260.p. 248."

Larson, Charles U. (2010). *Persuasion: Reception and responsibility.* Belmont, CA: Wadsworth-Thomson Learning, 2010.

Littlejohn, Stephen W. and Karen A. Foss. (2011). *Theories of human communication.* Long Grove, IL: Waveland Press, Inc.

Louv, Richard. (2008) *Last Child in the Woods: Saving our children from nature-deficit disorder.* Chapel Hill, North Carolina: Algonquin Books of Chapel Hill.

Maiteny, Paul T. (2002) "Mind in the Gap: summary of research exploring "inner" influences on pro-sustainability learning and behavior," *Environmental Education Research*, 8: 3, 299-306.

Moore, Kathleen Dean and Michael P. Nelson. (2010) "Toward a global consensus for ethical action," in Moore, Kathleen Dean and Michael P. Nelson, eds. (2010) *Moral ground: Ethical action for a planet in peril.* San Antonio, TX: Trinity University Press.

Rosenberg, Milton J., Carl I. Hovland, William J. McGuire, Robert P. Abelson, and Jack W. Brehm (1966). *Attitude organization and change: An analysis of consistency among attitude components.* New Haven: Yale University Press.

Saporito, Bill. (2011) "Refreshing Google," *Time Magazine*, 2-7-2011, pp. 48-49.

Williams, Jerry & Shaun Parkman. (2003). "On humans and environment: The role of consciousness in environmental problems," *Human Studies* 26: 449-460.

Zimbardo, P. G., & Leppe, M. R. (1991). *The psychology of attitude change and social influence*. New York: McGraw-Hill.

The Role of Education in a Sustainable Democracy

Michelle Williams
Jerry Williams

Introduction

We contend that the unsustainable present results from historic structural changes in the Western world that threaten the very institutions that have given us the greatest global standard of living in human history. Capitalism has been a tremendous liberating force over the last 400 years. It has broken feudal bonds, spawned democracy, and provided incentive for public education. The increasing levels of economic inequality found in modern capitalism, however, threaten not only the environment but also the very basis of human progress. We argue that if we are to reach a sustainable future, the democratic process must be disconnected from the interests of the economic elite, and must be informed by an educational system loosened from the constraints of political control. In the following section, we address the interactive and paradoxical relationship between capitalism, human environmental impact, democracy, and education. In the concluding section, we draw upon pragmatist philosophy and suggest three ways in which educators can facilitate democracy and promote a sustainable future.

Capitalism and Human Progress

When sociologists speak of the average characteristics of a society they are often accused of overgeneralization. Average income, for example, means very little to real individuals as they live their everyday likes. What matters more is their actual income. To speak about the impact of capitalism upon the human condition, however, we must seek to understand its overall impact. When we do so, we find that capitalism has produced both dramatic winners and losers, but that on average humans do better now than in the past. Marx (1977), an outspoken critic of capitalism pointed out that no other economic system to date has done so much to advance the human cause.

Contributing to the fall of feudalism, capitalism according to Marx, has decreased human control over other humans, and provided increased control over nature and natural resources (Marx and Engels, 1964). Historical evidence for these assertions is found in the rise of democracies in the 19th century, 20th century public education, and the affluence of modern industrial societies. Such gains are not the whole story however. Capitalism is not a static system; the increased wellbeing of the 19th and 20th centuries is presently at risk (Janmaat, 2008). Increasing economic inequality is a threat to both democracy and education. In the end, it also shatters any hopes we might have about a sustainable society.

Figure 1 illustrates the impact of increasing inequality as relates to democracy, education, and environmental impact. The impact of increasing inequality noted on the X axis predicts increased environmental impact, decreased democracy, and an educational system that is increasingly limited by powerful economic and political elites. As a result, democracy and education, the social institutions that might control environmental exploitation, find themselves unable to do so. An unsustainable future is the result. In what follows we address in more detail the impact of inequality upon environmental impact, democracy, and education.

Inequality

In the United States Economic inequality has dramatically increased over the last 30 years. For example, in 1979 the top 1% of U. S. households earned 8.9% of all income earned in the United States (Inequality, 2011). In 2007 the top 1% earned 23.5%. Similarly, during the period 1979 to 2008, real income of the top 5% of U.S. families increased by 73% while the lowest 20%

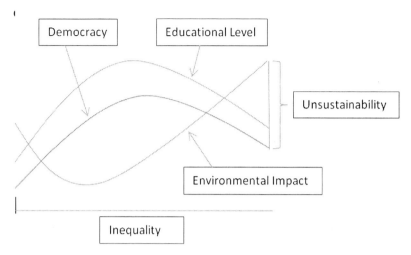

Figure 1. *Inequality and Unsustainability.*

Wealth is also quite unevenly distributed. In 2007 the richest 1% of American households owned 33.8% of the entire nation's wealth, that is, everything that can be privately owned. This is more wealth than is owned by the bottom 90% of Americans combined (Inequality, 2011).

It is not important for our purposes to comment about economic fairness or about the relative merits of inequality. Davis and Moore (1945), for example, argue that economic inequality provides incentive for innovation and risk taking. Our purpose is to simply point out that inequality at the level now seen in the United States directly threatens the possibility of a sustainable future. This is so because it increases human environmental impact, threatens our democracy, and hampers our educational systems.

Environmental Impact

The ability to make value from nature is perhaps the most striking feature of the capitalist system. The affluence or modern America is an outcome of nature transformed by capitalism. The profit motive linked with economic competition provides incentive for entrepreneurs to innovate and take risks. Without this incentive, it is unlikely that we would have seen the rapid pace of pharmaceutical development, the development of personal computers, or the ample supply of food we see in grocery stores. All value, however, is linked in some way to an environmental resource (Marx, 1978). Competition and the pursuit of profit, then, directly impact the environment. Schnaiberg and Gould (2000) point out that capitalism leads directly to a "treadmill of production," the ever increasing exploitation of nature in the pursuit of profit. Figure 1 illustrates how this treadmill impacts the environment. Paradoxically in its early phase, capitalism actually decreases the absolute level of environmental damage done by humans. This is so because capitalism creates enough value to make overuse activities such as unsustainable farming and wood gathering resulting in deforestation less common. Quite quickly, however, competition and the pursuit of profit – the "treadmill of production" escalate the impact of humans upon the environment.

Democracy

As Figure 1 also indicates, capitalism has had a historic and intimate relationship with the rise of democratic societies. Before the rise of 16th century mercantilism in the 16th century, markets were strictly controlled by royalty (Braudel, 1992). Additionally, control of agricultural production and trade were quite easily managed by monarchies because fixed capital existed primarily in the form of tillable land, a productive asset concentrated in the hands of a very powerful few. The rise of capitalism changed all this. The crown could no longer easily control economic production. A shift of power began then that eventually culminated in the democratic revolutions of the 19th and 20th centuries.

The level of democracy in society is very closely linked to economic inequality. Historically this is easy to see. As just mentioned, the rise of capitalism broke open the economic inequality associated with feudalism thus spreading income and wealth more broadly among the capitalist class. The result was a democratic revolution that lasted well into the 20th century. This historic relationship between inequality and democracy should, however, give us reason to pause. As pointed out earlier, economic inequality in the United States is dramatically on the rise. This unprecedented accumulation of wealth has resulted in some quite undemocratic changes in American life. For example, federal elections are now largely funded by large corporations and the economic elite The recent Citizens United Supreme Court decision is likely to make this even more the case as nearly unlimited corporate money can now flow directly into the hands of candidates seeking election. The risk, of course, is that political offices will now increasingly be open to the highest bidder. Often, these bidders are those who have a direct interest in the exploitation of natural resources. For this reason, making progress toward a sustainable future is seriously in jeopardy.

Education

Historically, public education has largely been under the control of local governments. As a result, schools were to some extent insulated from state and federal political control and therefore the impact of "big money" in American politics. However, concurrent with rising inequality in the United States during the late 20th century, this situation has changed. During the period 1990 to 2004, federal spending on public education more than doubled (United States Department Education 2011). While the federal contributions is outweighed by state and local funding, it is important to note that federal funding also often carries some element of control. In an era of tight budgets local school boards have been more likely to accept outside control in order to make ends meet.

In addition to control provided by federal funding, local schools have also been saddled with legal expectations from lawmakers, lawmakers that in many cases owe their positions to powerful interest as we have just argued. The national No Child Left Behind

Act (2002) is an example of this type of control (Hursh, 2007) The original intent of NCLB was to decrease outcome inequalities in the nation's schools by making schools "accountable" for student achievement (NCLB, 2002; Hursh, 2007). Since its enactment, NCLB has provided a significant mechanism for legislative control of education. Legislators and policy makers now have the ability to mandate curriculum by controlling what is contained on the test and therefore what is taught in schools. Additionally, standardized testing not only restricts what is taught but also limits the teaching of higher order teaching skills such as critical thinking (Hursh, 2007). As we will see in the concluding section, such skills are the backbone of a participatory democracy and a direct challenge to powerful interests who often have a vested interest in environmentally unsustainable activities.

Conclusion

We propose that in spite of its current deficits, our educational system holds the only key to creating a sustainable future. This is so because no other social institution has the comparable ability to transform the social landscape. Along those lines, Dewey (1916) described education as the means to the social continuity of life. He stated "it is the aim of a progressive education to take part in correcting unfair privilege and unfair deprivation, not to perpetuate them" (p. 89). Similarly, Freire (2007), Matthews (1998), and Noddings (2005) argued that dialogue and problem solving are necessary in order to create a democratic and civil society. We suggest that this is also true in regard to the creation of a sustainable future. More recently, Samanci (2010) suggested that elementary schools focus on student-centered learning through the formation of a democratic classroom environment. In this chapter we offer three important steps for educators as they facilitate learning that promotes both democracy and sustainability.

If a sustainable future is possible, it must first promote robust communication. Dewey (1897), Freire (2007), and Noddings (2002) refer to the importance of communication or dialogue. This includes listening, showing genuine respect, and commitment to learning and gaining information. The health of our democracy depends on participation; students must practice participation in our schools (Noddings, 2005). The experience of working together in a democratic learning environment leads to adults who are able to work together to solve problems. Good teachers involve students in cooperative learning activities and thus create a capacity for associative living. Students learn to listen, respect others, express themselves, resolve conflict, and solve problems. This is an important step for developing adults who will be able and willing to create a sustainable future.

A second step toward an education that leads to a sustainable future is what Freire (2007) refers to as "problem posing." Problem posing involves students discovering problems and taking steps to solve the problems. This would be in contrast to the traditional teacher who deposits or "banks" knowledge into the minds of students. Dewey (1897) described a school where students were involved in their own learning, not just solving but discovering problems. He emphasized that it is impossible to use authoritarian methods to educate democratic citizens. Teachers partner with students and guide them through the discovery of meaning and the application of what they have learned. Dewey (1916) suggested five steps involved in this discovery: 1) continuous activity (learning) for which one is interested, 2) a problem involved in the interest that stimulates thought, 3) ability to make observations concerning the problem, 4) suggesting and developing solutions, and 5) opportunity to apply and test the solutions. Students today must be given the opportunities to pose problems and develop the solutions to create a sustainable future.

Finally, it is important for educators to provide opportunities for students to serve others. Dewey (1900) discussed the importance of introducing and training children as members of the community. He spoke of saturating them with a spirit of service and stated it was the "best guaranty of a larger society which is worthy, lovely, and harmonious" (p. 27-28). Likewise,

Noddings (2002) referred to the importance of teaching children to "care for other human beings, and all must find an ultimate concern in center of self, for intimate others, for associates/acquaintances, for distant others, for animals, for plants and the physical environment, for objects and instruments, and for ideas." (p. 94). Through this developing sense of concern and the experience of serving others, these children will develop into adults who are concerned and committed to a sustainable future where the previously mentioned inequalities are diminished.

The previously paragraphs are beginning steps to transforming the world which Freire (1998) defines as denouncing the dehumanization process and announcing a dream of a new society. As educators provide opportunities for students to work cooperatively and dialogue together, pose problems and develop solutions, and show concern and service to others, they are facilitating democracy and promoting a sustainable world.

In this age of high-stakes testing and political unrest, educators are faced with pressure to teach to the test and resort to what Freire (2007) refers to as "banking." However, we must remember that there is more to education than test scores and grades. Education is and should be about living. (Dewey, 1916). Dewey stated:

> As a society becomes more enlightened, it realizes that it is responsible not to transmit and conserve the whole of existing achievements, but only such as to make for a better future society. The school is its chief agency for the accomplishment of this end. (p. 18)

We must provide students with an education that prepares them for life in a democratic community.

References

Braudel, F. (1992). *Civilization and Capitalism, 15th-18th century.* Berkeley: University of California Press.

Davis, K. & Moore, W. E. (1945). Some Principles of Stratification. *American Sociological Review,* 10(2): 242-249.

Dewey, J. (1897). My Pedagogic Creed. *The School Journal,* LIV(3): 77-80.

Dewey, J. (1900). *School and Society.* Chicago: The University of Chicago Press.

Dewey, J. (1916). *Democracy in Education: An Introduction to the Philosophy of Education.* New York: McMIllan.

Freire, P. (1998). *Pedagogy of Freedom: Ethics, Democracy, and Civic Courage.* Lantham, MD: Rowman and Littlefield Publishers, Inc.

Freire, P. (2007). *Pedagogy of the oppressed: 30th anniversary edition.* New York: Continuum.

Hursh, D. (2007) Exacerbating inequality: the failed promise of the no child left behind act. *Race, Ethnicity, and Education,* 10(3) 295-308.

Inequality, W. G. O. E. (2011). "http://extremeinequality.org."

Janmaat, J. G. (2008). Socio-Economic Inequality and Cultural Fragmentation in Western Societies. *Comparative Sociology,*7(2): 179-214.

Marx, K. (1977). *Capital : a critique of political economy.* New York: Vintage Books.

Marx, K. (1978). *Alienated Labor. Karl Marx: Selected Writings.* Oxford: Oxford University Press: 73-112.

Marx, K. & Engels, F. (1964). *The communist manifesto.* New York: Washington Square Press.

Matthews, D. (1998). Afterthoughts. *Kettering Review,* Fall 1998: 74-75.

NCLB (2002). No child left behind act.

Noddings, N. (2002). *Educating moral people: A caring alternative to character education.* New York: Teachers College Press.

Noddings, N. (2005). What does it mean to educate the whole child? *Educational Leadership,* 63(1): 8-13.

Samanci, O. (2010) Democracy education in elementary schools. *The Social Studies,* 101, 30-33.

Schnaiberg, A. & Gould, K.A. (2000). *Environment and society: the enduring conflict.* Caldwell, N.J: Blackburn Press.

United States Department of Education. (2011). http://www2.ed.gov/about/overview/fed/10facts/edlite-chart.html

German and American Paths to Sustainability

Louise E. Stoehr

Every society will have to tread its own path to sustainable development. The difficulties and challenges that come up along the way are different for each society and so quite different formulas for this transformation process will be required. The first steps have been taken, but a long way lies before us (Weiland, 2007, p.303).

Introduction

What is it about two cultures that prompts them to view each other in certain ways? Negative terms—for example, "Environmental contaminators. Gas-guzzling vehicles. Uncontrollable air polluters. Energy squanderers" (Schmiedicke, 2010) —are often used in German media reports on environmental issues in the United States. This seems surprising because behind the obvious differences in size (for example, the United States has a population of about 300 million versus about 82 million in Germany), the similarities in Western lifestyle are overwhelming: both countries are established democratic nations that afford their citizens a high standard of living. More importantly, since the end of the Second World War, both the United States and Germany have experienced industrial expansion and considerable economic growth, making the United States the world's largest economy and Germany the world's fourth largest (Geoghegan, 2010, p. 104). And, as a consequence, both countries have in common serious environmental problems.

What sets the United States and Germany apart from each other in terms of their respective approaches to sustainable development? In light of the similarities between the countries, the answer to this question may be surprising in its emphasis on two opposing models at the foundation of social and cultural norms: the model of competition in the United States versus the model of consensus in Germany. The current result for sustainability is that the emphasis on individualism has let the United States fall behind countries like Germany, whose consensus model makes it easier for the government to effect change.

Different Steps: Cultural Norms of Consensus and Competition

Culture can be defined comprehensively as the set of "values, beliefs, customs, traditions, symbols, norms, and institutions—combining to create the overarching frames that shape how humans perceive reality" (Assadourian, 2010, p. 8). In short, culture determines who we as a society are. Just as important as what a culture is like now, however, is how it has become that way. The cultures of Germany and the United States in the eighteenth and nineteenth centuries were shaped by the Industrial Revolution, which focused on continuous growth of income and profit. A primary characteristic of the culture that grew out of the Industrial Revolution is what Weiland calls the "Promethean Principle," that is, a strong belief in the infinite gift of human invention to overcome all obstacles (Weiland, 2007, p. 35). Despite a similar economic history, the two countries now have taken steps in different directions: The trust in human invention—in technology—to solve all problems is still the driving force behind American approaches to sustainability, while Germany is basing its decisions about environmental problems on the precautionary principle.

Simply stated, the precautionary principle places responsibility on the proponent of an activity for proving that the activity presents no threat to human health, health of other species, or the environment in general. For example, documented evidence regarding the absolute safety of a genetically modified plant would be required *before* permission would be granted to introduce the new product to the agricultural community. The resulting new approach is called "ecological modernization" because it strives to solve or prevent environmental problems (ecology) through societal change and technological innovation (modernization).

The specifics of the political framework within which such societal change and technological innovation unfolds may offer an explanation of the different ecological approaches. Germany is a social democracy and a multi-party parliamentary republic where consensus is essential for effective governing. In contrast, the United States' two-party system is based on a model of competition, characterized by explicit rivalries.

More specifically, German citizens embrace "the active and formative role of the state, which considers itself to be the representative of the general well-being" (Weiland, 2007, p. 294) The government's role as a caretaker of the general welfare is written into the German Constitution with Article 14.2: "Property entails obligations" (Das Grundgesetz/The Basic Law). In other words, the letter of the law holds everybody with power, including economic power, responsible for contributing to the common interest. In contrast, in the United States government regulation is usually viewed as an intrusion on the rights of individuals and corporations. Steven Hill reduces the differences between the two political systems to "inclusion vs. exclusion and consensus building vs. power-over adversarial politics" (Hill, 2010, p. 267).

Thinking in terms of "consensus" versus "competition" offers a promising model for further understanding the different national responses to the sustainability crisis. In the big picture, the consensus-competition model suggests explanations for a wide array of social and political issues, ranging from the role of science to worker productivity and taxation—ultimately, these are also lifestyle issues that impact sustainability.

Science is valued differently. Wieland suggests that in Germany expert knowledge (but not the opinion of special interest groups) is sought on matters of science and technology. But she sees the role of science in the American political debate as "not an objective authority to settle a matter by realizing the truth" (Weiland, 2007, p. 94). She explains: "As in no other country, science in the USA is a politicized arena that is subject to the laws of competition" (Weiland, 2007, p. 94).

The culture of a society is reflected in the daily lives of its people, and the routines of these daily lives have a direct impact on the environment. Examining employees' productivity, workers in the United States are currently twice as productive per hour as they were in 1970, yet these more productive workers now work an average of 1880 hours annually, or 180 hours more than in 1970 (Schor 2010, p. 92). Schor describes people who work long hours as "time poor," (Schor 2010, p. 93) a condition which encourages resource-intensive, consumer-oriented activities, such as living in larger suburban homes, eating out, and purchasing packaged foods (Schor 2010, p. 93; Geoghegan 2010, p. 63). These lifestyle choices are often justified in the name of individualism, which has become, as Bill McKibben argues, a major problem in the United States as "the hyper-individualism"—"the idea that everything works best if we think not a whit about the common interest. In the end, that has damaged our society, our climate and our private lives" (McKibben, 2009)

German workers, on the other hand, work fewer hours and pay more taxes—with perplexing results from an American perspective: German workers are even more productive than their American counterparts (McKibben, 2007, p. 223), even though they enjoy more holidays, have a minimum four-week vacation, and work fewer hours per week. The less competitive lifestyle leads to a reduced need for convenience products; more time to repair, reuse, and recycle; and the use of more environmentally-friendly forms of transportation. The differences in transportation modalities combined with peoples' homes as a rule being smaller and better weather-proofed, results in Germans using "about half as much energy per capita as Americans" (McKibben, 2007, p. 222). In respect to social issues that incur cost, for example, poverty rates are low. The United States suffers an overall poverty rate of 17% compared to Germany's 7.5% (McKibben, 2007, p. 222). In sum, not only do Germans live in a country that ranks among the top ten on the quality of life index (the United States ranks thirteenth) (McKibben, 2007, p. 224), de Graaf argues that the shorter working hours enjoyed by Germans contribute to their "conscientious consumer habits, and proper environmental stewardship" (de Graaf, 2010, p. 174-175).

The differences in American and German lifestyles and cultural norms of competition versus consensus correspond to different attitudes toward ecological issues. According to McKibben, more than twice as many Europeans as Americans "believe that environmental protection is an immediate and urgent problem" (McKibben, 2007, p. 225). It is no surprise that each country is taking different steps toward achieving sustainable development.

Different Paths: Comparative Examination of Sustainable Development

The different steps toward sustainable development indeed suggest that both countries pursue different paths. In the United States, environmentalism began as a grassroots movement, consistent with the American notion of the self-reliant citizen who actively participates in creating societal change. In contrast, large-scale environmental protection in Germany began on the initiative of Chancellor Willy Brandt in 1969 as an attempt to reign in the unlimited growth that had characterized the immediate post-Second World War years, create better living conditions, and improve the quality of the environment. Since then, the German government has played an active role in establishing precautionary guidelines and formulating modern environmental policy.

In the case of the United States, however, Weiland argues that the competitive nature of American politics has contributed to the inability to establish the precautionary principle as a guiding principle in American environmental policy (Weiland, 2007, p. 224). Commencing in the late 1970s, the grass-roots environmental movement slowly lost momentum. When Ronald

Reagan became president in 1980, many of the country's newly-established environmental regulations were relaxed. Since 1980, the United States has increased oil consumption by 21%; during the same period Germany's oil consumption decreased by 20% (Hill, 2010, p. 180). Although President Bill Clinton signed the 1997 Kyoto Protocol, the United States Senate refused to ratify the treaty, and Clinton's successor, George W. Bush, likewise refused to honor the treaty. The United States has emerged as the largest per capital polluter in the world.

Bill McKibben suggests the only way to a sustainable future is "massive investment in green energy" (McKibben, 2010, p. 70). That is precisely what the German government has done by supporting renewable energies and energy efficiency (German Missions in the United States). First, it invested in the burgeoning solar energy industry and established the "100,000 rooftops program," which offered subsidies to individuals who invested in photovoltaic rooftop systems, and secondly it passed the Renewable Energies Act (EEG) in 1999, which requires providers of electricity to purchase electricity from renewable energy sources at fixed prices (Bode, Dohmen, Jung, Krumrey, & Schwägerl, 2010, p. 91) The investment has paid off. Germany is now the world leader in solar power (Michel, 2008). In September 2010, Chancellor Merkel's government announced an ambitious energy plan for Germany with the goal of achieving 80% percent of all gross electricity consumption from renewable energy sources by 2050 (German Missions in the United States; Has, 2010/2011, p. 13; Bode, Dohmen, Jung, Krumrey, & Schwägerl, 2010, p. 90).

The United States, conversely, has remained focused on old technologies, concentrating its efforts on further development of nuclear energy and extraction of fossil fuels. The Department of Energy has spent twice as much for research and development on nuclear energy, and three times as much on coal as it invested in research and development on solar energy (Hill, 2010, p. 167). Jeffrey H. Michel, an American engineer living in Germany, outlines impediments in the United States that inhibit full realization of renewable energy potential. These include the lack of a long-term national renewable energy policy and the absence of greenhouse gas reduction targets, meaning that there is no economic motivation for lowering emissions by using alternative energy sources (Michel, 2008).

Hill reinforces the argument that ecological investment is also economic. He describes the positive effects that "cap and trade" policies have had on environmental quality and job creation in Germany. Setting a finite limit on carbon dioxide emissions has reduced Germany's carbon footprint, and "many of the new technologies and emerging energy industries have *contributed* to job creation and stimulated Europe's economy" (Hill, 2010, p. 177-178). The German newsmagazine *Der Spiegel* reports that in northern Germany, for example, as the ship building industry has seen fewer and fewer contracts, the employees—carpenters, electricians, pipe fitters, sheet metal workers, machinists, and mechatronics engineers—at the Nordseewerken shipyard have transferred their manufacturing skills to renewable energy jobs, now producing wind turbines (Grill, 2010, p. 94).

Despite lack of similar government support, the United States is beginning to invest more in renewable energies, though with some German participation. A joint venture of Chevron Energy Solutions and Solar Millennium, LLC (California Energy Commission), the Blythe Solar Power Project, is a 1,000 megawatt solar project being built on public land near Riverside, California. It is the largest solar project in the world (Hast, 2010/2011, p. 12). Solar Millennium, however, is a German company that specializes in parabolic trough power plants (Solar Millennium, AG). German leadership in renewable energy projects in the United States is not limited to solar energy. Texas is home to the Horse Hollow wind energy farm, the largest in the world. In fact, it is the largest wind farm installed by Siemens Wind Power, a German company, in 2006 (Siemens).

Part of the secret of success are not only large-scale government or private-industry projects, but also simple measures that add up to large savings when these measures become the cultural norm. Ubiquitous in Germany, but virtually unheard of in the United States, are such features as a start button or motion sensor to begin the steps of escalators in public buildings rolling; toilets with two flush levers, one for more and one for less water, allowing the user to determine how much to flush. Tankless water heaters, an expensive novelty in the United States, are the norm in Germany. Of course, incentives may encourage sustainability also because they help turn certain behaviors into culturally accepted norms. For example, "passive housing" is a more recent construct introduced in Germany that has been shown to use $1/20^{th}$ of the energy required of a conventional housing structure, while costing less than 10% more to build.

However, as Hill points out, "in the United States, passive housing doesn't exist; in fact, the advanced windows and heat-exchange ventilation systems needed to make passive houses work properly are not even commercially available" (Hill, 2010, p. 172). There are no federal regulations requiring a minimum level of energy efficiency for new constructions. The voluntary Leadership in Energy and Environmental Design (LEED) guidelines are not followed by 99% of builders in the United States. The result is that the average building in the United States uses about a third more energy than an otherwise equivalent building in Germany (Hill, 2010, p. 175).

Different Steps, Different Ways, One Goal: Outlook

Germany and the United States seem to be on different paths toward sustainability. In his book *Europe's Promise*, Hill summaries the differences eloquently, explaining that in Germany "sustainability is part of the system; i.e., sustainability isn't just a set of building standards, but is part of an entire system of design, an entire system of culture, living styles, activities that the community engages in" (Hill, 2010, p. 175). At the same time, however, both countries still share the goal: sustainability.

The differences, after all, do not mean that we cannot achieve an American system that is just as sustainable. The United States was once a champion of conservation; we have learned how to get more productivity from the same amount of available energy. In fact, since 1970, the United States has met 75% of its new energy needs through greater efficiency rather than new energy supplies (Margonelli, 2007). We can do this again by making extensive use of existing technologies and conservation practices. Margonelli argues that we need "leadership willing to enact tough energy standards and eliminate the perverse incentives (such as tax credits for big vehicles) that encourage us to squander fuel."

Assuming that competition and individualism describe American society, the appropriate path for the United States is to take stronger individual initiative that builds on American achievements and learns from its weaknesses. An appeal to this effect has been issued forth in *Diagnosis Earth*: "To address global climate change, we will need action at all levels of society, from individual choices to international agreements, from industry's technological solutions to government policy. Each and every one of us can be a part of the climate solution" (Anderegg, 2010, p. 32). A return to grass-roots effort, the appeal is followed by four concrete suggestions—"be informed," "be active in our democracy," "live conscientiously," and "teach others"—which may be specific to American democracy but may also be something Germans can learn from.

References

Anderegg, W. R. L. Prall, J. W., Harold, J., Schneider, S.H. 2010. Expert credibility in climate change. PNAS (Proceedings of the National Academy of Sciences) 107 (27): 12107-9.

Assadourian, E. (2010). The Rise and Rall of Consumer Cultures. In W. Institute, *2010 State of the World: Transforming Cultures - From Consumerism to Sustainability* (pp. 3-20). New York: W. W. Norton.

Bode, K., Dohmen, F., Jung, A., Krumrey, K., & Schwägerl, C. (2010, September 20). Öko um jeden Preis. *Der Spiegel* , 88-97.

Breakthrough Institute. (n.d.). *Soaking up the Sun: Solar Power in Germany and Japan.* Retrieved from http://thebreakthrough.org/blog/2009/04/soaking_up_the_sun_solar_power.shtml

California Energy Commission. (n.d.). *(Solar Millennium) Blythe Solar Power Project.* Retrieved from California Energy Commission Website: http://www.energy.ca.gov/sitingcases/solar_millennium_blythe/

de Graaf, J. (2010). Reducing Work Time as a Path to Sustainability. In W. Institute, *2010 State of the World: Transforming Cultures - From Consumerism to Sustainability* (pp. 173-177). New York: W. W. Norton.

Edwards, A. R. (2005). *The Sustainability Revolution: Portrait of a Paradigm Shift.* Gabriola Island, BC, Canada: New Society Publishers.

Ehrenfeld, J. R. (2008). *Sustainability by Design: A Subversive Strategy for Transforming our Consumer Culture.* New Haven and London: Yale University Press.

Geoghegan, T. (2010). *Were You Born on the Wrong Continent? How the European Model can Help You Get a Life.* New York and London: The New Press.

German Missions in the United States. (n.d.). *Energy Plan.* Retrieved from http://www.germany.info/Vertretung/usa/en/__pr/P__Wash/2010/09/07__EnergyPlan__PR.html

Grill, M. (2010, September 20). Wind statt Waffen. *Der Spiegel* , 94.

Hast, A. (2010/2011, Winter). Chancellor Merkel's Plans to Increase Share of Sustainable Energy to 80% by 2050. *German World* , p. 13.

Hast, A. (2010/2011, Winter). Deutsches Unternehmen baut
3000-Negawatt-Kraftwerk, das zwei Millionen Haushalte versorgen
soll. *German World* , p. 12.

Hill, S. (2010). *Europe's Promise: Why the European Way is the Best
Hope in an Insecure Age.* Berkeley and Los Angeles, California:
University of California Press.

Margonelli, L. (2007, June 3). Myths About That $3.18 Per Gallon. *The
Washington Post* .

McKibben, B. (2007). *Deep Economy: The Wealth of Communities and
the Durable Future.* New York, New York: Henry Holt.

McKibben, B. (2009, March 23). Together, We Save the Planet. *The
Nation.* McKibben, B. (2010). *Eaarth: Making a Life On a Tough
New Planet.* New York, New York: (de Graaf, 2010)Henry Holt.

Michel, J. H. (2008). *The Case for Renewable Feed-In Tariffs.* EUEC
Energy & Environment Conference, Tucson, Arizona.

Newman, P. Building the Cities of the Future. In W. Institute, *2010 State
of the World: Transforming Cultures - From Consumerism to
Sustainability* (pp. 133-137). New York: W. W. Norton.

Schmiedicke, P. (Narrator). (2010) Wind of Change: Interessante
Projekte rund um Sonne, Wind und Wasser. [Television series
episode]. *Im Grünen.* Stuttgart, Germany: Südwestrundfunk.

Schor, J. (2010). Sustainable Work Schedules for All. In W. Institute,
*2010 State of the World: Transforming Cultures - From
Consumerism to Sustainability* (pp. 91-95). New York: W. W.
Norton.

Siemens. (n.d.). *References - Siemens.* Retrieved from Siemens Energy
Web site: http://www.energy.siemens.com/br/en/power-genera-
tion/renewables/wind-power/references.htm

Solar Millennium, AG. (n.d.). *Solar Millennium AG - We are Developing the Future*. Retrieved from Solar Millennium AG Company Web site: http://www.solarmillennium.de/index,lang2.html

Weiland, S. (2007). *Politik der Ideen: Nachhaltige Entwicklung in Deutschland, Großbritannien und den USA*. Wiesbaden, Germany: VS Verlag für Sozialwissenschaften.

DESPERATE QUEST
A Poet Looks at Sustainability

Ken Lauter

PREFACE – *PLEASE! SOMEBODY TALK ME DOWN!*

Desperation is probably not the most congenial term to introduce into a conversation on sustainability. So, with apologies to the other contributors to this volume who may have a more optimistic outlook— not to mention better credentials on the subject than mine— I must first issue a *caveat:* I seriously doubt that sustainability can be achieved in the "developed" countries of the world, much less in the Third World; that is, not with the speed, precision, political will, and coordination necessary to prevent massive ecological and climate disruption, and consequently a virtual collapse of the corporate "civilization" that has come to dominate the globe over the past several centuries. [1]

---

1   For more hopeful views, see: Janine Benyus, *Biomimicry: Innovation Inspired by Nature* (William Morrow & Company, 1997); Eric A. Davison, *You Can't Eat GNP: Economics as if Ecology Mattered* (Perseus Publishing, 2000); Paul Hawken, *Blessed Unrest - How the Largest Movement In the World Came Into Being and Why No One Saw it Coming* (Viking Press, 2007) and *Natural Capitalism: Creating the Next Industrial Revolution* (Little Brown and Co. 1999); David Korten, *Agenda for a New Economy: From Phantom Wealth to Real Wealth – A Declaration of Independence from Wall Street* (Berrett-Koehler Publishers, 2nd edition, 2010); Bill McKibben, *Deep Economy: The Wealth of Communities and the Durable Future* (St. Martin's Griffin, 2007); Harvey Franklin Wasserman, *SOLARTOPIA! Our Green-Powered Earth, A.D. 2030* (publisher unknown); Donald Worster, *Nature's Economy: the Roots of Ecology* (Sierra Club Books, 1977). [f.n. continued on next page.]

In fact, just thinking about "sustainability" for very long makes my head feel like it's about to explode. This is not an effort to be funny— it's a simple fact. I said as much to Dr. Jerry Williams when he invited me to contribute to this volume. Actually, the way I put it to him was more like: "The word *sustainability* triggers a rush of factoids in my brain that jostle each other madly for a while before dissolving into incomprehensibility." I thought that would stop Jerry in his tracks. For reasons of his own, however, he wouldn't take no for an answer— so he bears at least part of the responsibility for the dark, rambling nature of these remarks.

Why elaborate on such a dour vision? First, I wanted to see if I could talk myself out of my funk. As Rachel Maddow says: "Please, somebody, talk me down!" To which, my muse whispered in my ear: *Fat chance— but worth a try.* I suppose that's a confession that I still harbor a few grains of hope that humanity will come to its senses at one second before midnight and pull off the greatest comeback since the day the Buffalo Bills, trailing 38-3 late in the game, beat the Houston Oilers, 41-38. It was almost a miracle. Ah yes, *miracles!* That is precisely what is needed in these desperate times— and, of course, precisely what we're not about to get.

The explosion of such literature in our time is both reassuring and disturbing. For instance, have any of the G-8 heads of state read any of it? If so, some of their policy stances seem hypocritical or obtuse; if not, they are dangerously naïve. Either way, the implications for a sustainable future are not good.

PART I – THINKING LIKE AN ENGINEER

It is much too late for sustainable development;
what we need is sustainable retreat.

James Lovelock
The Revenge of Gaia: Earth's Climate in Crisis and the Fate of Humanity
(Basic Books, 2006)

* * *

The scale of our enterprise is now bumping up against the scale of the planet. The most difficult transition is not from oil to solar power. The most difficult transition is a mental one: from a world where the answer to every problem is growth to a world where we have to be mature and accept the idea that we're going to have to focus on resilience, stability, and security.

Bill McKibben
The Progressive, Dec. 2010-Jan. 2011

* * *

We are the only species without full employment.

Paul Hawken
(paraphrasing theologian Matthew Fox)
"Natural Capitalism," *Mother Jones*, March/April, 1997

The main focus of my life for the past half-century has been poetry, but I've always had a strong interest in scientific thought, and as an undergraduate (in the Stone Age) I minored in engineering. So the engineering model of problem-solving comes naturally to me, and rightly or wrongly the whole arena of environmental degradation and sustainability first hit me as something to be "solved."

Thus, in my first pass at this essay, I decided to brush up on the solutions currently floating around. I dutifully gathered about 150 articles, most from journalism, a few from technical reports, eventually reading about a third of them— but the data storms they evoked became unendurable. Each of the generally hopeful books cited in the footnote to my preface exemplify the "engineering model" to one degree or another, but as powerfully imagined and eloquent as such works sometimes are, I am not terribly comforted by them. Why? Because even the best of them seemed to be grasping at straws— ingenious ones in some cases, but straws nevertheless.

The negative sides of the argument, however, hit home for me with great force. Please indulge me, then, but we need to know the devil in all his guises, so I must itemize a few of these horrors. (I have not fact-checked or sourced most of them because they are readily available in multiple publications and websites.)

— Earth's atmosphere is already well above 350 ppm of CO2 with no sign that the West's major powers fully comprehend that lethal fact, much less are likely to do what is needed to deal with it.

— The most recent estimate of sea-level rise due to global warming: *five feet within ten years.* Goodbye New York, Amsterdam, New Orleans, Bangladesh, etc.

— The International Union for Conservation of Nature predicts: "extinction for almost half the world's coral reef species, a third of amphibians, and a quarter of mammals" in a few decades.

— "Satellite data gathered over the past 10 years have shown... that the growth of marine phytoplankton— *the basis of the entire ocean food chain*— is being adversely affected by rising sea temperatures." (italics added) – Steve Connor, "Climate Change is Killing the Oceans' Microscopic 'Lungs.' " *The Independent / UK* - 12/7/06

— Global water consumption is doubling every 20 years. Currently, a billion or more people have no access to safe drinking water.

— Within two decades, the disappearance of the glaciers in the Himalayas may disrupt the water supply of tens of millions of Asians.

— Rising silt levels at Glen Canyon Dam and Hoover Dam, combined with falling water levels from a drought now in its second decade, may disrupt water and electrical supplies throughout most of the American Southwest by the year 2025.

— World population will "taper off" at nine or ten billion in the next century, with the slums constituting the fastest growing demographic within this growth. The U.S. is projected to hit 600 million or so, roughly *twice* our present brood, by the year 2100.

— The so-called free-trade thrust of the global economy is impoverishing millions of traditional farming communities, shattering local economies, poisoning local ecologies, and fostering brutal dictatorships in the process. (See Naomi Klein's brilliant and massively documented *The Shock Doctrine: The Rise of Disaster Capitalism.* Metropolitan Books, 2007)

— The UN says "human trafficking" (slavery) is the world's fastest growing illegal industry and will soon surpass drug trafficking, which will make it the world's largest criminal enterprise. There may be 30 million souls enslaved around the globe— a figure that does not include those who are trapped in brutalizing labor out of the sheer need for survival.

— *"Over 50 billion food-animals are raised and slaughtered every year...* [italics added] Grazing and growing feed for livestock now occupy 70 percent of all agricultural land and 30 percent of the ice-free terrestrial surface of the planet... meat production is predicted to double... [by] 2050." – Ronnie Cummins, *Organic Consumers Association Newsletter* #260, January 20, 2011

— Nearly 20% of Americans (50 million+ people) are "food insecure," and yet more than a third of American adults are obese. Meanwhile world wide, some 24,000 children *per day* die from starvation or preventable disease. (You do the math for an annual figure.)

— Organic farms are the fastest growing segment of American agriculture; but of the 2.2 million farms in the U.S. only some 14,000 are certified organic— less than *one percent.* Moreover, 125,000 Big Ag factories (they are *not* farms) produce 75% of all foodstuffs delivered to American consumers.

— Eighty-five percent of the 82,000 chemicals registered for use in the United States have never been tested for toxicity.

—There were some 45,000 abandoned houses in Detroit as of 2010.

— Light pollution obscures the sky above 2/3 of the world; 20% of people on earth can no longer see the Milky Way.

— By 2020, data processing centers and telecom networks will consume more electric power than France, Germany, Canada, and Brazil combined— much of it supplied by coal-fired plants. (Greenpeace Newsletter, Spring, 2011)

— When Reagan was president, there were approximately 300 lobbyists with offices in Washington DC; today there are some 35,000.

— In the Savings and Loan scandal of the 1980s, the Justice Department sent some 1,000 "banksters" to prison. In the recent Wall Street/Real Estate mega-scandal that nearly imploded the global economy, *none* of the financial barons responsible has been indicted, much less convicted of any crime. In fact, many have been given multi-million-dollar bonuses.

— Millions of hard-working Americans have been evicted from their homes through absolutely no fault of their own; and in the coming years millions more will be.

— Millions of hard-working Americans are a paycheck away from financial ruin due to a corrupt, zealot-filled, and cowardly federal government's failure to do what virtually every other Western democracy has: provide universal health care.

— The military-industrial complex reigns supreme in American politics, maintaining perhaps a thousand military bases around the world, devouring a full 60% of the federal budget, while prosecuting two meaningless, barbaric wars— even as it is tempted to start a third.

— In the congressional races, the candidate who spends the most wins roughly 90% of the time.

— The recent Supreme Court decision in *Citizens United,* giving corporations unlimited power over elections via anonymous cash contribution, has created what some have called a political "super-organism." The only way to rectify this problem is evidently to amend the Constitution— a slow, arduous process with an uncertain outcome and which could quite possibly be subverted into making things worse. In short, proto-fascism is already upon us and threatens to become the full-blown version via Fox News, the Tea Party, and billionaire ghouls like the Koch brothers.

* * *

One could continue *ad infinitum, ad nauseam*. I go to this irritating length only to drive home the obvious: it's not just the raw number of crisis points that is the real problem— it's that they are so diverse and interconnected. You could put out literally thousands of these fires, and the general conflagration would continue. Which is to say that the barriers to sustainability are both vast and complex and are therefore unlikely to yield to anything less than vast and complex remedies. The corollary is that no industrial society or city on earth is now or has ever been close to achieving genuine sustainability. We are all eating our seed corn.

Move horizontally or vertically in surveying the current unsustainable civilization (or should we call it anti-sustainable?) and you quickly realize that there is virtually *nothing* untouched by destructive theory and practice today— from food production to child care, from transportation systems to dietary habits, from construction standards to marital/living arrangements, from energy sources to media revolutions— how could we have lost our way on so many fronts, so completely, and so fast (in evolutionary terms)?

In fact, my strongest intuition, verging on the mystical, is that sustainability once lost can never be regained. How many legends of a "fall," of "original sin," are there across the cultures of this planet? Such mythologies all render the same verdict: something in human social practice became fatally dysfunctional in the far distant past.[2]   Therefore, the attempt to "rebuild"

---

2 Exactly what caused this dysfunction is the key question, of course, but too large to address here. The only fully plausible answer I have encountered is a theory of brain types and their bio-social implications, summarized for the general reader in *How Is Your Brain Like A Zebra: A New Human Neurotypology* (Xlibris, 2008) by Dr. Judith Lauter, Director of the Human Neuroscience Laboratory at Stephen F. Austin State University. A second volume extending the theory into human history, politics, and social evolution is in progress, with the working title *Neural Rainbow – the Center, the Perimeter, and the Brain, a Neuroethological Theory of Human Nature*. My fondest wish for readers of *Toward a Livable World* is that they could become acquainted with the vision embodied in these works.

human sustainability within the biosphere is trying to redress in a comparative blink of an eye what the dominant human societies have perpetrated on us all over the last five to ten thousand years. I am certainly not alone in this outlook. For example, University of Texas journalism professor Robert Jensen, in an article with the uplifting title "The Delusion Revolution: We're on the Road to Extinction and in Denial," provides the following overview of our dilemma:

> We're in trouble, on all fronts, and the trouble is wider and deeper than most of us have been willing to acknowledge. We should struggle to build a road on which we can walk through those troubles— if such a road is possible— but I doubt it's going to look like any path we had previously envisioned, nor is it likely to lead anywhere close to where most of us thought we were going... The agricultural revolution set us on a road to destruction. The industrial revolution ramped up our speed. The delusional revolution has prevented us from coming to terms with the reality of where we are and where we are heading.
>
> - AlterNet.com, Aug. 15, 2008

In spite of its gloom, I find Jensen's critique exhilarating, almost inspirational in a weird sort of way. His three "revolutions" cover an enormous subject with elegant fatalism, a diagnosis of startling clarity and humility. His synthesis makes me feel that we can at least define the full scope of the threat— which is obviously necessary if we are to confront and somehow deal with it.

If we are to deal with it... At that sentence, several months ago, I gave up hope on ever completing this essay. The engineering model had led me to a dead end. Depressed and exhausted, I saw that my muse had been right all along. I hadn't talked myself down. So I told Jerry I couldn't contribute. My frustration boiled over into a poem.

The Offering

There is a mythic bird—poised
on the edge of the day
after tomorrow. He may be

the one Wallace Stevens saw,
a creature with fire-feathers
dangling down— or he may be

an heir of the huge vultures
on the walls of Çatal Höyük.
I approach the bird slowly

offering the food called
sustainability— fresh, raw,
undigested. The large bird

treads the ground, hard,
eyeing me warily— but
without fear or forgiveness.

He sniffs at the offering
then turns away. He peers up
at the gathering clouds, as if

he sees something
up there—
something I cannot see.

Note - Çatal Höyük was a Neolithic village in Anatolia (modern day
Turkey), dating to 7,500 BC. see Rianne Eisler, *The Chalice and the
Blade – Our History, Our Future* (Harper & Row, 1988). Stevens'
bird appears in the poem "Of Mere Being."

PART II – THINKING LIKE A POET

The poetry of earth is never dead.

John Keats - in a letter

"There is a sanctuary in the mind made of poetry
and music and laughter."

C.D. Wright - *One with Others*

The mechanistic, algebraic engineering model had utterly failed to let me see much, if anything, of the inner nature of sustainability— of what its deepest essence is, of what it would take to transform our grossly unsustainable present world into something with a future.[3] The "mythic bird" first spurned my "offering" (our good intentions to create sustainable systems) and then left me peering into an ominously occluded future (the clouds). An entirely different approach was obviously needed— needed desperately. So I turned the quest toward poetry.

Here is a theory of poetry. It isn't original with me, but I will

_____

3   The Gaia theory of James Lovelock and Lynn Margulis is a kind of engineering model, in that it derives fundamentally from physics. However, Lovelock's strict definition of Gaia is "geo-physiology," which he regards as so complex and powerful as to be beyond the reach of any literal "geo-engineering" (such as seeding clouds with minerals to create more shade and therefore retard global warming.) Moreover, in *The Revenge of Gaia: Why the Earth is Fighting Back - and How we Can Still Save Humanity* (Basic Books, 2006) Lovelock believes that the earth's feedback loops have already triggered a near-catastrophic "fever" that will last a century or more even if atmospheric pollution fell to zero immediately. Bill McKibben advances a similar premise in *Eaarth: Making a Life on a Tough New Planet* (St. Martin's Griffin, 2011) but concludes we can and must swiftly take significant measures to mitigate the damage.

Wary of the kind of cult thinking they have inadvertently inspired, Lovelock and Margulis are adamant that the "Gaia" of their hypothesis is strictly a scientific shorthand, with no mythic or anthropomorphic implications whatsoever. That is, although Gaia was a Greek earth goddess and the Roman goddess of marriage, she is not posited as a conscious, supernatural entity. In short, these two revolutionary scientists are wrestling with something much larger than "pagan" mythology or its latter-day counterparts.

try to focus it in a slightly new way.[4] Regardless of its theme, style, or form, every poem— perhaps at a level below language, older than language— seeks something of which words are only "a fitful portal" on what Wallace Stevens called "a blessed rage for order." I think that in Stevens' mind, the word *order* can be legitimately taken as a synonym for *sustainability.*

Another example from Stevens comes in "Not Ideas About the Thing But the Thing Itself," one of the last poems he wrote before his death. Just as the narrator is waking up one morning at the end of winter, he hears "a scrawny cry" coming from an unknown bird outside his window. This modest sound of spring and renewal quickly leads him to a visionary moment. The bird's cry, he realizes, is a part of the life of the whole solar system, of the earth swinging closer to "the colossal sun, / Surrounded by its choral rings." As such, the birdsong seems to the poet "like / A new knowledge of reality." I would argue that this "new knowledge" is also nothing less than a perception of sustainability— which, we notice, occurs on both a grand, cosmic scale (sun and planets) and an intimate, personal scale (scrawny birds and people waking from sleep).

I'm suggesting that great poems— and some merely good ones—are often essentially a quest for sustainable consciousness, an image of life "in balance," an indirect articulation, perhaps, of the Yin and Yang of Asian thought. Other kinds of poetry, both ancient and modern, also exist which do *not* focus on the earth's bounty and our relation to it in positive ways.[5] Nevertheless, a

---

4   One highly original and provocative version of the theory was formulated by my mentor Donald Hall (U.S. Poet Laureate 2005-06) in the essay: "Goatfoot, Milktongue, Twinbird: the psychic origins of poetic form," in *Field*, Fall, 1973. Hall hypothesized that poetry arose from the intersection of infant cognitive development ("Milktongue"), infant motor development ("Twinbird"), and the chanting/dancing/story-telling ceremonies around the campfire of our evolutionary forbearers ("Goatfoot"). Other proponents of Romantic theory offer something similar though less vivid—see M.H. Abrams, *Natural Supernaturalism: Tradition and Revolution in Romantic Literature* (W.W. Norton & Company, 1971); Harold Bloom, *The Visionary Company: a Reading of English Romantic Poetry* (Cornell University Press, 1971).

large body of earth-loving visionary power can be traced well back into the history of English poetry. Milton called this power "the Paradise within," which could bless Adam and Eve, after they were banished from Eden. In his long poem *The Prelude*, Wordsworth tried to match Milton's prophetic power, calling his own moments of clairvoyance "spots of time," when the cosmos seemed to speak to him directly. In his most famous ode, he wrote:

> There was a time when meadow, grove, and stream,
> The earth, and every common sight
> To me did seem
> Appareled in celestial light . . .

from "Ode: Intimations of Immortality," *Wordsworth: Selected Works*
(Oxford University Press, 1969)

These lines express a sense of sacramental sustainability, and there are hundreds of similarly rhapsodic overtures in Wordsworth— "My heart leaps up when I behold / A rainbow in the sky," for instance. But even as Wordsworth and Coleridge were ushering in the Romantic Movement with their revolutionary *Lyrical Ballads* (1798),[6] the heavens over England were rapidly

---

5 The anti-earth poetics derive ultimately from Judeo-Christian-Platonic asceticism, which taught that the material world is corrupt, the things of the flesh sinful, and only Spirit is a pure avenue to ultimate truth and salvation (if not necessarily to happiness). The Bible's admonition to multiply and *subdue* the earth is the most blatant expression of this premise. Such a sensibility, instead of celebrating our bond with the biosphere, subliminally fears nature and sees humankind as separate from and in conflict with it. In fact, while working on this essay, I found to my great surprise and dismay that some of my favorite poets— like William Blake, Robert Frost and Dylan Thomas— belong for the most part to this camp.

6 Wordsworth's famous Preface to the *Ballads* called for the use of the "real language" of society in poetry, instead of high, flowery rhetoric from the past. This aesthetic prevailed world-wide for the next two centuries (with some eccentric exceptions) and helped inspire the Environmental Movement, whose pioneers (Muir, et al.) were well read in the Romantic poets. Other arenas were also influenced, including psychology— see Theodore Rozak, *The Voice of the Earth – an Exploration of Ecopsychology* (Simon & Schuster, 1992).

losing their "celestial" aspect. Over Birmingham, Manchester, and London, the skies were blackening with coal smoke from locomotives and factories— the "Dark Satanic Mills," in Blake's words—which were filled with a displaced agrarian population, including young children, whose 14-hour days usually ended in cramped, unheated, unlighted tenements, where the only drinking water available often carried typhoid.[7]

Blake, Wordsworth, Coleridge, Byron, Keats, and Shelley were all appalled by this spectacle— and their poetry is suffused with their multi-layered response. In short, the Romantic "return to nature"— and away from the elegant classicism of the 18th century— was at least in part a recoil from the loss of ecological sanity (sustainability) accelerated by the Industrial Revolution. In an age when the orthodox Christian god was manifestly failing to redeem "meadow, grove, and stream" from industrialism's assault, these poets worshipped the Imagination as a force that could effectively substitute for divine intervention.

Somewhat later, Mathew Arnold would proclaim: "the future of poetry is immense." For Arnold and many poets of the latter 19th century, their art was nothing less than a new and better kind of religion. How would the new religion work?

Each poet's answer was highly idiosyncratic and changed over time, but Keats is a prime example. He coined the term "negative capability" for the poet's power to imaginatively enter the consciousness of things outside your self— a sparrow, a cloud, a horse, a Grecian urn, or a human being.

I believe he should have called this power *positive* capability, but in any case a yearning for a more serene union of the human and natural realms is found in an astonishing range of poets, including some who are different in every other way. For instance, Walt Whitman was a vatic voice of roaring egomania

---

7   Such grotesque conditions were exposed first by Frederic Engles in his renowned *Conditions of the English Working Class* in 1844 and subsequently by Henry Mayhew in *London Labour and the London Poor* (1884).

and extremely long, strident lines of free verse:

> O to be self-balanced for contingencies
> To confront night, storms, hunger, ridicule, accidents,
> rebuffs, as the trees and animals do.

from *Whitman - Selections from Leaves of Grass*
(Dell Publishing Co. 1959), Leslie Fiedler, ed.

The great Emily Dickinson couldn't be further from Whitman, publicly, personally, and poetically. He was an autodidact and hyper-social vagabond bard who quickly became a national poetic icon. She was an avid student of biology in her brief time at Amherst Academy and Mount Holyoke Female Seminary, but was greatly misunderstood and virtually unpublished in her lifetime. Stylistically, the contrast between these two literary giants is just as sharp. Her short, rhymed, metered lines were modeled on hymns— in fact, she parodied the Holy Trinity in a tribute to the vivid life found in her own backyard garden:

> In the name of the Bee—
> And of the Butterfly—
> And of the Breeze— Amen!

The Compete Poems of Emily Dickinson
(Little Brown and Company, 1960), Thomas H. Johnson, ed.

Referring to bees, butterflies, and breezes as sacraments (even ironically) would have been heresy to Gerard Manly Hopkins, the Catholic convert who became a Jesuit priest; but Hopkins penned one quatrain with a world-famous last line that expresses a kind of pagan gusto and adoration of nature that Dickinson would have loved:

> What would the world be, once bereft
> Of wet and of wildness? Let them be left,
> O let them be left, wildness and wet;
> Long live the weeds and the wilderness yet.

from "Inversnaid," *Gerard Manley Hopkins: Poems and Prose*
(Penguin Books, 1971), W.H. Gardner, ed.

Dickinson is rarely this effusive, but can be just as forceful in acknowledging an existential awareness of nature's ultimate inviolability and priority over all things— including governments, human language, and by extension even poetry itself.

> We pass, and She abides.
> We conjugate her skill
> While She creates and federates
> Without a syllable.

Although he was cold to both Whitman and Dickinson, and barely warm to Hopkins, T. S. Eliot— in his typically dry, analytic way— praised the 17th century "metaphysical" poets like John Donne, by describing their intellectual equipoise as the ability to hold two contradictory ideas in their minds at once—a kind of sustainability in Newton's sense of "equal and opposite forces," like the centrifugal-centripetal gravitational tensions keeping planets in a steady orbit instead of collapsing into each other or flying apart.

And yet Eliot also called writing a poem "turning blood into ink," the systole-diastole pumping of the mind/body into thought, in a sustainable biorhythm. And what is Eliot's *The Wasteland* but the 20th century's greatest poetic dirge for the lack of a sane and durable cultural balance in the Western World? (The poem's beautiful conclusion suggests that things are otherwise in the East, however, and Eliot later found some kind of peace in Anglican Christianity, a conversion of dubious benefit to his poetry.)

A poet about as far removed as possible from any of those mentioned thus far (except maybe Blake), Theodore Roethke produced a large body of verse emanating from a mystical, sensual vision of nature. In his hypnotic, deeply mysterious poem, *The Lost Son,* Roethke tells the reader of "a lively understandable spirit" which "once entertained you"— and which "will come again," if you can only learn to "be still" and "wait." This was perhaps a distant allusion to the Milton sonnet ending: "They also serve who only stand and wait," but it clearly registers a note of sustainable consciousness that doesn't derive from abstract reason or engineering.

Closer to our own time, Kay Ryan (U.S. Poet Laureate, 2011) in her short poem "Patience," speculates:

> it is possible
> that waiting
> is sustainable
> a place with
> its own harvests.

from *Say Uncle* (Grove Press, 2000)

This kind of spiritual harvest was also noted by the Kentucky poet/farmer/activist Wendell Berry. In "A Discipline," written in response to the "blazing cocoon" of nuclear war looming over the world at the time, he sang:

> O gaze into the fire
> and be consumed with man's despair
> and be still and wait. And then see
> the world go on with patient work
> of seasons, embroidering birdsong
> upon itself as for a wedding...

from *Openings*
(Harcourt Brace Jovanovich, Inc.1968)

Like the advocates of Gaia theory, Berry posits here that the biosphere will remain fully functional (and ultimately self-sustaining) no matter what human damage is inflicted on it. Gaia is larger, wiser, and more resilient than human "civilization" ever was or could be, and Berry's invocation of nuclear Armageddon smoothly giving way to an earth still doing the "patient work / of seasons" reads like a miniature version of the "world without us" in the documentary film and book with that title.[8]

In any case, it seems to me that all the poets cited above

---

8   Alan Weisman, *The World Without Us* (St. Martin's Press, 2007)

were engaged at some level in the kind of quest I had in mind in the title of this piece— a desperate search for a point of natural stability. To flesh out the picture, I will now look briefly at some complete poems by four contemporary poets.

If there were one poet who could talk me down, it might be **William Stafford** (U.S. Poet Laureate, 1970). Stafford was astonishingly prolific. (There are some 3,000 poems of his poems in print, and he supposedly wrote one every day!) He was also a man of tremendous integrity, as indicated by his taking a pacifist stance during World War II.

In his poem "Near," Stafford describes his style as "Talking along in this not quite prose way," and his calm voice generates poems of congenial strangeness, offering an earthy, avuncular comfort that rarely strains to become self-proclaimed "wisdom." But although Stafford's poems are clear, modest, and serene on the surface, they sometimes have their own kind of grand ambition and disturbing intimation. Here, for instance, is one that may contain an allegory of the poet/shaman/storyteller's role in evolutionary history and in discovering modes of sustainability.

> In the White Sky
>
> Many things in the world have
> already happened. You can
> go back and tell about them.
> They are part of what we
> own as we speed along
> through the white sky.
>
> But many things in the world
> haven't yet happened. You help
> them by thinking and writing and acting.
> When they begin, you greet them
> or stop them. You come along
> and sustain the new things.

Once in the white sky there was
a beginning, and I happened to notice
and almost glimpsed what to do.
But now I have come far
to here, and it is away back there.
Some days, I think about it.

from *The Darkness Around Us Is Deep*
(HarperPerennial, 1993), Robert Bly, ed.

Why are we speeding through the sky here—and why is it that ominous *white?* Is the sun going nova, is the light pale from air pollution? Stafford doesn't say; but like him, we need to "think about it" if we are to sustain new things, old things, or anything at all.

I began with one of Stafford's most ambitious and unnerving poems only to contrast it with what I take to be the major strain in his work, which is almost always veering toward a perception of biosphere and our place in it that is fundamentally positive.[9] Here is a beautiful case in point.

Assurance

You will never be alone, you hear so deep
a sound when autumn comes. Yellow
pulls across the hills and thrums
or the silence after lightning before it says
its names— and then the cloud's wide-mouthed
apologies. You were aimed from birth:
you will never be alone. Rain

will come, a gutter filled, an Amazon
long aisles— you never heard so deep a sound,

---

9 There are literally dozens of Stafford's poems revealing this "biosphere-positive" sensibility. However, to my knowledge, he never used the word *biosphere.* He preferred terms like *earth, home,* and sometimes simply *the world,* which in his poem "Earth Dweller," he calls "our only friend."

moss on rock, and years. You turn your head—
That's what the silence meant: you're not alone.
The whole wide world pours down.

from *The Way It Is – New & Selected Poems* (Gray Wolf Press, 1998)

I can't imagine a quieter, more understated articulation of the aesthetics of sustainability. It is contained, however, in one of Stafford's typical, if mostly implied, quotidian narrative structures— a lone man or woman's impressions and musings on a fall day, presumably out of doors. What we overhear in the poem are the speaker's spontaneous half-thoughts triggered by his senses, memories, and deepest longings as he watches the approaching thunderclouds and then the welcome commencement of the rain.

Nothing else "happens" in the poem. That limited dramatic backdrop, however, takes us on an amazing journey— from lonely isolation to communion with the planet, a conversation with Gaia herself if you will. Within this larger arc are several sub-journeys— from impersonal, cosmic silence to "talk" with meteorological forces (lightning and thunder); from human, domestic receptacles of rain (the full gutter) to the greatest "gutter" in earth's entire water-cycle, the Amazon River; from birth's blank slate of animal anonymity (pure genetics set in physiological motion) and the promise of infinite possibility to a sense of the realized destiny and social comfort that every human being longs for from his or her earliest moment of self awareness in infancy: *You were aimed at birth; / you will never be alone.*

How daring but astonishingly right is the verb "aimed" here. As a poet myself, I'm damned jealous— and as someone trained in lit crit, if space permitted, I would love to analyze the poem's technique, particularly its array of metaphors that slide from one to another so effortlessly. How for example, does Stafford get away with telling us that the clouds *apologize?* (And for what, we wonder?) What exactly is the *sound* of "moss on rock, and years"? I think this paradoxical metaphor is not just a clever turn of phrase, but a key to the whole poem. Can an ant literally hear moss growing? Can the planet, in its mediation of geological time, somehow "hear" us and other animals crawling around on its skin, or sense something like sound when another planet swings closely by?

Stafford leaves this poem open to such interrogation, without insisting that it be made. Read it again, slowly, aloud. Your own questions for it will come— or not. No pressure. The other side of that coin is that even in the age of impending ecological and social chaos, Stafford's voice is stable, sane, and yes, assuring. For a brief moment, in its sheer verbal energy and serenity, this poem *does* talk me down.

Stafford's subdued acceptance of earth's bounty— and its ecological limits— doesn't mean that he lacks passion, and even outrage, at the damage being done by the loss of sustainability. He can, in fact, be vehement and rudely didactic at times. A good case is point is this poem:

Weeds in Vacant Lots

We know that it's our fault, these effluent suburbs
the great population spill that we are, and our trash
that thickets of scrub will try to contain.
Return, wilderness; what we held
for a while we will give back. Singly
as we depart we will bequeath our temporary
vainglorious, posturing conquests— back to
the pampas grass, the forgiving vines
 that embrace auto carcasses, refrigerators and
their spilled treasure, the bulldozed
garbage of our civilization.

We know that it's us, the stink
in the sky; the machine that can't stop:
"We are coming; we will bury you."
But we leave space where we can— any place left vacant
fills with volunteers bivouacking till their time
arrives. The great soft hope of the milkweed
explodes, and the wind carries its parachutes

and salvation wherever development hesitates
or allows, even for a season, an opening
for our ultimate friends, these quiet
relentless, healing adversaries.

from *Even In Quiet Places* (Confluence Press, 1996)

Nothing subdued here! The poem bludgeons us with an almost unbearable load of guilt and sorrow stemming from the abuses of laissez faire industrialism. Stafford's exhausting catalogue of eco-insults includes "effluent suburbs," "population spill," "auto carcasses," "bulldozed / garbage," a "stink / in the sky," and perhaps most ominously "the machine that can't stop." That "machine" might be thought of in purely political terms as global capitalism or the "free" trade system mediated (read enforced) by the World Bank, IMF, and if necessary, killer drones. One of the most dreaded ambassadors of this kind of thinking is a *real* machine, though, that appears in the poem: the bulldozer.

However, I would argue that the machine is by extension the sustainability crisis as we have come to know it in the past half century. What insight or perspective on the crisis does the poem contain? In a maneuver that only a poet as emotionally grounded and subtle as Stafford could pull off, "Weeds in a Vacant Lot" does almost as much as "Assurance" to give us a sense of patient tolerance of the world as it is, and even of a modest hope.

Stafford does this by subverting the two common nouns in the title—*weeds* and *vacant*. In ordinary usage, these terms convey unmistakably negative denotations and connotations. Weeds are uninvited, undesirable, uncontrolled, ugly. They "invade" lawns and gardens and deserve the Roundup we eagerly murder them with. Similarly, a vacant thing is an empty, abandoned thing— drained of meaning and utility. A vacant mind is an idle, unreflective, immature mind, perhaps even a retarded one.

So the poem begins with a hugely negative impulse. It then proceeds to systematically undermine that impulse *at the same time* that it unfolds the negative side of its theme even further.

After three full lines of relentless, negative battering, the poem spins around and we suddenly get a surprising, compact reversal: "Return, wilderness." It's worth noting that this imperative does not end with an exclamation mark— as it would have in Walt Whitman. In any case, the commanding phrase lands like a left jab to the jaw— and more or less stops the 'unstoppable' machine in its tracks. The phrase is surely also an allusion to Hopkins' "long live the weeds and the wilderness yet" — except that it celebrates the weeds in close, among us, not somewhere "out there" where civilization hasn't yet landed on the soil.

From here on, the negative sway of the poem will be met with a positive one that prevents Stafford's efforts from seeming like a mere rant or "tree-hugger" lament. First, comes "pampas grass. " ("I am the grass. Let me work" wrote Sandburg, and Stafford agrees.) This great plant of the Argentinean pampas is the antithesis of a weed— an image of vast, wild vegetation that (at least temporarily) would seem to be beyond the reach of our "vainglorious, posturing conquests" (like Roundup). Then those "forgiving vines" arrive, another wild growth that actually "embraces" our junked cars, as if forgiving us our trespasses against Mother Earth— by covering them over, returning them to a jungle state, "greening" them if you will.

In the concluding stanza, this reversal continues. The vacancy of the title is now replaced with *space*— an open, free, cool word as opposed to the claustrophobic sense of heat and confinement of an urban vacant lot. Extending the change even further, Stafford drolly suggests that we intentionally leave empty lots wherever and whenever we can, because they will attract "volunteers" who will "bivouac" on the open, unoccupied ground "till their time / arrives."

The poem's deepest intuitions now emerge, as the image of a patient camping troop introduces what can only be called a military metaphor— more than a little surprising from a life-long pacifist like Stafford— and an undeclared war dominates the rest of the poem. The dirt of the vacant lot is seen as a landing zone for any army of the "great soft hope of milkweed" which will "explode," not like bombs but as parachutes of "salvation." That is, the only ordinance in Gaia's arsenal is her sheer *fertility*— represented here by the swirling descent of millions of seeds in their silky, wispy white parachutes.

Given the chance, these "paratroopers" will turn the dead vacant lot back into living ground. Yes, they are weeds— which is to say life. So the invading forces are no threat, no cause for fear or triggering of sirens. They are the diametric opposite: "our ultimate friends... quiet / relentless, healing adversaries." *Adversaries*? Of what or whom? Not of Gaia or the vacant lot, but rather of the "machine," the proponents of endless and therefore unsustainable growth whose mantra is "We are coming; we will bury you."

So Stafford renders a daring (and perhaps desperate) conceit: the war waged by humans against life on this planet, as brutal and omnipresent as it is, may ultimately be won not by a counter violence but by bringers of "great, soft hope" who, in their very softness and silent arrivals, are as relentless as weeds. Perhaps we could even say that the return of sturdy new plant communities and animal life in the blast zone of the Chernobyl explosion, much earlier than biologists predicted, is a kind of vindication of Stafford's prophesy in "Weeds in a Vacant Lot."

I leave Stafford with an unlikely comparison: e. e. cummings. Cummings' avant-garde experimental forms and lush lyricism mark him as following a totally different path from Stafford's "not quite prose" way. And yet in "La Guerre" (i.e., World War I) one of the earlier poet's most memorable efforts, he presents a vision of the assault upon the biosphere in terms much like that in "Weeds." Cummings begins the poem with "the bigness of cannon" and ends it with a long, passionate call to "O sweet spontaneous / earth" who, he says, will always respond to war of any kind and its "prurient philosophers" in the same way:

> thou answerest
> them only with
>   spring

* * *

The large body of poetry that **Gary Snyder** has produced over the past half century is a cornucopia of meditations on the natural world, his work sharpened by experiences in mountain-climbing, logging jobs, merchant ship crews, translating Asian verse, and practicing Zen Buddhism, as well as his years as a professor of literature. Here is a Snyder poem that traces a river's history out of and then back into a sustainable mode— but by an incredibly ironic means. (The 'redds' in the last line are salmon, and the italicized note at the end of the poem is Snyder's.)

To the Liking of Salmon

Spawning salmon dark and jerky
Just below the surface ripple
Shallow lower Yuba

River bed—old mining gravels
Mimicking a glacier outflow
Perfect for the redds below Parks Bar.

*(how hydraulic mining made the Yuba Goldfields
like a post glacial river in Alaska)*

from *Danger on Peaks* (Shoemaker Hoard, 2005)

With his degree in anthropology and sometimes referred to as "The Poet Laureate of Deep Ecology," Snyder often displays both a dazzling simplicity and a haunting depth— and, as in this next case, an abruptly registered humility in the face of the self-sufficiency of nature.

Pine Tree Tops

In the blue night
frost haze, the sky glows
with the moon
pine tree tops
bend snow-blue, fade

into sky, frost, starlight,
the creak of boots.
rabbit tracks, deer tracks,
what do we know.

from *No Nature – New and Selected Poems*
(Pantheon Books, 1992)

Finally, in "Prayer for the Great Family" (in the same volume) modeled on a Mohawk ceremonial chant, Snyder acknowledges the ecological wisdom of the many indigenous cultures of North America.   This poem is emblematic of the spiritual stance we must somehow regain if the word "sustainable" is ever to become a real guide of socio-political priorities. It begins like this:

Gratitude to Mother Earth, sailing through night and day—
and to her soil: rich rare and sweet
in our minds so be it.

The poem continues with salutations to Air, Wild Beings, Water, Sun, and the Great Sky. These entities may be mythic deities in the Mohawk pantheon— but they are also indispensable variables in any equation spelling out sustainability in the modern world.

* * *

I turn next to one of my own poems. In it, like Snyder, I seek an image of cultural-ecological balance in the voices of indigenous people, in this case ancestral forbears of today's Hopi, Navajo, Hualapai, Southern Paiute, and Havasupai. The setting is the Grand Canyon, at a place called Unkar Delta, a wide alluvial bank on the Colorado River, with rich soil and enough sunlight to sustain (that word again!) crops like corn, beans, and squash.

The site of major archeological excavations, Unkar has yielded thousands of artifacts (pottery shards, textiles, sandals, stone tools, etc.) and before the arrival of any European in North America it was inhabited by native peoples for a very long period. When midsummer heat ended one growing season down in the canyon, these tribes went up to the cooler plateaus on the north rim to plant crops and bring the harvest down to the delta in the late fall.

On Unkar Delta

We plow the ground.
We drop the seed.
We go to the river.
We bring the water
to green corn rows
calling the Corn God
and the River God
to bless our crop.
The season turns.

We climb to the rim.
We plow the ground.
We drop the seed.
We fill the *ollas*
with snow water
and bring it to the corn
calling the Corn God
and the Snow God
to bless our crop.
The season turns.

We climb back down.
We plow the ground.
We drop the seed.
We do this at Unkar—
for one thousand years.

from *Grand Canyon Days* (Xlibris, 2011)

*   *   *

I will end with a poem by my wife, Judy Lauter, because it creates a strong, beautiful sense of planetary peace and tranquility— qualities intrinsic to any possible world of sustainability.

Trees Sleep, Too

Across the lake, birds
dip and rise against
the trees I can still see.

The lake's silken, shining
surface reflects the evening
sky that shares its color.

The darkening sky lets coolness
down, the lake's waters
release coolness up

to meet in middle air to make
a breeze that stirs
the trees around the lake,

a sighing and relaxing
in the leaves, the chlorophyll
factories shutting down

now, the sugar made
and stored away, and all
the night to rest.

The bio-cycle of sunlight-to-chlorophyll-to-sugar in tree metabolism is a perfect symbol of sustainability in the natural world. The speaker connects this process to birds, water, trees, the evening breeze, and a nightfall that seems to bless (a restful "sleep"). The web of life here is presented with the kind of scientific precision Emily Dickinson enjoyed so much— and in exactly the sense that Lovelock meant by "geo-physiology." That is, there is a temperature differential at sundown between water and land which actually *creates* the evening breeze; it in turn creates a kind of lullaby for the leaves, letting them "sigh and relax" for the night (that is, stop their photosynthesis). The organic and inorganic engaged in a cosmic dance.

This linkage of nature to feelings of abundance, ripeness, and restfulness gives the poem its kinetic energy and sense of serene joy. But for me the best stroke is the use of the word *factory*. The term reverberates rather harshly, since it is diction from an entirely different realm of language than that of the rest of the poem. "Factory" has connotations of machinery, assembly lines, time clocks, paymasters, etc. — all of which are totally absent from the world of trees, lakes, and birds. That very absence, however, is the covert theme of the poem. Nature's factories *need none of those things.* Its factories are entirely self-sustaining— and there is nothing at all desperate in their means of achieving that state.

Epilogue
COINCIDENCES, CONFESSIONS, QUALIFICATIONS

Coincidences
Ironically, in the same week that I was invited to contribute to this volume, I discovered the book *Can Poetry Save the Earth? — A Field Guide to Nature Poems* (Yale University Press, 2009) by John Felstiner. Great, I thought— this guy has done half my work for me! The title's half-serious, half-wistful rhetorical question locates the solace of poetry in the context of our unfolding planetary crisis—and the book did help me find some prime examples of eco-poetry, particularly in Dickinson and Snyder.[10]

Felstiner's survey of more than fifty poets is fresh and nuanced, celebrating in a meticulous prose both their craft and their insights on our current ecological crisis. He ends the book with this query: "Can Poetry Save the Earth? For sure, person by person, our earthly challenge hangs on the sense and spirit that poems can awaken." That strikes an appropriate note of humility in addressing such a vast subject— poetry's influence is

---

10   The book is enhanced by a unique selection of color photographs, from Blake's *Creation*, which depicts the madly abstract Urizen (Blake's version of Jehovah) attempting to geometrically measure the cosmos, to a child's two-part, colored-chalk picture heartbreakingly called *Yucky Pollution, Shiny Pretty*.

finite, its blessings a necessary but not sufficient element in any reconstitution of a sane and sustainable world.

Confessions
I began my writing life trying to take up W. H. Auden's challenge to poets, in his elegy for W.B. Yeats:

> Follow poet, follow right
> To the bottom of the night
> With your unconstraining voice
> Still persuade us to rejoice.

Today, the bottom of the night seems darker than I ever imagined— and it has become much harder for me to persuade myself to rejoice, much less to persuade anyone else. So, no, I haven't talked myself down. To the contrary, I still fear, as a friend put it recently, that we are probably "an evolutionary dead-end species."

And yet, I also fervently believe with Keats that the poetry of earth is never dead, with Stafford that the earth "speaks everything to us," and with C.D. Wright that there is a sanctuary in the mind made of poetry and music and laughter. There *are* consolations, very real ones, in what Robinson Jeffers called "the honey of peace in old poems. "

I further believe that the ethos of sustainability found at the heart of the greatest poems of the English language can contribute to a wide range of redemptive environmental efforts. As Paul Hawken points out, there are literally millions of such projects underway now, large and small, around the globe, and I could just as well have begun this essay with a catalogue of them. I say hail and godspeed to everyone involved in such endeavors— with the hope that the labors of the community of poets will increasingly reinforce their efforts.

Qualifications
However, I feel obligated to say that I find nothing in poetry, not in mine certainly, nor that of any other poet, living or dead, in

any language, nothing that seems to embody a truly sustainable, ecological consciousness that even remotely approximates the sensibility of pre-industrial indigenous populations and some of their present-day heirs–from the Hopi and Tohono O'odham of the desert Southwest, to the Australian aboriginals, the Pumé of Venezuela, the pygmy people of Africa, and the Yanomami of South America.[11]

Of course, we must constantly guard against idealizing or trivializing the complex ethnographies of these cultures, and so I acknowledge that some of the ancient, tribal cultures around the world have participated in the on-going "Holocene Extinction" as well as intra-tribal violence. But we can still look to the tribal peoples who have historically demonstrated a graceful, instinctive grasp of Gaia's intentions, habits, and (above all) needs that have been lost to modernity. Taking that look in a serious way is one of the last, best hopes for us as a species of learning again how to say:

In our minds, so be it.

---

11   See Frank Waters, *The Book of the Hopi* (Viking Press, 1963); Gary Paul Nabhan, *A Naturalist in Papago Indian [Tohono O'odham] Territory* (North Point Press,1982); Harvey Arden, *Dreamkeepers: A Spirit-Journey into Aboriginal Australia* (HarperCollins Perennial, 1994); Pei lin Yu, *Hungry Lightning: Notes of a Woman Anthropologist in Venezuela* (University of New Mexico Press, 1997); Jean-Pierre Hallet, *Congo Kitabu* (Random House, 1964); Louis Sarno, *Songs from the Forest – My Life Among the Ba-Benjelle Pygmies* (Penguin Books, 1993) and the CD *Echoes of the Forest – Music of the Central African Pygmies* (Ellipsis Arts, 1995); Colin Turnbull, *The Forest People* (Simon & Schuster, 1961); Dennison Berwick, *Savages: The Life and Killing of the Yanomami* [Kindle Edition] (Voyage Press, 2009); Kenneth Good and David Chanoff, *Into The Heart: One Man's Pursuit of Love and Knowledge Among the Yanomami* (Addison-Wesley Publishing Company, 1997).

CHAPTER III

Communities

Sustainable Communities

Jerry Williams

Introduction

Horton, Kansas like much of the rural Midwest is just not what it once was. Founded in 1985 by the Rock Island Railroad, Horton was a company town. By locating two large locomotive repair shops in midst of the tall-grass plains, the railroad provided an impressive, something from nothing, start to this little prairie town. In the years that followed, large-scale farming took hold of Horton. With topsoil in places approaching thirty feet deep, there seemed no end in sight for the prospects of locals; there were jobs and lots of them. No one worried much about the future.

Today Horton boasts 1,800 residents, less than half of what it once was, and a poverty rate that is more than double the national average. The railroad is gone and the railroad shops have been converted into light manufacturing firms. At $9.25 per hour they provide about the best wages in the county. Farming continues but few seriously try to make a living at it. Over coffee at the Charger Stop, local farmers sometimes joke about wishing polygamy was legal. They laugh, "that way I could have more than one wife with a job to support the farm."

The decline of rural communities in the United States is well documented. In fact, between 1990 and 2000, two out of five U.S. counties declined in population (Census 2000). All places like Horton can tell stories about the specific reasons for their decline. For Horton it was the loss of the railroad and the advent of industrial agriculture. For others it might be the decline of the steel industry, or the collapse of fishing, or the end of the timber economy. What all these places have in common is that for one reason or another the global economy has passed them by. Once dependent upon local production, they now find no convincing economic rationale to continue, but they do. Perhaps from inertia, or the stubbornness of having no other choice, generation after generation they continue, mired in poverty and a host of social problems.

We start with this picture of rural communities to make the point that sustainability is not an abstract idea; rather, human beings live in real places, with real histories, and real problems. If sustainability is to be more than an abstract idea, it must address the spirit of these communities by speaking about what matters to them. In what follows, we argue the unsustainable present is at least in part created because we treat communities and the individuals who comprise them as abstract variables in a larger economic calculus. Divorced from the particularities of place, culture, and belief, our communities have become disposable dormitories for faceless, interchangeable laborers.

If human life is to be sustainable, communities must be re-embedded in their own particular landscapes, cultural traditions, and beliefs. By treating communities as abstract producers of globally traded products, or as consumers of goods produced in distant places, the environmental damage created by humans is itself made abstract and as a result no one's responsibility. To achieve sustainability, the real and particular features of real and particular communities must be included in the conversation. Let us now consider how local communities and the people who comprise them have come to be abstractions in the modern world.

The Past - From Particular to Abstract

At the turn of the twentieth century local communities were indeed particular places. Towns like Horton and cities like Chicago had unique social characters with unique community lives. Particular communities are those that are embedded in a specific local environment and depend upon specific local resources. Because the environment is not the same everywhere, these communities and their social institutions, beliefs, and ideas often took on unique dimensions. In theory, a truly particular community is one that is completely isolated from other communities, and with no trade from abroad must learn to live with the resources that are near. In a particular society both abundance and scarcity are experienced firsthand. For example, if such a community over farms their agricultural land, they one day must face the consequences.

For the sake of historical accuracy we must readily admit that few communities have ever been completely isolated. Pre-Columbian trade networks in the Americas, for example, were comprised of a robust trade in metals used for ceremonial purposes (Townsend, Sharp et al. 2004). Even this somewhat small scale level of trade, however, led to what we can call abstractness in local communities. By this we refer to a means of social existence that is not directly linked to a particular environmental niche. To continue this example, Pre-Columbian trade in the Americas gradually led to community specialization. Some communities, for example became regional ceremonial centers producing highly prized ceremonial objects, yet others produced flint for tool manufacturing.

The key to understanding what abstractness means in this context is to keep in mind that once a community becomes economically oriented toward trade, environmental cues about sustainability become harder to hear. If a community depends upon the production of goods for exchange with a neighboring community for the agricultural goods it produces, individual labor and local environment resources become abstract in the sense that they are no longer linked to my particular needs. Rather, their value is linked to other people in other places about which I have no direct knowledge. Abstractness in this sense severs communities from the particular environmental niches in which they came about; thus, it makes overuse and environmental damage much more likely.

Perhaps the most important story to be told about American communities in the 20th century is that, although they were once relatively particular places, they are now largely abstractions. The current system of global economic exchange has helped to assure this. This is why even the most rural communities in America are today almost homogenous with all others. In contrast, not too long ago these communities had distinct regional dialects, food preferences, and ways of being. In their place we now find one-size-fits-all "industrial parks," fast food restaurants, and Wal-Mart stores. More importantly, gone also are the connections these communities once had to their local environments. Far from a romantic or idealized connection, communities had a pragmatic interest in preserving local streams and agriculture. Without these resources the community could not continue.

Today American communities exist in a world in which the nature of production and value accumulation are obfuscated by global trade. On a daily basis, we buy products made all over the world by people will never meet. These anonymous people seem familiar however; they are people just like us. Living and producing in the same global market, we ourselves are mere abstractions, anonymous consumers producing anonymous goods disconnected from our histories, places, and beliefs. Even our educational systems are implements of abstraction. Once controlled by local school boards, schools are now increasingly producers of abstract knowledge assessed by standardized tests emphasizing science and mathematics because they are thought to be the engines of economic competition.

The Future - From the Abstract to the Particular

Enmeshed in a competitive world economic system that has produced a high level of abstraction, local communities are faced with a challenging future. How can they move from the nameless, ahistorical, and placeless reality of "big box retail" to a one-size-does-not-fit-all livable community? The answer, we believe, is in creating and maintaining a meaningful life of the community that is deeply embedded in the specifics of local geography, history, culture, and values.

The non-abstract life of the community is first and foremost a shared life. It is you and I – all of us, engaged by, and sometimes constrained by the mutual life of people being together in a particular place. That is, the life of the community is not simply the aggregate of individuals pursing their own individual interests. To use a term coined by Robert Putman (2000), to live in a community is not to "bowl alone." Community life is also not the life of institutions. Institutions such as corporations are created for community life not community life for the benefit of corporations. This is why corporate "big box retail" is so devastating to small communities. By making the life of the corporation (its needs, motives, and means) the major organizing principle of community life, the values and cares of each of us are obscured by our institutionally sanctioned role as "worker" and "consumer." All of this is to say that real community life is composed of human relationships, not the abstract roles provided us by unimaginably large and complex corporations. Further, because the life of the community is founded in the relationships of real people, it at its best is highly particular, based in history, culture, and specificity of place.

Revitalizing the life of the community is key to changing our communities from abstract and unsustainable places to viable and particular communities. This shift starts with a change in vision. That is, we must change how we look at the very places we live. Imagine yourself on a summer vacation in the United States. With no particular plan, you start to drive. Along the way you pick places to visit. You select Brunswick, Georgia to taste Brunswick stew; you spend a night in Daytona, Florida to enjoy the beaches; and you make your way to San Francisco to walk through China Town. Now use your tourist vision to see the town in which you live. Without doubt you will not see retail strip developments, or big box retail. Rather, you will look for the places, people and things that make your community particular, and as a result, because you are a resident, you will discover what makes you a particular and unique person. This is how community life is born.

By first discovering the real and particular features of the places we live, we can then start to make decisions that foster the life of the community and thereby discover our own identities.

The second step toward rebuilding community life is more complicated than simply recognizing uniqueness. It also requires action. To be a community it is necessary to retrain our thinking and perspective to think about community first. Let us look at our educational system as an example.

Our communities are home to schools of varying quality and educational outcomes. Matthew Crawford (2009) suggests that what is true of all of these schools is the education provided there is of a particularly abstract type. The focus of American education, according to Crawford, is to produce college bound "knowledge workers," workers that have a generic set of skills who are capable of working in a variety of settings and in a variety of places. To the extent that this is true, community life takes second seat to the institutional needs of society. As a result, our students are trained not to see possibilities for community transformation that are present in their own communities. This is ironic. Community tax dollars are spent on educational systems that are institutionally biased against healthy community life.

If local educational systems are to support community life, they must be much more closely tied to what the community needs and can produce. By knowing local history, culture, values, and the specifics of place, our educational systems must teach students the skills necessary to revive the places they live. Educational reform toward vocational programs and small business entrepreneurship are examples of programs that can benefit local communities. When these programs are tied to government policies that support local investment and the ready availability of capital, they can quickly transform local economies. This will never happen, however, if we continue to teach our children to be abstract knowledge workers in a global system that values only global production and hyper consumerism.

Conclusion

Here we have described in general detail the historical and economic processes that have served together to damage local communities in the United States by transforming their residents into abstractions - workers and producers in a global economic system. We have asserted that healthy communities are the centerpiece of a sustainable future and that if progress is to be made we will need to change the way we see our own communities. We will also need to refocus our educational systems in a way that produces young people with the skills and desire to revitalize our declining community landscape. In the essays the follow we explore these contentions in more detail.

References

Census (2000). "U.S. Census, http://www.census.gov/."

Crawford, M. B. (2009). *Shop class as soulcraft : an inquiry into the value of work*. New York, Penguin Press.

Putnam, R. D. (2000). *Bowling alone : the collapse and revival of American community*. New York, Simon & Schuster.

Townsend, R. F., R. V. Sharp, et al. (2004). *Hero, hawk, and open hand : American Indian art of the ancient Midwest and South*. Chicago New Haven, Art Institute of Chicago ; In Association with Yale University Press.

CREATING SUSTAINABLE CITIES[1]

Alex Garvin

Sustainable cities must satisfy "the needs of the present without compromising the ability of future generations to meet their own needs." This definition of sustainability was first enunciated by the Brundtland Commission (1987) in *Our Common Future*. It is an opaque definition. What are the "needs" of a contemporary city, or the "needs" its inhabitants will face in the future? How do we meet the first without "compromising the ability of future generations to meet their own needs"?

The Brundtland Commission does not answer these questions. Instead, it poses challenges that include dealing with an exploding population, potential shortages of resources (particularly land, food and energy), threatened species and ecosystems, etc... Then, assuming there is agreement on the nature of these challenges and the methods of meeting them, it calls for action to preserve species and ecosystems (by segregating land and people), enact legislation to minimize the role of parochial interests (by transferring power from local communities to international institutions), and maximize global resources (by regulating what individuals and businesses can do).

For nearly a quarter of a century, many self-designated "environmentalists" have agreed that these identified challenges are real and that their proposed action program is necessary. They are dumbfounded that much of the world's population does not share their concerns and that many governments are unwilling to enact the necessary legislation to make their proposed program a reality.

1 I would like to thank Matthew Goldstein for his invaluable comments and suggestions, which helped me to make this a particularly convincing essay.

These "environmentalists," so often willing to shoulder the world's problems, are often blind to the fact that the impracticality of their program is a detriment to gaining widespread approval of the goals they have identified for achieving sustainability. Although they believe their program is the very essence of sustainability, they should have long ago perceived that what they are proposing was unsustainable. Their definition is too narrow and excludes too many other objectives. It is so narrow and exclusive that they cannot get most of the world to accept it, as proven by the many failures of the Kyoto Protocol and the unwillingness of so many American legislators to impose a cap-and-trade program throughout the United States.

The first deficiency of the traditional "environmentalist" program is that it assumes people are not part of nature and that their activities are not natural, because they believe that, by definition, human action is always deleterious to other species. The omnipresence of human beings, however, means that there is not an ecosystem on this planet that has not already been affected, directly or indirectly, by humanity. Therefore, no current or future condition of the "natural" order can be considered truly sustainable unless it includes the people and their activities.

Its second deficiency is that it assumes stasis is the standard condition for nature, absent intervention by people. On one hand, many environmentalists posit that any desirable world is one that existed prior to its corruption by an intruder; on the other hand, it takes for granted that mutation is bad. No systems, human or natural, are free from change for very long. Whether in the form of evolution or economic development, change is an undeniable constant and driving force for adaptation and growth.

The third problem this ideology poses is that it promotes generalized goals that may or may not be applicable to every location. Transit-oriented development may be an easily achieved and appropriate objective in Chicago or New York, but far too expensive and difficult to create in hills around Boulder, Colorado, or grasslands around Lincoln, Nebraska. Moreover, residents of most low-density suburbs are unalterably opposed to high-rise construction replacing one-family houses. Forcing these communities to accept higher densities is not only inappropriate, it is also far too difficult to achieve politically.

Let me assure you: I am not a proponent of environmental degradation. I have simply been trying to shake you up enough to think about what sustainability means and take the opportunity to suggest how we can create more sustainable cities.

The difficulty with this traditional "environmentalism" is that it calls for the establishment of a sustainable version of nature that will be accepted by a docile population. That goal is untenable and unreachable. There is no line between humanity and nature. Useful, realistic criteria for sustainability can only be developed through an understanding and acceptance of the deep and abiding links between people and nature.

If we realize that meeting humanity's contemporary and future needs means recognizing people's role as an integral part of the ecosystem, then genuine environmentalists must accept and adjust to continuing change. Thus, creating sustainable cities means adopting policies that are based on their continuing evolution.

Rather than search for the requirements of a sustainable, continually changing global ecosystem that merely "accepts" human beings, we should be seeking to define the requirements of a sustainable human habitat. The broader definition must include six aspects of sustainability: environmental, functional, financial, social, aesthetic, and political.

An **environmentally sustainable** human habitat is one with an easily available supply of healthy air and water, with large, predominantly natural areas ("patches") that contain a wide range of self-perpetuating flora and fauna, connected by corridors that can be used by those species going from one natural area to another (Forman 1995). Maintaining ecosystems through creative landscape management and design provides direct benefits to human development. The foliage in those areas exchanges carbon dioxide for oxygen, muffles noise, and lowers ambient temperatures during hot summers. The ground in such areas retains and filters storm water and vehicular runoff, and in so doing reduces the need for water treatment facilities. Human beings are among the users of both the natural areas and the corridors; so are birds, reptiles, fungi, and flora.

A **functionally sustainable** human habitat requires an infrastructure that supplies the daily demands of its people and businesses and a public realm that accommodates whatever activities they choose to engage in during their lifetimes. Changing tastes and the ravages of time mean that maintenance will eventually be necessary to preserve and continually improve functionality. The infrastructure of transportation networks, water supply and distribution, and waste collection and disposal is not only expensive to create but requires ongoing, expensive stewardship. It has to be continually adjusted to changing quantities and locations of users. The same is true of the public realm - the fundamental element of any human habitat: streets, squares, parks, and public buildings. This public realm is the framework within which common human activities take place. The difference between the infrastructure and public realms necessary to support human settlements is that each component of the infrastructure deals with a single function, such as supplying water or disposing waste, while an effective public realm must be multi-functional. A fine street, for example, is more than a corridor for moving trucks, buses, and automobiles. It is also where people encounter one another, move around, shop, do business, play, or just wander. Unlike infrastructure, which is relatively inadaptable to changing populations, the public realm must be continually adjusted. The unpaved streets that served the horse and buggy world of the 19th century must be paved, electrically lighted, and provide access to telephone and internet service in the 21st century.

Residents of Greece, Ireland, Portugal, and even the United States are learning that their habitat must be **financially**

sustainable. During the first decade of the 21st century, their governments had been spending on services and investments in amounts greater than the revenues they were collecting. By the end of that decade, lenders who had sustained that spending were now threatening to stop providing further funds unless they balanced their budgets.

It is easy to say expenditures should match revenues. But that misses the point. Many of the expenditures are as important to meet needs of future generations as they are to meet present needs. That requires spending far beyond current revenues. New York City did not pay all at once for the Croton Reservoir and Aqueduct System that brought water to New York City. The 1834 New York State legislature (and referendum voters the following year) approved borrowing the necessary funds. They sold long-term bonds. Debt service on those bonds came from fees and taxes collected on an annual basis. New couples do the same when they use money from a long-term mortgage to purchase a new house with bedrooms for as yet unborn children. Like the governments that use annual revenues to retire the bonds, these families make monthly payments until the mortgage has been paid down.

There has always been a very simple way to determine whether expenditures on human habitats are sustainable. When those expenditures add sufficient value to that habitat, its occupants are able to produce additional goods and services and use the resultant increase in revenues to pay for the investment. Borrowing to be repaid from that additional value is clearly sustainable. Chicago, Atlanta, and other American cities do this all the time. They call it tax increment financing.

Just as Frederick Law Olmsted (1997) provided a convincing rationale for environmental sustainability, he provided a convincing rationale for **social sustainability**. Explaining what he was trying to do in the design of New York's Central Park, he wrote of the importance of bringing together rich and poor, young and old, "each individual adding by his mere presence to the pleasure of all others."

There are human habitats, like Switzerland, that have been socially sustainable for centuries. But, as Orson Welles says in the movie The Third Man: "In Italy, for thirty years under the Borgias, they had warfare, terror, murder and bloodshed, but they produced Michelangelo, Leonardo da Vinci, and the Renaissance. In Switzerland they had brotherly love, they had five hundred years of democracy and peace – and what did that produce? The cuckoo clock."

Even in Switzerland, cuckoo clocks by themselves are not enough to sustain human habitats. **Aesthetic sustainability** is manifest in every corner of the country. Whether one is in Geneva, Zurich, Lausanne, or anywhere in Switzerland, however, the environment provides continually changing, fascinating experiences that are never the same a week, a month, or a year later. It includes habitats that are as aesthetically satisfying to residents as they are to the millions of tourists who go there to experience them.

There are always proposals to make different human habitats more livable. Some proposals, however, are not **politically sustainable**. A section of highway in Maryland, financed by the National Interstate and Defense Highways Act of 1956 (Public Law 84-627) is a good example. The interstate highway network had overwhelming public approval because it made production of good and services easier, cheaper, and accessible to an increasing population. The highways, however, did not always affect communities for the better. Sometimes, they diverted traffic from main streets in small towns, in the process eliminating their customers and causing stores to go out of business. They also displaced thousands of people and their jobs.

General approval of the system by most people was not enough. For any leg of the proposed interstate highway system to be built, it had to be politically sustainable. In 1968, Barbara Mikulski, later U. S. Senator from Maryland, organized community opposition to a proposed 16-lane section of interstate highway I-95 that was to have passed through Fells Point, the Polish-

American neighborhood of Baltimore in which she lived. At a local meeting, she explained: "I jumped up on a table and I cried, 'The British couldn't take Fells Point... and goddamn if we'll let the State Roads Commission take Fells Point" (McNichol 2006). Mikulski helped to put together a coalition that included residents of the predominantly African-American neighborhood of Rosemont, which also would have been dismembered by the highway. They won the battle and kept the highway from passing through their neighborhoods. The system itself, however, went ahead because in most places it was politically sustainable.

By now you must be wondering whether there is a model one can use for creating sustainable cities. There is. You can get there by a car or a train. It isn't far, far away, or over the rainbow. It's Manhattan and it's environmentally, functionally, financially, socially, aesthetically, and politically sustainable.

Manhattan is home to a huge range of species. More than 325 different kinds of birds have been observed in the 842 acres of Central Park alone, including House Wrens, Downy Woodpeckers, Wood Thrushes, Gray Catbirds, White-breasted Nuthatches.... not just pigeons and sparrows (McCabe 2011). New Yorkers keep improving Manhattan's natural environment. Since the early 1960s, the city has added a 5-mile-long Hudson River Park, 36 acres of parkland in Battery Park City, and more than 500 plazas covering 3.5 million square feet of privately-owned, public open space (Garvin 2010, p.50-51; Kayden 2000). Its GreenStreets Program is responsible for transforming dozens of traffic triangles into islands of nature (Garvin 2010, p.44). Mayor Michael Bloomberg's PlaNYC has initiated planting one million trees. This year, on the 350-foot-long block where I live, for example, nine street trees have been added to the fourteen that were already there.

There are few cities that function as well or are as livable. Tourists from all over the world find their way around its numbered streets and avenues. They may be confused when they get on the subway, but it brings millions of people to and from work every day. The water supply system, initiated in the 19th century, remains one of the finest in any metropolis. Consumers usually find stores that sell what they are looking for quickly, easily, and for a reasonable price. In fact, New Yorkers invented the expression: "I can get it for you wholesale."

When it comes to financial sustainability, Manhattan is legendary. Its businesses and residents pay the taxes that support expenditures on the Island and billions more in the four other boroughs.

Manhattan is one of the most socially sustainable islands anywhere, teaming with the languages and cultures of the world. It is host to immigrant students from more than 180 nations. Its residents speak more than 140 languages. Nearly two-thirds of its population has at least one parent who was born outside the United States. It is a testament to how a completely diverse population can live together.

Tens of millions of tourists travel to Manhattan to experience its theaters, museums, concerts, restaurants, retail stores, and much, much more. They will tell you about all the wonderful experiences you can have there. They keep coming back, too.

Politics in Manhattan are legendary, having produced such diverse figures as Theodore Roosevelt, Fiorello LaGuardia, Adam Clayton Powell Jr., and Daniel Patrick Moynihan. Three of its last six mayors have either seriously considered or actually competed to be the Democratic or Republican Party's candidate for President. Manhattan has had twelve community boards since Borough President (and later Mayor) Robert F. Wagner Jr. established them in 1951. The reason for adding a community approval layer to the city's decision-making system was that residents were increasingly unhappy with proposals for their neighborhood. Their opposition was slowing down and sometimes preventing public approval. The involvement of the community in the development process increased the political sustainability of proposals in every Manhattan neighborhood. They became the model for establishment of similar neighborhood entities throughout the city and later throughout the country.

Can we create sustainable cities? Of course; to do so, however, we need to expand our conception of sustainability and seriously consider emulating the sustainable elements of Manhattan.

References

Brundtland Commission. (The World Commission on Environment and Development), *Our Common Future* (Oxford: Oxford University Press, 1987), 8.

Forman, R.T.T. *Land Mosaics – The Ecology of Landscapes and Regions*, (Cambridge: Cambridge University Press, 1995).

Garvin, A. *Public Parks: The Key To Livable Communities*, (New York: W. W. Norton, 2010),

Garvin, op. cit., 44.

Kayden, J.S. *Privately Owned Public Open Space* (New York: Wiley, 2000).

McCabe, R. A. *The Ramble in Central Park – A Wilderness West of Fifth*, (New York: Abbeville Press Publishers, 2011), 57.

McNichol, D. *The Incredible Story of the U.S. Interstate System*, (New York: Sterling Publishing Co. Inc, 2006), 157.

Olmsted,F. L. "Public Parks and the Enlargement of Towns," in Charles E. Beveridge and Carolyn F. Hoffman, eds., *The Papers of Frederick Law Olmsted,* Supplementary Series, vol. 1: *The Writings on Public Parks, Parkways, and Park Systems* (Balitimore: Johns Hopkins University Press, 1997), 186.

Sustainable Communities:
Social Connectedness and Social Capital

Kathleen Belanger

What is Community?

If the term "sustainable" is difficult to define, the term "community" may be even more amorphous. Community is derived from the Latin word, communis or common (Webster). It can refer to a place (a city, town village), a society with common laws, or people with similar interests. Depending on one's view of life and its purpose(s), a community can include those in the past and those in the future. We may think of our ancestors as part of our community, care for their memories and their burial spaces, live our own lives to honor them. We may view our progeny as those who will carry on our traditions, and treasure those to come enough to leave them resources to live happily instead of burdens and challenges. Our communities can focus solely on our own space, or we can envision our community to be interdependent with other geographic communities. As Peter Block suggests, "The social fabric of community comes from an expanding shared sense of belonging. It is shaped by the idea that only when we are connected and care for the well-being of the whole that a civil and democratic society is created." We seem faced with the puzzle of where to draw our community's boundaries so that we can belong, be cared for, experience well-being.

Community and Well-being

If our communities are places to belong, be cared for and experience well-being, it will help to understand what the terms "belonging", being "cared for" and "well-being" refer to. Wendell Berry describes the mistaken notion that economic development is the primary measure of well-being, and ultimately asks "What are people for?" (Berry, p. 123). If well-being refers only to a growing economy, then the outmigration of people from rural to urban centers, i.e. from one community to a different one, is sensible. From a purely economic point of view, to challenge this process of "hallowing out the middle" (Carr & Kefalas, 2009), or draining rural America of its brightest young men and women, is to challenge our own well-being, at least economically. Certainly well-being infers an economy sufficient to support and sustain life. However, when does a stronger economy actually translate into reduced well-being? McKibben (2007) suggests that our efforts to grow our economy, i.e. produce more, have actually resulted in reduced quality of life in economically wealthy countries, while jeopardizing life itself in other countries and even our own future. If our common good includes care for not only our current economy, but our farmland and system of sustainable food supply (Berry, p. 124), i.e. for "our common future" (Brundtland, 1987), then our view of community has to encompass both rural and urban partnership, global partnerships, and a variety of partnerships across various systems. Our boundaries of belonging have to extend to include a variety of ecosystems in order for any of them to be "cared for."

Community Transformation and Social Capital

That is precisely the task necessary for sustainability: to shift our parochial or provincial view of our community, i.e. a view of community that sees only our own "province" or "parish" to the more accurate one of interdependence. Shifting our view is more, however, than just changing the boundaries of the target systems. It also includes substantial transformation and the creation of social capital.

Social capital refers to resources available by membership in a social network (Bourdieu, 1991; Portes, 1998) that include trust and norms (Coleman, 1990; Portes, 1998; Putnam, 2000; Putnam, Feldstein & Cohen, 2004)) and that result in outcomes that would not otherwise be possible (Coleman, 1990; Putnam, Feldstein & Cohen, 2004).

Increasing Awareness

The first step in developing a social network of trust and shared norms related to sustainability is increasing awareness. Universities, and particularly the arts and sciences, are places in which students leave their childhood communities and encounter new information, new problems to solve, develop new norms and new relationships. Introducing issues related to sustainability in the curriculum, either as specific courses or addressed within courses, raises awareness for individuals and for the university community. There is already material within science courses that raises awareness of the interdependence of ecosystems, but philosophy, poetry and literature, sociology, political science, etc. include numerous examples of questions raised about the value of individual vs. collective action and its impact on sustainability. John Donne, for example, in Meditation XVII provides a memorable treatise on our interdependence: "No man is an island...", while the field of ethics, and particularly environmental ethics target the nature of man's relationship with his environment. Are more money in the bank, a larger home, or vacations ethical if our children's children would live shorter lives because of increased exposure to chemicals in food we import. And are our ethical perspectives the same if we apply them close to home, if the Asian "factory girls" (Chang, 2008) who make it possible for us to consume so much with so little economic cost were part of our own community?   Social Work requires practitioners to understand the "person in environment" (Karls & O'Keefe, 2008) and all accredited programs require content and practice related to community change (Educational Policy 2.1.10; CSWE, 2010), a perfect setting for engaging students in sustainability.

Developing a Language of Promise

Increasing awareness includes not only understanding

the challenges related to sustainability, but also developing a language that makes action possible, promoting hope and possibility rather than despair, and unity rather than division. Kretzmann and McKnight (2005a, 2005b) suggest that successful community development requires rejection of the deficit model of development, instead focusing on assets, on the strengths of individuals and their relationships to the whole. When members of a potential community understand that they have contributions they can make to the well-being of the whole community, they are more likely to join in efforts and connect with other members to create positive change. The university is also the ideal place to develop networks to focus on not just challenges, but possibilities for sustainability with a language of hope and empowerment. In fact, universities are already engaging students in these discussions, as evidenced by the development of the Ecovillage at Ithaca and centers engaged in transformative, inclusionary action around the United States and abroad.

Developing Bonds

Putnam et al. (2003) refer to bonding social capital as a kind of "sociological SuperGlue" (p.2.) Many universities understand the importance of providing the ability to form tight-knit groups for incoming students, within dorms, fraternities and sororities, clubs, etc. Universities are the place to form life-long relationships. Many relationships are centered on altruistic endeavors which provide students with experience and help promote civic engagement. Sustainable community development projects can be the center of a student's experience in higher education, while leaving a legacy of positive change and lasting friendships. With the advent of the internet, of discussion groups, of social networking, bonding is possible across distances. People meet each other and marry through internet connections. Can we not develop strong international bonds related to such an important issue?

Constructing Bridges

Bridging capital, according to Putnam et al. (2003) is the "sociological WD-40", or the "grease" that connects tight-knit groups to work together. Again, universities are perfect communities to bridge, from faculty to students, from one student group to another, from past to future. A university can provide the opportunity to bridge subject areas and fields of interest that are concerned with sustainability, and through distance education bring experts into the classroom. A university can bridge geographic distances, particularly in online education, uniting students anywhere in the world in a collaborative learning environment. These bridges can then build smaller bonded communities of change. International certificates and exchange programs create these kinds of bonded communities while bridging cultures and distance.

The University as the Agent for Creating and Implementing Solutions

Interconnectedness is personal. The university can begin these conversations, and achieve successes in sustainability by engaging its students and faculty, by inviting them to participate in small groups of promise in which the issue of sustainability becomes personal. It can suspend authority to allow small groups to create change, and highlight those accomplishments toward sustainability. It can encourage movements from within, focused on possibilities we have yet to imagine, and engage directly within its own geographic region with citizens, business, public and non-profit human service workers and recipients, home owners and the homeless, to create sustainable food supplies and sustainable regional work. It can bridge the small successes to build larger ones, and connect those with the world around us. Between June of 2010 and February of 2011, Wael Ghonim, a Google marketing manager, created a community in Egypt through Facebook, committed and strong enough to overthrow a 30-year regime. Communities make all things possible.

References

Berry, W. (1990). *What are people for?* New York: Farrar, Straus & Giroux.

Block, P. (2008). *Community: The structure of belonging.* San Francisco: Berrett-Koehler.

Bourdieu, P. (1991). The forms of capital. In J. G. Richardson (Ed.), *Handbook of theory and research for the sociology of education.* New York: Greenwood.

Brundtland, G./World Commission on Environment and Development. (1987). *Our common future.* Oxford: Oxford Univ. Press.

Carr, P. & Kefalas, M. (2009). *Hollowing out the middle: The rural brain drain and what it means for America.* Boston, MA: Beacon Press.

Chang, L. (2008). *Factory girls: From village to city in a changing China.* New York: Spiegel & Grau.

Coleman, J. (1990). *Foundations of social theory.* Cambridge, MA: Harvard University.

Council on Social Work Education (CSWE). (2010). *Educational Policy and Accreditation Standards.* http://www.cswe.org/File. aspx?id=13780.

Karls J. & O'Keefe M., National Association of Social Workers (2008). *Person-in-Environment System Manual, 2nd Ed.* Washington, DC: NASW Press

Kretzmann, J. & McKnight, J., (2005). *Discovering Community Power: A Guide toMobilizing Local Assets and Your Organization's Capacity.* Evanston, IL: AssetBased Community Development Institute in cooperation with the Kellogg Foundation.

Kretzmann, J., McKnight, J., & Green, M. (2005). *Hidden Treasures: Building Community Connections.* Evanston, IL: Asset-Based Community Development Institute.

McKibben, B. (2007). *Deep economy: The wealth of communities and the durable future.* NY: Henry Holt & Co.

Portes, A. (1998). *Social capital: Its origins and applications in modern sociology.* Annual Review of Sociology, 24, 1-24.

Putnam, R. (2000). *Bowling alone.* New York: Simon & Schuster.

Putnam, R., Feldstein, L. & Cohen, D. (2003). *Better Together: Restoring the American Community.* New York: Simon & Schuster.

The Role of Faith in a Sustainable Future

Jerry Williams
Maya Lemon

Introduction

Religion is perhaps the most difficult aspect of human societies to reconcile with scientifically informed conversations about sustainability. As a key part of many American's self-identity, Christianity is a powerful force in human affairs yet it often remains outside the public debate about the environment. This is in part true because over the last 300 or so years faith and science have been embroiled in a battle to define what constitutes truth (Dewey 1920). For many, this battle has led them to abandon faith altogether. The declining incidence of religious practice in the Western World is evidence of this. For others, the battle has been resolved by adopting a scientific sounding approach to religion (for example "creation science") thus attempting to make mainstream science only one of many competing answers to some very nagging problems. For adherents of this latter approach, scientific claims about the environment are automatically suspect because they are thought to be inherently antithetical to religious perspectives.

Recently the debate about religion has intensified. Speaking about conflict in human societies, Daniel Dennett's (2006:296) recent book *Breaking the Spell: Religion as a Natural Phenomenon* takes a dismissive tone in respect to religion. He states

"...either way, your declarations of your deeply held views are posturing that are out of place, part of the problem, not part of the solution, and we others will just have to work around you as best we can."

To the current public conversation about sustainability,

religion is often at best seen as unimportant, and at worst as part of the problem. What is not in question, however, is that for many in America, faith is a central concern, perhaps even "THE" central concern in everyday life. Here we argue that while many versions of modern Christianity are openly hostile to scientific environmentalism, other social justice oriented perspectives might actually help to bring about sustainability by including care for the environment as an expression of faith and Christian responsibility. We examine the role of faith in sustainability by first looking at ways in which the Judeo-Christian tradition has contributed to environmental degradation. Next we address social movements that seek to reframe environmental concern as a necessary part of the Christian experience.

Faith as Part of the Problem

Many writers have commented about Christianity's role in the environmental crisis (McKibben 1990). It is not possible to fully address these discussions here. However, it is apparent that at least two cultural themes linked to Judeo-Christian tradition contribute to unsustainability in modern, American life. The first is dualism and the second is otherworldly asceticism.

Christianity was not the first or only religion to posit dualism as a real feature of the human experience. Simply put, dualism refers to the notion that human beings are vested not only with a physical body, but also a spiritual side that transcends the body. Much of Christian doctrine rests upon this foundation (Williams 2008). From this perspective, the corrupted and inherently dark physical world is seen as in opposition to the spiritual realm of God. That is, dualism has led humans to think of think of themselves as altogether different from nature, and that nature is corrupt and therefore rightly subject to human control. The result of this way of thinking is that humans are thought not to be bound by natural limits. Sociologists refer to this as "human exemptionalism" (Catton and Dunlap 1978). The consequences of this are obvious. If humans do not see themselves as bound by natural limits, transcending those limits is a certainty given our scientifically informed technology. No doubt, our unsustainable future is at least in part caused by our willingness to see human beings as distinct from nature, an idea that is at least in part of a product of the Judeo-Christian perspective.

Otherworldly Asceticism

Many versions of the Christian tradition result in what Max Weber called otherworldliness. This otherworldliness may also be in part responsible for our unsustainable present. Max Weber (1958, 148), speaking of the Baptist tradition, argues that such groups follow "a sincere repudiation of the world and its interests...." By doing so, adherents hope to gain rewards in the afterlife as a reward for making the right choices on here on earth. Otherworldliness treats thinking about this world and its problems as at best unnecessary, at worst as sin. For this reason, problems like global warming, ozone depletion, and species extinction are not commonly seen as a reason for concern by believers. Even if such problems create "this worldly" difficulties for believers, these concerns can simply be explained away as a natural part of being human life as we wait for better things to come after death.

Taken together, human exemptionalism and otherworldly asceticism can be thought of as a "latent ideology" for environmental exploitation. That is, in an unintended fashion these ideas derived from Judeo-Christian religious tradition, provide an apologetic for the continued exploitation of the environment. Simply put, it is convenient for those who exploit the environment to do so in the context of social norms that see nature as something dark and corrupt and at the same time as something not worthy of concern. While faith is not directly responsible for environmental destruction, certain versions of faith nevertheless provide a cultural ideology for its continuance.

Faith as Part of the Solution

Despite the ways in which organized religion, and Christianity in particular, is often portrayed as part of the environmental "problem," current social movements structured around the integration of religion and environmentalism suggest that religion has the potential to be an integral part of the success of environmental movements for social change. The following section addresses religious organizations actively pursuing social change through environmental protection and preservation. We first discuss the role of interfaith movements, then exclusively Christian organizations, and finally focus on the factors that lend to the overall effectiveness of these organizations.

Interfaith Organizations

Interfaith organizations structured around environmental protection and preservation tend to base their involvement around two central framing issues, the connection between all major religions and the environment, and the need to find a comprehensive means of addressing the potential threats and realities related to global climate change. The use of religious texts supports the connection between religion and environment is paired with the assertion that climate change is occurring and that people of religious faith have an obligation to address these changes. Organizations such as the Forum on Religion and Ecology go so far as to suggest that rational knowledge derived from science or law does not provide humans with the will to enact change and that religious, ethical, or spiritual involvement is critical to addressing complex the environmental issues of our time (Forum on Religion and Ecology 2011).

Interfaith organizations have uniquely transcended religious and cultural boundaries in their work, bringing together Moslem mosques and Protestant farmers, Jewish congregations and Christian organizers (Renewal 2007). This particular aspect of interfaith organizations is key to their success because it allows these organizations to gain access to more diverse constituent bases. Due to the scale which these organizations are able to mobilize, many of these organizations are national, such as Interfaith Power and Light and the Renewal Project, or even international, such as the United Religions Initiative. The pluralistic aspect of these organizations allows them to transcend religious and cultural barriers in favor of a common cause. These organizations have played an important part in current environmental movements for social change and promise to continue doing so in the future.

The Christian Environmental Movement

By virtue of the fact that Christian environmental organizations only work within one set of religious doctrine, the Christian environmental movement is more specific and detailed in its discussion of the Church's obligation to environmental justice than most interfaith organizations are able to be. Christian environmental organizations tend to discuss their involvement primarily the context of a biblical and religious mandate. This mandate is generally discussed in terms of stewardship, and relies heavily upon the ways in which the natural world is discussed particularly in the book of Genesis but also in the bible as a whole. The Green Bible does an excellent job providing a support Christian biblical commitment and demonstrates the biblical connection to the environment.

The Green Bible highlights all passages in the Bible that relate to God's care for creation in green ink, emphasizing the importance of the environment to a biblical God. Using the Bible, the single most important text to all Christian denominations, serves as a way to frame this issue as a central part of the identity and mission of the Church and insures that members will feel a moral and religious obligation to involvement in this movement.

Christian environmental organizations are uniquely positioned to have a huge impact on the religious environmental movement that secular or other religious organizations might not be able to exercise to the same degree. In particular, activist Mathew Sleeth points out that although the evangelical church has come late to this issue, as an institution they wield considerable political and economic weight making them crucial to the success and progress of the movement (Renewal 2007).

The Effectiveness of Religious Environmental Movements

There are several central ways in which the effectiveness of religious environmental organizations can be discussed. Examination of the specific projects of environmental religious groups reveals that, as longstanding far-reaching institutions, religious groups seem especially willing to take on long-term projects.

Many of the projects examined for this research are not set up to come to maturation for many years and represent a commitment of time and resources. This does not present and issue however, due to the fact that religious organizations work within the assumption that the goals and missions of their particular groups will be carried forward into the far future. This results in an expectation that religious environmental involvement is not a fad but part of the future for these religious institutions. The work done by Greenfaith Interfaith Environmental Coalition is an example of the longevity a religious organization can provide. This group helps religious congregations conduct energy audits and install solar panels and other energy saving appliances in their places of worship. These changes represent ways in which the beliefs of religious congregations can instigate changes in the structure of these organizations.

Bloc recruitment is another positive aspect of religious environmental organizations. Because most religions operate as a religious 'body', involvement of individuals within the 'body' frequently facilitates easy and effective recruitment of the group as well.

As with both Christian and Interfaith organizations, issues such as global climate change, poverty, and hunger, continue to be framing issues for these movements. The ways in which care for the earth and its people is built into the fabric of most major religious institutions makes these issues particularly salient for people across different religious and spiritual walks of life.

Conclusion

Here we have attempted to layout an argument that illustrates a legitimate place for religion in the discourse about sustainability. The path forward is not an easy one. Much of American culture and faith strongly adheres to human exemptionalism, and otherworldly asceticism. The Christian environmental movement, however, does illustrate that the faithful can widen their conceptions of faith in ways that include a sustainable future. It is also important to point out that while many conceptions of faith have been quite dismissive to the environmental cause, the same is also true of the view scientific environmentalism has of religion.

Both views are shortsighted. No matter one's particular religious belief of scientific conviction the unsustainable present requires attention. To make sustainability a real possibility, we will need to find ways to promote reconciliation of many different and divergent perspectives.

References

Catton, W. R., Jr. and R. E. Dunlap (1978). "Environmental Sociology: A New Paradigm." *The American Sociologist* 13(1): 41-49.

Dennett, D. C. (2006). *Breaking the spell : religion as a natural phenomenon*. New York, Viking.

Dewey, J. (1920). *Reconstruction in Philosophy*. Boston, Beacon Press.

Forum on Religion and Ecology
http://www.religionandecology.org/ retrieved: February 18, 2011.

Forum on Religion and Ecology at Yale
http://fore.research.yale.edu/ Retrieved: February 18, 2011

McKibben, B. (1990). *The end of nature*. New York, Anchor Books.

Renewal: Stories from America's Religious-Environmental Movement. Produced/Directed Marty Ostrow and Terry Kay Rockefeller. Fine Cut Productions, 2007.

Williams, J. (2008). "Thinking as Natural: Another Look at Human Exemptionalism." *Human Ecology Review* 14(2): 130-139.

Weber, M. (1958). *The Protestant Ethic and the Spirit of Capitailism.* Blacksburg, VA, Wilder.

Multiculturalism and Globalization: Case Studies from Three Ethnicities

Herman Wright, Jr., Wilma Cordova, Jeffery E. Roth, William Forbes

This essay will summarize case studies of three cultures and their efforts to not only persevere but thrive in the face of global change. So much of white society is embedded in the global economy that it is easy for many to accept Thomas Friedman's (2005) positive outlook on the process. Despite the 2008 recession, advances continue in both developing nation living standards and global technology. Yet African-American, Hispanic, and Native American cultures (among others around the globe) can have centuries-old customs and artifacts erased in the development process. Our state university in East Texas is assisting with projects that highlight threats and opportunities posed to these three cultures.

African-American heritage

East Texas, also known as the 'Pineywoods,' exhibits a cultural landscape more like the South than the West. Almost 5,000 schools were built throughout the South from 1920-35 to promote African-American education, through the generosity of Julius Rosenwald (Ascoli 2006). East Texas was home to 500 of these Rosenwald Schools. Many today are documented on a National Trust for Historic Preservation list but, critically, locations and building conditions are not always identified. Thus, efforts to find old school buildings based on corresponding place names can result in no remaining building, decomposing structures, and buildings still in use as storage units - sometimes with no memory of the building's use held by nearby residents.

Other aspects of African-American heritage such as cemeteries and churches can be found with overgrown vegetation and little to no maintenance (Galland 2007). In some cases cemeteries were desecrated during insensitive road construction or urban expansion efforts as late as the 1950s, 60s, and 70s. The Stephen F. Austin State University Geography Club (undergraduate students led by Dr. Jeffery Roth) has initiated efforts to locate unmarked graves and remove brush at two such African-American cemeteries. It has also located sites of seven Rosenwald Schools in Nacogdoches County, one holding an almost intact building – a candidate for restoration and state historical marker status. Their efforts were described in a poster that won first prize at the Association of American Geographers 2008 national meeting in Boston.

Herman Wright, Jr., a health care executive for 25 years, moved from Los Angeles to East Texas in 2005. He became part of the latest migration of African Americans back to the South. Herman came home to take care of his ailing father and took over the family ranch, deeded to his father's grandfather, Benjamin Wright, in 1874. The nearby community of Mount Union offers a cross-family and cross-racial story of multiple relationships that reflect the closeness of the community and the lack of social mobility that has kept people on the land for well over a century.

Herman traces his history back to Sherrod and Alexander Wright, two teenage Scottish brothers who fought with Andrew Jackson's army at the Battle of New Orleans at the end of the War of 1812. They moved to Texas, where they acquired land from the Mexican government and then served in the Army of the Republic of Texas, which brought Texas independence in 1836.

Herman's research reveals that slaves were bought, presumably by Sherrod and Alexander. Benjamin Wright, bi-racial and called a mulatto on the 1870 census, was deeded half of Sherrod and Alexander Wright's 4,000 acre land grant upon emancipation. Most of that land is still possessed by descendents of slave families, all deeded land in the 1870s.

Early African American leaders of Mount Union, James and Rachel Frazier, were born in Virginia in 1819 and 1824. They came to Texas with their daughter Mariah, born in Louisiana in 1850, the probable date of their purchase as slaves by Sherrod Wright or his descendents.

James and Rachel never apparently owned land, as they were elderly by the time of emancipation. However, their daughter Mariah became Benjamin Wright's first wife around the time the couple bought land in 1874. This land is the ranch Herman operates today, living in the restored home of Benjamin and Mariah. Herman is a descendent of Benjamin and Mary Jane Wright. Mary Jane was Benjamin's second wife, after Mariah. The ranch was honored in 2006 as Family Land Heritage Property by the State of Texas for being in continuous agricultural operation for over 100 years.

Such continuous land ownership is not as common as it could be in the South. Sitton (2005), among others, tracks the history of Texas freedom colonies, from emancipation to modern day status. Jobs became available in the 1940s, after the Depression and before and during World War II. Herman notes that the great migration that saw many blacks move north also happened from Mt Union westward - to Houston and ultimately to California. The Civil Rights Movement in the 1950s and 1960s further created social mobility and people moved away from the land and the community.

Mt Union today honors the legacy of James and Rachel Frazier as its founders. Today most of the 2,000 acres that was the original Sherrod and Alexander Wright League is still owned by the descendents of the original slave families. That is a testament to James and Rachel's instructions, which are still on the lips of descendents to make sure land is always owned by family members. It is also a testament to the fact that, after children were educated and migrated around the world, their success and wealth translated to family land ownership. In 2019, the community will celebrate the 200th anniversary of the birth of James Frazier.

Herman Wright, Jr. formed a non-profit organization in 2006, The Long Black Line.Org, to tell this story of land ownership and the powerful messages of family wealth creation. The story of The Long Black Line is the history of these African American rural communities formed after Emancipation. The history of communities like Mt Union can be told through their cemeteries, churches, schools, and land.

In 2012, The Long Black Line Organization will concentrate its research on four of these historic communities. Jasper County has four standing Rosenwald School buildings constructed in the 1920s. The county has the highest concentration of these existing depression-era school structures of any county in Texas. The Long Black Line.Org has contributed funding to local schools to support historical research on these communities. The Long Black Line.Org partners with the Jasper County Museum, conducting quarterly tours of these historic communities, their schools, cemeteries, and churches. Stephen F. Austin State University is partnering with The Long Black Line Organization to help facilitate, publicize, and research such efforts.

Hispanic heritage

Miguel Montiel, Tomas Atencio, and Tony Mares (2009), in their recent book Resolana, suggest cross-cultural solutions to globalization's effect on historical culture and traditional knowledge. "Resolana" is a Spanish term derived from resol, the reflection of the sun. Used for centuries in northern New Mexico, the term often refers to the sunny side of buildings where meetings take place. Much like the pragmatic philosophers, the authors indicate that wisdom is not unique to educated people and is improved locally through everyday community critique.

Atencio summarizes the economic history of his home region, northern New Mexico. Indo-Hispanic subsistence agriculture dominated since the 1500s, then changed through introduction of the railroad in the 1880s and later a service economy centered on technology (Los Alamos Laboratory) and tourism (Santa Fe,

Taos). This process left many long-term residents behind as highly educated and wealthy Anglos moved in. Traditional village values of reciprocity, sharing, communalism, and connection with nature declined. Atencio revitalized community values in his hometown of Dixon. A building was converted to La Academia de la Nueva Raza, designed as a kind of "Plato's Academy for Hispanics." This 1970s effort evolved into the current Resolana Service Learning Documentation Center, a community library that documents and incorporates traditional knowledge into internal and outreach activities. These efforts also reconnected communities with elders' storytelling through a local journal, Entre Verde y Seco (Between Green and Dry).Such movements revive what Michel Foucault (1980) calls "subjugated knowledge" and Atencio refers to as "el oro del barrio."Recovering traditional knowledge evokes Paolo Freire's (1970) "praxis" learning or everyday life experience. Freire himself visited the project and left with a positive impression.

Like Herman Wright, Jr., Atencio works from a personal sense of place or "querencia" – local family documents date back to the 1700s. Like the German Thomas Abt's *Progress without Loss of Soul* (1989) or Bill McKibben's *Deep Economy* (2007), Atencio's ultimate goal is a "la vidabuena y sana y alegre" or a good, healthy, happy life, based on broad values. He sees a future "non zero-sum world," where benefits of globalization are not necessarily offset by someone else's costs (winners and losers).

Miguel Montiel notes important differences among Hispanic groups. Mexican nationals can feel like outsiders among Chicanos. Northern New Mexicans emphasize they are Spanish and not Mexican. Educated Mexicans can more easily deal with adversity than less-educated, second generation urban Chicanos who are losing the Spanish language. The individualistic culture of the US tends to dilute Chicano "tribalism." There is a need to strike a balance between culture and career, between Friedman's "Lexus and the Olive Tree" (1999). Hispanics will soon lose minority status in states like Texas, and it's important not to discriminate like the previous majority. Montiel suggests new leaders are more likely to come from newer immigrants. Tony Mares contrasts cultural preservation (museums) with living, expanding, and interacting cultures.

Stephen F. Austin State University (SFA) in East Texas is working with the northern New Mexico community of El Cerrito to help preserve its heritage and participate in events that perpetuate community values. The history of the remote community was profiled by cultural-historical geographer Dick Nostrand (2003). A geography field school is proposed by SFA faculty member, former Nostrand student, and local landowner Dr. Jeffery Roth. He will involve students in community ditch digging. This seemingly simple, labor-intensive practice is actually a critical form of cultural preservation. Centuries-old acequias, or canals, often fill in from natural or human-intensified erosion. Other activities include maintaining the old school building and replanting fruit trees that formerly lined canals and ditches. Such efforts involve numerous local and outside individuals to help maintain this centuries-old, living and working landscape.

Another effort involves engaging students in researching community assets in East Texas colonias, "interior US" versions of squatter communities that are more typical along the US-Mexico border. Such poor communities can be, especially to Anglos who investigate further, surprisingly family-oriented and populated by members with significant leadership qualities. They tend to build social and political capital over time, evolving from shacks with corrugated tin roofs into more permanent villages, eventually gaining infrastructure such as power, sewer, and water lines (Cordova 2004). One of the better resources on Hispanic and other US immigrants is the recently updated anthology, edited by Ines Miyares and Christopher Airriess (2007), Contemporary Ethnic Geographies in America. It highlights issues of cultural preservation within disruptive processes of migration and urbanization of Hispanics, Native Americans, and others.

American Indian Heritage

On the topic of sustainability, no group could be more appropriate to mention than the American Indians of East Texas, the Caddo. Unlike more nomadic tribes to the west, the Caddo essentially practiced sustainable agriculture for 1,000 years, from approximately 800 to 1800 AD. The introduction of maize (corn) helped build their civilization to its peak from roughly 1000 to 1400 AD, allowing trade with Mesoamerican cultures to the south and the development of intricate pottery and industries such as salt production (Perttula 1992, Smith 1995).

The Caddo lived in long, linear villages stretching along rich bottomland forests of East Texas. In the prehistoric period and similar to other Mississippian cultures to the southeast, they built ceremonial centers with temple and burial mounds. When Texas became independent from Mexico in the 1830s, Governor Mirabeau Lamar had the Caddo people, along with the Cherokee (more recent transplants), moved to Oklahoma. The Caddo still attach important cultural significance to East Texas sites and revisit on a regular basis.

Today mound centers are found in many locations in East Texas. One of the best understood mound center is located at Caddo Mounds State Historic Site, just west of Alto, Texas. Although there is only one mound remaining at Washington Square in downtown Nacogdoches, Stephen F. Austin State University is helping the Caddo establish a cultural center in one of the original university buildings there. The University also preserves Caddo artifacts from this and other sites at their certified archaeology laboratory. Students also volunteer with Caddo Culture Day, an autumn ceremonial event at the State Historic Site.

Another American Indian project underway is an eco-cultural restoration project in Mexico's Sierra Madre Occidental. The Chiricahua Apache formerly ranged from southern Arizona and New Mexico into northwestern Mexico's Sierra Madre mountain range, bordering the Mexican states of Chihuahua and Sonora. Although Apaches were removed from the area with the surrender of Geronimo in the 1880s, descendents of the Chiricahua living today in Fort Sill, Oklahoma and Mescalero, New Mexico attach great cultural significance to Sierra Madre sites (Goodwin and Goodwin 2000, Opler 1941). The Sierra Azul (Blue Mountains), located in the Rio Gavilan watershed west of Nuevo Casas Grandes, Chihuahua, are especially important.

Traditional Chiricahua dance groups, organized by Berle and Aryliss Kanseah of Mescalero, visited the Sierra Azul area in recent decades to perform ceremonial rituals. Berle's son is carrying on their dance tradition in New Mexico, organizing ceremonies associated with the coming of age ritual for teenage women, one of the most important Apache events. However, the Mexican site where ceremonies were performed has degraded over time through ecological processes changing much of the West over the past 100 years - grazing, fire suppression, and brush encroachment on grasslands, which increases erosion and can dry up formerly wet areas.

Stephen F. Austin State University is generating a grant proposal to facilitate Chiricahua Apaches not only revisiting the Mexican ceremonial site, but allowing Apache youth to get involved in restoration of the area's cienega (wet meadow) and surrounding pine-oak grasslands.

Conclusion

The cultural heritage of all three major groups, African-American, Hispanic, and Native American, is under threat from changes brought by modern culture. Some changes happened decades or even centuries earlier, while others continue to occur in both urban and rural settings. We are so embedded in modern (mostly Anglo) culture that it is easy to miss impacts before it is too late. We often miss opportunities to work together and not only preserve artifacts, but engage in living landscapes that carry on traditions. In this way, universities can provide a unique societal niche, working at the heart of sustainability, to facilitate the sustenance of not only economies, but the integrated whole of environments, societies, and cultures.

References

Abt, T. 1989. *Progress without Loss of Soul: Toward a Wholistic Approach to Modernization Planning*. New York: Chiron Publications.

Ascoli, P. 2006. *Julius Rosenwald*. Bloomington: Indiana University Press.

Cordova, W. 2004. Life in a Colonia: Identifying Community Assets. In, *Rural social work: Building and sustaining community assets*. T. L. Scales & C. L. Streeter, eds. Pacific Grove, CA: Brooks/Cole.

Freire, Paulo. 1970. *Pedagogy of the oppressed*. New York: Herder and Herder.

Friedman, T. 2005. *The World is Flat: a Brief History of the Twenty-First Century*. New York: Farrar, Straus, and Giroux.

Friedman, T. 1999. *The Lexus and the Olive Tree: Understanding Globalization*. New York: Farrar, Straus, and Giroux.

Foucault, M. 1980. *Power/Knowledge, selected interviews and other writings 1972-1977, by Michel Foucault*. Gordon, C., ed. Hertfordshire: Harvester Wheatsheaf.

Galland, C. 2007. *Love Cemetery: Unburying the Secret History of Slaves*. New York: Harper One.

Goodwin, G., N. Goodwin. 2000. *Apache Diaries: A Father-Son Journey*. Lincoln: University of Nebraska Press.

McKibben, B. 2007. *Deep Economy: The Wealth of Communities and the Durable Future*. New York: Henry Holt Books.

Miyares, I. M., C. A. Airriess, eds. 2007. *Contemporary Ethnic Geographies in America*. Lanham, MD: Rowman and Littlefield.

Montiel, M., T. Atencio, E.A. Mares. 2009. *Resolana: Emerging Chicano Dialogues on Community and Globalization.* Tucson, Arizona: University of Arizona Press

Nostrand, R. L. 2003. *El Cerrito, New Mexico: Eight Generations in a Spanish Village.* Norman: University of Oklahoma Press.

Opler, M. E. 1941. *An Apache Life-Way: The Economic, Social, and Religious Institutions of the Chiricahua Indians.* Chicago: University of Chicago Press.

Perttula, T. K. 1992. *The Caddo Nation: Archaeological and Ethnohistoric Perspectives.* Austin: University of Texas Press.

Sitton, T. 2005. *Freedom Colonies.* Austin: University of Texas Press.

Smith, F. T. 1995. *The Caddo Indians.* College Station: Texas A&M University Press.

Sense of Place and Expandable Community Boundaries

William Forbes

Defining communities and our attachment to them is a critical component to sustainability. Despite the most common perception of a community as a small town or neighborhood, communities can vary greatly in both geographic scale and membership (e.g., scientific, corporate, biological communities). Defining relationships between various communities can help increase care for sustainability and our sense of place in the world. Within the social sciences, geography has traditionally addressed these relationships, especially in regards to understanding international issues, historical human-environment relations, and more recently political ecology (how power relations influence landscape change).

Aldo Leopold, co-founder of numerous fields such as wildlife ecology, restoration ecology, and wilderness preservation, is one of the most famous leaders in conservation history. His essay "The Land Ethic" became a founding concept of the US environmental movement in the 1960s. The main idea was that government regulations and incentives were not enough to foster adequate conservation in the face of the juggernaut of modernization. The appropriate next step in the natural progression of ethics through human history, progressively outward over time from individual to family to larger communities of village, state, and nation, would now include the biotic community (Leopold 1949).

The rationale for Leopold's call to expand our circle of ethics has, if anything, increased since he wrote the piece. Many people think that extinction is natural, and thus conservationists' concern over endangered species is narrowly focused. Harvard biologist

E.O. Wilson (2002) and others now estimate that the current global rate of species extinction is 100 to 1,000 times the natural background rate. The primary cause is human alteration of habitats, with our spread of invasive species the secondary cause. Our effects are so great that some are calling for giving humans our own geological period, the anthropocene. The five previous mass extinctions (440, 370, 250, 210, and 65 million years ago, respectively) were caused by physical agents such as atmospheric change and asteroids. We are the first biological "weapon of mass extinction" in the 4.6 billion year history of the earth.

You may ask, isn't the majority of this mass extinction occurring elsewhere on the planet? Yes, it is, especially in tropical forests renowned for their biodiversity. Wilson found that one tree in the Peruvian Amazon contained more species of ants than exist in all of the United Kingdom. Yet here is the crux of this essay. The world is more connected globally than ever before, not just through communication over cell phones and internet, but through networks (or communities) of consumption.

Just one example is the recent US movement to make ethanol from corn. The American farm community obligingly responded to the rise in demand (and price) by growing more corn. Corn replaced lower priced soybeans in their fields, yet there was still a global market for soybeans. Who grows more soybeans in response? Brazilian farmers do, pushing westward into Amazon rainforest to increase their agricultural capacity. Thus a seemingly benign effort to develop ethanol as an alternative fuel has the unintended result in no small loss of biodiversity– extinction is forever. Expanding our boundaries of care to global locations of conservation and consumption is the next logical step in the evolution of ethics, over half a century after Leopold's call for extension of a land ethic.

Douglas MacCleery (2000) proposes an adaptation of Leopold's land ethic. US citizens comprise approximately 5% of the world's population yet use roughly 30% of its resources. MacCleery suggests adoption of a domestic land ethic is inadequate without adoption of a corresponding consumption ethic. He points out that, since the first Earth Day in 1970, the average US family size decreased 16%, while the average family house size increased 48%. Meanwhile, federal timber harvest declined and lumber export from Quebec to the US tripled.

MacCleery suggests a consumption ethic along the lines of Leopold's land ethic, whereby a community stigma surrounds individuals with blatantly high consumption habits. He cites evidence, as Leopold did with the land ethic, that such an ethic does not currently exist:

> A suburban dweller with a small family who lives in a 4,000 square-foot home, owns three or four cars, commutes to work alone in a gas guzzling sport utility vehicle (even though public transportation is available), and otherwise leads a highly resource consumptive lifestyle is still (if otherwise decent) a respected member of society. Indeed, her/his social status in the community may even be enhanced by virtue of that consumption.

This is not to place all the blame for overconsumption on the US. Most developed nations export their cultural and environmental impacts as we do, although some seem more concerned about it. Nations like Switzerland and the United Kingdom have more connections with Fair Trade programs, in which developing nation farmers receive fair prices for their produce, often bypassing the middleman in trade linkages. The City of Bristol, west of London, officially declared itself a Fair Trade community (Barnett et al. 2010).

Programs like Fair Trade can make a huge difference overseas. Of the 18 million residents of the West African nation of the Ivory Coast (Cote D'Ivoire), approximately 7 million depend directly on export of cacao beans (used to make chocolate). A 5% change in the global price of cacao beans can make a critical difference in marginal returns to small farmers. Small farmers worldwide are increasingly linked to community cooperatives to gain legal and political lobbying power and better market access to compete with larger, industrial farm producers.

US farm subsidies are a sensitive subject for developing nations, as the US has recommended they drop government subsidies over recent decades to improve free market competition and efficiency. At the same time, we are maintaining our subsidies that allow our corporate farms to outcompete developing nation small farm communities for access to markets. President Bush tried to reduce our farm subsidies, partly in response to pressure from Latin American leaders, but was unsuccessful - the US farm lobby is one of the strongest groups in Washington.

Linking consumers and producers in new communities could be influential, but changes in big producer and retailer consumption habits can further ramp up the scale of change. A Mexican subsidiary of Pepsi recently decided to buy corn directly from a nearby farm cooperative in Jalisco state, rather than go through middlemen, for its snack food division. It was a win-win situation, as the local farm community received guaranteed prices and had less reason to immigrate to the US. Pepsi not only received corn at lower transportation costs but used the farmers to test development of sunflower oil to replace more environmentally-impacting palm oil imported from Africa and Asia (Strom 2011).

The same subsidiary was buying potatoes, as much as 22% of the Mexico potato market, causing wild swings in market prices – so it stabilized the market by using guaranteed prices for growers to develop new varieties more suitable to Mexico's subtropical and tropical climates. Wal-Mart has made similar changes in demanding more environmentally-friendly labeling and packaging from their community of 100,000 suppliers, making a large difference globally.

The global community of media outlets likes to portray economy and environment at odds with each other, as controversy sells news. While this can be the case with specific firms or business sectors facing ecological constraints, environmental quality and economic benefits often coalesce on a broader, public scale. The US Environmental Protection Agency conducted a retroactive cost/benefit analysis of the Clean Air Act between 1970 and 1990. The costs were striking – over $520 billion; however, the benefits were even more shocking – over $22 trillion – a net benefit of over $21 trillion, largely due to reduced medical costs (EPA 1997).

Thus, changing the geographic scale of community boundaries can greatly change the results of your assessment. Changing the temporal scale of your assessment can also change perspectives. UCLA geographer Jared Diamond (2005) documented the decline of several past civilizations in his recent book "Collapse."

Much of the unsustainable nature of those cultures resulted from failure to adapt to change. In many cases cultures continued to use the same livelihood strategies regardless of their location or conditions. There is little doubt that some internal complacency or conflict set in. Perhaps they did not heed military or ecological warnings, or they did not develop appropriate technology to adapt in a timely manner. Even some of the most famous civilizations, including the Aztecs and Incas, dominated their regions for only 100-150 years.

However, there are numerous examples of past civilizations lasting half a millennium or more, much longer than our modern society has evolved since the industrial revolution two centuries ago. Some of these longer-lived societies even occurred in the very same places we live in now. The Caddo lived near the site of our university for approximately 1,000 years, adapting and improving their more sedentary agricultural lifestyle through introduction of corn (maize). Thus, our present-day communities can develop a certain hubris or overconfidence regarding the quality and probable longevity of its dominance.

After giving in to arguments for anthropocentrism, Leopold (1937) thought about such grandiose self-confidence when contemplating chronological layers of culture in the US Southwest:

Granting that the earth is for man—there is still a

> question: what man? Did not the cliff dwellers who
> tilled and irrigated these our valleys think that they
> were the pinnacle of creation—that these valleys were
> made for them? Undoubtedly. And then the Pueblos?
> Yes. And then the Spaniards? Not only thought so, but
> said so. And now we Americans? Ours beyond a doubt!
> ...Five races—five cultures—have flourished here. We
> may truthfully say of our four predecessors that they
> left the earth alive, undamaged. Is it possibly a proper
> question for us to consider what the sixth shall say
> about us?

Carl Sauer, a contemporary of Leopold and perhaps the most famous geographer of the 20th Century, studied agricultural hearths - sites of first domestication of wild plants - as one aspect of his research (Sauer 1952). Studies in his field reveal that Andean agricultural communities have been growing potatoes for about 8,000 years. Peruvians developed thousands of potato varieties over this time to help them adapt to varying climate and topography. They also practice intercropping, mixing various crops in one field to not only vary diet, but decrease risk if some crops fail.

German explorer and renowned geographer Alexander von Humboldt (1852) was one of the first to document the impact of outside markets on such long-standing local subsistence agriculture in the early 1800s, when he noticed disruption of the sustainability of Venezuelan oyster beds by introduction of outside markets and scaling up of production. This theme is one of the more popular research tracks of recent decades in geography. A sense of place, derived over centuries if not millenniums, can be disrupted by the very powerful outside forces of neo-colonial powers and capitalist markets.

Michael Watts (1983) analyzed the role of Nigerian export farming in the Sahel, changing practices away from long resilient subsistence cattle grazing to cash crops. Prices fluctuated greatly as droughts came to the region in the early 1970s. Already marginal farming failed and famine resulted on a scale not seen before. Modern-day examples exist in places like Yemen, where the stimulant qat was recently promoted as a cash crop to replace subsistence agriculture. Farmers not only flooded the market, dropping prices, but the water-intensive qat drained limited water supplies, leaving farmers with losses and disruption of subsistence systems that had lasted centuries (Worth 2009).

Thus by expanding our community boundaries internationally and inter-generationally, we can learn lessons that may help us think about longer-term resilience of our own locally adapted agriculture. Many US consumers and farmers are linking in a movement called Community Supported Agriculture (CSA). This effort helps link demand for local, often organic crops with supply provided by local niche farmers. Studies are showing a trend towards increasing number and decreasing size of farms in Iowa, a reverse of the trend of recent decades towards large-scale, industrial agriculture. There is such a demand that, not only Austin-based Whole Foods, but even giant retailers like Wal-Mart are entering the organic produce market.

The movement also offers a mode through which one can partially withdraw from the global economy, with all its fluctuating prices, unseen impacts, and high carbon footprint. Such local-global hybrid economies may be the future trend "Reverse Corps," where subsistence farmers from developing nations visit to help us build resilient subsistence agriculture to augment our cash economies. Payments equivalent to Peace Corps volunteer stipends would likely be welcome. Better yet, students may interview elders who grew up on local farms. When interviewing locals to determine the site of Leopold's 1909 East Texas field camp, an informant who grew up on a farm across the Sabine River in Louisiana, ten miles from the nearest town, stated that her mother went to the store once a month.

The notoriously footloose nature of Americans (far more mobile in changing residences than Europeans) could be offset by programs such as ESL – "Ecology as a Second Language." New suburbanites, or Hispanic migrants for that matter, would learn the local flora and fauna along with community recycling, waste, and energy systems. Community pride in local sense of place would expand to encompass not only figures in local history but those in the biotic community.

Americans are also notoriously poor at geography. The National Geographic Society (2006) noted that 44% of young Americans could not locate any of the following four nations on a map: Iran, Iraq, Israel, or Saudi Arabia. The good news is that US scores are slowly increasing over time, with the help of the Society's education programs. The Society website has the subtitle: "Inspiring people to care about the planet since 1888."

Sense of place does not necessarily have to be enhanced by expanding boundaries of care. The Botanical Research Institute of Texas recently held a workshop for teachers titled, Mapping Your Sense of Place. Facilitator Mark Baldwin had participants begin by focusing on a 1 meter by 1 meter piece of ground, describing what they saw – grass species, passing insects, underground tree roots, falling seeds, overhanging branches, and remnants of civilization such as bricks or trash. The inward focus on narrowed boundaries helped alter perspective and give the participant a new mode of analyzing the local landscape with no particular agenda in mind.

The Botanical Research Institute of Texas (2007) also has a project at the other end of the spatial spectrum, its Andes to Amazon Project in southeastern Peru. Botanists look for new species in the backcountry of some of the world's most diverse flora - diversity enhanced by the Amazon rainforest meeting the eastern slopes of the Andes, with its elevation-based ecological zones described by von Humboldt in the early 1800s. Botanists not only work with biotic communities but human communities, scheming on how to build local agricultural systems in an Amazon landscape filled with relative newcomers from the highlands. Given the unknown global impact of US subdivisions, mitigation could be aligned not just locally but globally, to projects such as the Andes to Amazon, even involving subdivision residents in face-to-face interaction and overseas internships.

Perhaps building sense of place and sustainable communities is based on a tension between these two forces: creativity enhanced by having no particular agenda, an open mind; countered by the notion that we live during a special time in earth's history, when for the first time one species can not only alter the course of the planet's biotic community, but realize that it is doing so. Expanding the geographic boundaries of our intimacy offers unknown possibilities.

References

Barnett, C., P. Cloke, N. Clarke, A. Malpass. 2010. *Globalizing Responsibility: The Political Rationalities of Ethical Consumption.* RGS-IBG Book Series. John Wiley and Sons.

Botanical Research Institute of Texas. 2007. Andes to Amazon Project Update. *Iridos*, Vol. 18, No. 1, pp. 12-13.

Diamond, J. 2005. *Collapse: How Societies Choose to Fail or Succeed.* New York: Penguin Group.

Environmental Protection Agency. 1997. *The Benefits of the Clean Air Act, 1970 to 1990.* Washington, D.C.: EPA Office of Policy, Planning, and Evaluation.

Humboldt, A. 1852. *Personal Narrative of Travels to the Equinoctial Regions of America.* London: Henry G. Bohn.

Leopold, A. 1949. *A Sand County Almanac and Sketches Here and There.* New York: Oxford University Press.

Leopold, A. 1937. Conservationist in Mexico. *American Forests* 43, 3 (March), p. 118-20, 146.

MacCleery, D.W. 2000. Aldo Leopold's Land Ethic: Is it Only Half a Loaf? *Journal of Forestry*, Vol. 98, No. 10, pp. 5-7.

National Geographic Society. 2006. *National Geographic-Roper Public Affairs 2006 Geographic Literacy Study.* Washington, D.C.: National Geographic Society.

Sauer, C. O. 1952. *Agricultural Origins and Dispersals.* New York: American Geographical Society.

Strom, S. 2011. For Pepsi, a Business Decision with Social Benefit. *New York Times*, February 21st.

Watts, M. J. 1983. *Silent Violence: Food, Famine, and Peasantry in Northern Nigeria.* Berkeley: University of California Press.

Wilson, E. O. 2002. *The Future of Life.* New York: Knopf.

Worth, R. F. 2009. Thirsty Plant Dries Out Yemen. *New York Times*, October 31st.

GLOBALIZATION, ENVIRONMENTAL JUSTICE, AND SUSTAINABILITY IN THE WORLD-SYSTEM: THE CASE OF E-WASTE IN GUIYU, CHINA

R. Scott Frey

The editors of *The Economist* (2007:14) magazine made several observations about globalization recently that are worth quoting because they raise important questions about environmental justice and sustainability in an increasingly globalized world. Sounding a bit like Marie Antoinette, the editors wrote:

> . . . the best way of recycling waste may well be to sell it, often to emerging markets. That is controversial, because of the suspicion that waste will be dumped, or that workers and the environment will be poorly protected. Yet recycling has economics of scale and the transport can be virtually free--filling up the containers that came to the West full of clothes and electronics and would otherwise return empty to China. What's more, those who are prepared to buy waste are likely to make good use of it.

Despite the internal consistency of their market logic and celebration of the current global system, globalization and environmental justice as well as sustainability can be seen as contradictory tendencies in the current world-system. Consider, for instance, the fact that centrality in the world-system allows some countries to export their environmental harms to other countries (Frey, 1998a, 1998b, 2006a, 2006b, in press). Such exports increase environmental injustice and reduce sustainability by putting humans and the environment in recipient countries at substantial risk. The specific case of e-waste exports to Guiyu, China is discussed in light of the contradictory tendencies mentioned. The discussion proceeds in several steps. Environmental justice and sustainability in the world-system are first examined. This is followed by a discussion of the e-waste trade in the world-system. The extent to which this trade has negative health, safety, and environmental consequences in Guiyu, China is outlined and the neo-liberal contention that such exports are economically beneficial to the core and periphery is critically examined. Policies proposed as solutions to the problem of e-waste traffic in Guiyu and the world-system are critically reviewed. The paper concludes with an assessment of the likelihood that existing "counter-hegemonic" globalization forces will overcome the tensions between globalization and environmental justice and sustainability.

ENVIRONMENTAL JUSTICE AND SUSTAINABILITY IN THE WORLD-SYSTEM

The world-system is a global economic system in which goods and services are produced for profit and the process of capital accumulation must be continuous if the system is to survive (see especially Wallerstein [2004] for the origins and nature of the world-system perspective and Harvey [2010] for a recent discussion of continuous capital accumulation under capitalist relations). Proponents of the perspective conceptualize the world-system as a three tiered system, consisting of a core, semi-periphery, and periphery.

The world-system is an open system that can be understood not only in "economic" terms but also in "physical or metabolic" terms: entry of energy and materials and exit of dissipated energy and material waste (Frey, 1998a; Hornborg, 2011; Martinez-Alier, 2009; Rice, 2007, 2009). In fact, the world-system and globalization itself can be described or understood in terms of a process of "ecological unequal exchange" (e.g., Hornborg, 2011; Rice, 2007, 2009; or a process of "accumulation by extraction and contamination"). Frey (2006a) has described the process of unequal ecological exchange in the following terms:

- Wealth (in the form of materials, energy, genetic diversity, and food and fiber) flows from the resource rich countries of the periphery to the industrialized countries of the core, resulting often in problems of resource depletion/degradation and pollution in the peripheral zones or the "resource extraction frontiers."

- The core displaces anti-wealth (entropy broadly defined) or appropriates carrying capacity or waste assimilation by transporting it to the global sinks or to the sinks of the periphery in the form of hazardous exports. In other words, global sinks and the peripheral zones of the world-system are essentially "waste-disposal frontiers."

This paper focuses on the transfer of hazards to the peripheral zones of the world-system, whether hazardous products, production processes, or wastes, with a focus on e-waste. Such hazards damage the environment and adversely affect human health through environmental and occupational exposure. Peripheral countries are particularly vulnerable to the risks posed by such hazards for several reasons: limited public awareness; a young, poorly trained, and unhealthy workforce; politically unresponsive state agencies; and inadequate risk assessment and management capabilities and infrastructure (e.g., Frey 2006a).

The core (consumers, states, and capital in various countries) benefits from the transfer of hazards to the periphery while the periphery bears the costs associated with such exports. Environmental justice and sustainability are enhanced in the core because environmental harms are displaced to the periphery, while such export practices increase environmental injustice and reduce sustainability in the periphery. Risks associated with hazardous exports or environmental harms are distributed in an unequal fashion within the periphery: some groups (especially the state and capital) are able to capture the benefits while others (those marginalized by gender, age, class, race/ethnicity, and geospatial location) bear the costs (see Frey, 2006a).

E-WASTE IN THE WORLD-SYSTEM

Nature and Scope of E-Waste

E-waste consists of discarded computers, cell phones, televisions, and other electrical and electronic products. (See Widmer et al. [2005] for a review of existing definitions of e-waste.) This waste is a byproduct of the information and communication technology-infrastructure underlying the world system's social metabolism. Globalization is dependent (or "symbiotic," to use Pellow's [2007:185] term) on information and communication technology, most notably the computer. It is the computer in conjunction with the internet (and the global transport system) that facilitates the transport of wealth to the core and anti-wealth to the periphery, whether it is the movement of bauxite and iron ore from Brazil by large ocean going vessels (Bunker and Ciccantell, 2005) or the recycling, incineration, and/or disposal of e-waste in China.

E-waste is growing more rapidly than other waste streams because the consumption of electronic products is growing at an astonishing pace. Increased consumption of electronic products is due to the constant development of new electronic products, planned obsolescence, and falling prices throughout the developed world. In 1975, for example, there was one computer per 1,000 population in the US, but in 2010 the number was over 800 computers per 1,000 population (United Nations, 2010). And it is expected that growth of computers will continue in the core and be overtaken by the developing countries in the next fifteen to twenty years (Yu et al., 2010a).

Anywhere from 30 to 50 million tons of e-waste are discarded each year in the world-system (according to the Basel Action Network and Silicon Valley Toxics Coalition [2002] and the United Nations Environment Programme [2009]). Every year, hundreds of thousands of old computers and mobile phones are dumped in landfills or burned in smelters. Thousands more are exported, often illegally, from Europe, the US, Japan and other industrialized countries, to countries in Africa and Asia (Bhutta, Oma, and Yang, 2010). Recipient countries include Bangladesh, China, India, Malaysia, Pakistan, the Philippines, and Vietnam in Asia and Ghana and Nigeria in West Africa. In fact, it is estimated that upwards of 80 percent of the US's e-waste is exported to these countries with 90 percent of the waste going to China (Grossman, 2006:Chapter 7).

E-waste follows a path of least resistance: it flows from the highly regulated core countries to low wage countries with limited health and environmental regulation. It is exported to countries for inexpensive, labor intensive recycling, incineration, and/or disposal (Basel Action Network and Silicon Valley Toxics Coalition, 2002; Nnorom, Osibanjo, and Ogwvegbul, 2011; Tsydenova and Bengtsson, 2011). Valuable materials extracted from computers include copper, lead, plastics, steel, and glass. The state and capital in China (and many peripheral countries) want the "recycling" industry for economic reasons, including the high demand for used parts and the high demand for materials for the growing manufacturing sector.

Guiyu Township in Guangdong Province is one of the major destinations for much of the e-waste entering China and it the largest e-waste recycling site in the world-system. (Taizhou city is the second largest site in China and it is located south of Shanghai.) Guiyu is 100 miles northwest of Guanghou and has a population of approximately 200,000 people in seventeen villages (the four main villages are Huamei, Longgang, Xianpeng, and Beilin). Once a rice producing area, Guiyu became an e-waste recycling center in the early 1990s, though its residents have a long history of waste collection stretching back to the early 20th Century when residents would collect duck feathers, scrap metal, and pig bones for sale. Guiyu is now home to an estimated 150,000 e-waste workers (including children, as well as commuters from nearby areas) engaged in e-waste recycling. Much of the e-waste recycling that takes place in Guiyu consists of the dismantling of computers and related accessories imported from the US, Japan, Canada, South Korea, Europe, and Taiwan (Basel Action Network and Silicon Valley Toxics Coalition, 2002; Grossman, 2006:Chapter 7; Sepulveda et al., 2010).

Steps in Dismantling Computers

Brokers based in Hong Kong and Taiwan sell the e-waste to recyclers through e-waste dealers in China who pay anywhere from 400 to 500 dollars or more per ton for computers (Grossman, 2006:Chapter 7). The cost depends on the composition of the e-waste (whether circuit boards, monitors, printers, or the like) and profit margins. Several steps are followed once the e-waste reaches its port of destination in Hong Kong or Shantou, China (see Basel Action Network and Silicon Valley Toxics Coalition, 2002; Grossman, 2006:Chaper 7; Tsydenova and Bengtsson, 2011:51-55):

- Computers are trucked in after they are unloaded from container ships in their port of destination.

- Cathode ray tubes are broken with hammers, exposing the toxic phosphor dust inside. The copper yokes are removed and sold to metal dealers.

- Circuit boards are cooked in woks over open charcoal fires to melt the lead solder, releasing toxic lead fumes. The lead solder is collected for metal dealers.

- Large pieces of plastic are melted into thin rods and cut into small granules and sold to factories that make low quality plastic goods.

- Wires are burned in open piles to melt the plastics to get at the copper and other metals inside.

- Acid baths are used to extract certain materials from microchips such as gold. Nitric and hydrochloric acids are used to release gold from plastic and other commodities and the acids are dumped into the local environment.

- Plastic casings are burned, creating dioxins and furans – which are extremely hazardous to human health.

- Unwanted leaded glass and other materials are dumped in ditches.

- Acids and dissolved heavy metals are dumped directly into local waterways.

Buyers from local factories and outside the area purchase the metals such as copper, gold, aluminum, steel, and other commodities and sell them locally and nationally.

Health and Environmental Risks Associated with Computer Dismantling

The average desktop computer contains valuable recyclable and hazardous materials. Aluminum, copper, gold, steel, and platinum, as well as the more toxic lead are the most valuable materials (e.g., Williams et al, 2008:Table 1, page 6447). Hazardous materials include heavy metals, brominated flame retardants, and many other toxic materials; lead and cadmium and mercury in circuit boards; lead oxide in CRTs; mercury in switches and flat screen monitors; cadmium in computer batteries; and persistent organic pollutants (dioxins, PVCs, and PAHs) in plastics (Nnorom, Osibanjo, and Ogwuegbu, 2011; Tsydenova and Bengtsson, 2011).

As noted above, materials are extracted in an unsafe fashion. Recycling practices release toxins from hazardous materials and generate new ones. Open air incineration is used to recover copper in wiring and acid baths are used to extract metals such as copper and gold. Waste is dumped in irrigation canals and other waterways, including the nearby Lianjiang River (Sepulveda et al., 2010; Tsydenova and Bengtsson, 2011). Working conditions are primitive and unsafe, and workers are exposed to toxic materials but little safety equipment is available. Labor conditions are grave for the workers: they work six day work weeks of twelve hours duration per day for limited pay and they have few rights. Child labor is quite common (Basel Action Network and Silicon Valley Toxics Coalition. 2002; Grossman, 2006:Chapter 7).

Available research indicates that human health and the environment are under assault in Guiyu (see the excellent reviews of the extant literature by Sepulveda et al. [2010] and Tsydenova and Bengtsson [2011]). The air, soil, and water of Guiyu are contaminated with a range of toxic materials, including lead, cadmium, PCBs, benzene, and so on (Bi et al., 2010, Tsydenova and Bengtsson, 2011). A study released in 2007 (Huo et al., 2007) found that a majority of the children sampled in Guiyu had blood levels of lead and cadmium many times higher than limits set by the US Centers for Disease Control and Prevention. A recent study (Yang et al., 2011) undertaken at the other major e-waste recycling site in China, Taizhou, indicates that air samples from the area contain toxic particulate matter that can induce human DNA damage. Exposure to these and related materials are extremely hazardous to human health and represent significant risks to other species, as well as the larger environment and surrounding human communities.

EVALUATING THE COSTS AND BENEFITS

Are the costs associated with the displacement of e-waste recycling to Guiyu offset by the economic and other benefits as proponents of neoliberalism (Grossman and Krueger, 1993, 1995) and some ecological modernization theorists (Mol, 2001) would suggest? After all, e-waste recycling employs at least 150,000 poor workers desperate for jobs in Guiyu. The materials and parts recovered are recycled and used domestically which reduces dependence on outside sources, reduces pollution associated with mining, provides needed capital for the economy, and reduces energy use and carbon dioxide emissions. In addition, import duties on some of the incoming goods provide a revenue stream for government (see Williams et al. [2008:6449-6450] for a discussion of the benefits of computer exports).

Answering the question raised above as noted elsewhere (Frey, 2006a) is problematic because it is difficult to identify, estimate, and value the costs and benefits (especially the costs) associated with hazards in monetary terms (see, e.g., Frey, McCormick, and Rosa, 2007; Williams et al., 2008). Despite suggestions and efforts to the contrary (e.g., Logan, 1991), there is no widely accepted factual or methodological basis for identifying, estimating, and valuing the costs and benefits associated with the flow of core hazards to the periphery. Even if the consequences of hazardous exports could be meaningfully identified and estimated, there remains the question of valuing them in monetary terms. Economists typically look to the marketplace for such a valuation, but adverse health, safety, environmental, and socio-economic consequences are not traded in the marketplace. Efforts have been made to deal with this problem by using either expert judgment or public preferences, but such techniques are deeply flawed (see Dietz, Frey, and Rosa, 2002; Foster, 2002a).

When he was Chief Economist of the World Bank, Lawrence Summers (1991) made the argument, much like the editors of *The Economist* mentioned above, that displacing environmental harms to peripheral areas makes economic sense. He wrote in a World Bank memo: "I think the economic logic behind dumping a load of toxic waste in the lowest-wage country is impeccable and we should face up to that." Environmental harms should be sent to poor areas because "measurements of the costs of health impairing pollution depend on the forgone earnings from increased morbidity and mortality. From this point of view a given amount of health impairing pollution should be done in the country with the lowest cost, which will be the country with the lowest wages."

As noted elsewhere (Foster, 2002b; Puckett, 2006), such reasoning undervalues nature and assumes that human life in the periphery is worth much less than in the core because of wage differentials. Although most costs occur in the periphery and most benefits are captured by the core and elites located in the periphery, the costs to the periphery are deemed acceptable because life is defined as worth so little. In sum, it can be argued convincingly that the costs associated with the transfer of e-waste to Guiyu, China (and elsewhere, for that matter) outweigh the benefits.

WHAT IS TO BE DONE? AND WHO SHOULD DO IT?

The Chinese government banned imports of toxic e-waste in 2002 and has created additional regulations since then (as recently as January 1, 2011 [Moxley, 2011]; see also Yu et al. [2010a] for a comprehensive review), but the e-waste continues to flow into the country and thousands of Chinese women continue to cook the core's circuit boards over charcoal burners and the blood lead levels of children remain high. This is a result of lax enforcement of regulations due to bribes and corruption. In turn, local government officials are evaluated by the central government in terms of overall economic growth in their areas, so there is a strong incentive for officials to protect e-waste activities since they contribute to the economic growth of the area. And, of course, China's growth machine requires large material inputs to sustain it and e-waste recycling is an important source for these materials (Grossman, 2006; Yu et al., 2010b:992-994, 999).

A number of actors have emerged to challenge e-waste recycling in China. These include Chinese government officials and Chinese NGOs. Pan Yue, Vice Minister of the Ministry of Environmental Protection (CMEP) of the People's Republic of China, has been an unwavering supporter of the environment at all levels (Byrnes, 2006). Pan has been very active in promoting partnerships between CMEP and various Chinese environmental

NGOs. It is increasingly clear that China (and other developing countries such as India) are going to be confronted with drastic increases in e-waste as domestic computer consumption increases in the next several decades which will further compound the e-waste problem in China and elsewhere (see Yu et al., 2010a for estimates of growth in computer consumption by different regions in the world-system).

What is being done to challenge e-waste exports to China and elsewhere in the world-system? The Basel Convention on the Control of Transboundary Movements of Hazardous Wastes and their Disposal (1989) is a multilateral agreement that was enacted in 1989 under the auspices of the United Nations Environment Programme (and its subsequent amendment to ban e-waste export in 1995 which has yet to be ratified). The Convention, signed by 170 countries, requires that a country can only ship hazardous wastes if it has received written consent from the recipient country. The Convention has been ineffective in stopping the trade for several interrelated reasons. The US, one of the world's largest e-waste exporters, has not signed the bill and thus the effectiveness of the Convention has been undercut. The Convention has been ineffective because illegal shipments of wastes are pervasive and a general lack of implementation at the border areas in China.

The United Nations Environment Programme (2005, 2009) and international NGOs, including Greenpeace International and Greenpeace China, Silicon Valley Toxics Coalition, the Basel Action Network, and others have been monitoring and studying export flows and actual conditions in and around the recycling centers in China and elsewhere (Basel Action Network and Silicon Valley Toxics Coalition, 2002). The Basel Action Network has been particularly active in pressuring state authorities in the developed countries to enforce higher standards (see Puckett, 2006; www.ban.org). The Basel Action Network, other international organizations, and analysts have made a number of specific recommendations for dealing with the e-waste problem (see, e.g., Grossman, 2006:Chapter 7; Nnorom, Osibanjo, and

Ogwuegbu, 2011; Pellow, 2007:203-224; Smith, Sonnenfeld, and Pellow, 2006; United Nations Environment Program, 2005, 2009; Yu et al., 2010b). A sampling of these recommendations are listed below:

- A fully implemented global regime should be developed to regulate the movement of computer waste.

- The next generation of computers should be constructed to reduce health, safety, and environmental impacts at the time of decommissioning and increase capacity to upgrade computers over time.

- End-of-life- electronics and greener design using fewer toxic materials and increased capacity for upgrades.

- Extended Producer Responsibility (EPR) as a new paradigm in waste management.

The European Union's Directive on Waste from Electrical and Electronic Equipment (WEEE), along with the RoHs Directive, were enacted into law in February 2003 and came into force in 2004. The Directives require manufacturers and importers in the European Union countries to take back their products from consumers and ensure safe waste disposal or safe recycling-reuse. Heavy metals (lead, mercury, cadmium, and chromium) and flame retardants (polybrominated biphenyls and polybrominated biphenyl ethers) were to be replaced with safer materials. The directives have not been fully implemented (European Commission. 2002; Geiser and Tickner, 2006).

After years of failure to address the issue of e-waste (see Stephenson, 2008), the US has moved forward in several areas. On November 15, 2010, President Obama issued a presidential proclamation on e-waste recycling and the creation of an Interagency Task Force of Agencies within the federal government "to prepare a national strategy for responsible electronics stewardship, including improvements to Federal procedures for managing electronic products." He indicated he wanted the Federal Government to lead (Anonymous, 2010). The report of the Task Force was released in July 2011. The Task Force identified four major goals, one of which centers on reducing "harm from US exports of e-waste and improve safe handling of used electronics in developing countries" through five specific actions (Interagency Task Force on Electronics Stewardship, 2011:2-3):

- Improve information on trade flows and handling of used electronics, and share data with Federal and international agencies, within the limits of existing legal authorities.

- Provide technical assistance and establish partnerships with developing countries to better manage used electronics.

- Work with exporters to explore how to incentivize and promote the safe handling of remanufactured, recycled, and used electronics at home and abroad.

- Propose regulatory changes to improve compliance with the existing regulation that governs the export of cathode ray tubes from used computer monitors and televisions that are destined for reuse and recycling.

- Support ratification of the Basel Convention on the Control of Transboundary Movements of Hazardous Wastes and their Disposal.

Two Democratic Representatives (Gene Green of Texas and Mike Thompson of California) introduced the Responsible Electronic Recycling Act in the US House of Representatives on June 22, 2011. The bill would ban the export of certain restricted electronic waste exports to developing countries. "The bill aims to stop U.S. companies from dumping dangerous old electronics on countries where they are broken apart or burned by workers using few safety precautions," said Texas Representative Gene Green. It is reported that several computer manufacturers support the bill (Miclat, 2011).

The Basel Action Network adopted a certification program in April 2010 called the e-Stewards Standard for Reasonable Recycling and Reuse of Electronic Equipment. The program referred to as e-Stewards Certification was established to facilitate responsible disposal of e-waste materials. Basel Action Network announced on July 5, 2011 that Intercon Solutions (a Chicago Heights, Illinois, electronics recycler) would be the first company denied BAN's e-Stewards certification, which aims to recognize e-waste recyclers operating responsibly (www.ban.org; www.e-stewards.org/certification-overview).

CONCLUDING THOUGHTS

Counter-hegemonic globalization or "globalization from below" in the form of transnational networks of NGOs remains one of the most viable means for curbing the adverse consequences associated with the transfer of hazardous processes to the periphery (see Frey, 2006a). Globalization from below may help reduce or mitigate the worst abuses associated with the displacement of computer recycling and other environmental harms to the periphery as suggested by the concrete actions that have occurred in China, the EU, and the US noted above. (See Yu et al., [2010a, b] and Williams et al. [2008] for a very insightful discussion of why the existing policies noted above are unlikely to solve the e-waste problem in China and elsewhere.) Stopping the core's appropriation of the periphery's carrying capacity is another matter, for this process is embedded in the structure of the current world-system. In other words, the process of "ecological unequal exchange" between the core and periphery is necessary for continued capital accumulation in the core. And it will be some time before environmental justice and sustainability are realized in the peripheral zones of the world-system because of the contradictory tendencies between accumulation in the core and the role of the periphery as resource extraction frontier and waste disposal frontier. To put it another way, the "metabolic rift" (Foster, Clark, and York, 2010) between the core and periphery is made invisible by globalization and the attendant market ideology espoused by proponents of the neo-liberal perspective, including the editors of *The Economist* cited at the beginning of this chapter.

References

Anonymous. 2010. "Obama Driving E-Waste Reform." *Electronics Weekly* (15 November) at www.electronicsweekly.com/.

Basel Action Network and Silicon Valley Toxics Coalition. 2002. *Exporting Harm: The High Tech Trashing of Asia.* Seattle: Basel Action Network.

Basel Convention on the Control of Transboundary Movements of Hazardous Wastes and their Disposal. 1989. Available at www. basel.int/text/documents.html.

Bhutta, M. Khurrum S., Adnan Omar, and Xiaozhe Yang. 2011. "Electronic Waste: A Growing Concern in Today's Environment." *Economics Research International* 2011:1-8.

Bi, Xinhi, Bernd R.T. Simoneit, Zhen Wang, Xinming Wang, Guoying Sheng, and Jiamo Fu. 2010. "The Major Components of Particles Emitted During Recycling of Waste Printed Circuit Boards in a Typical E-Waste Workshop in South China." *Atmospheric Environment* 44:4440-4445.

Bunker, Stephen G, and Paul S. Ciccantell. 2005. *Globalization and the Race for Resources.* Baltimore, MD: The Johns Hopkns University Press.

Byrnes, Sholto. 2006. "Person of the Year: The Man Making China Green." *New Statesman* (18 December) at www. newstatesman.com.

Dietz, Thomas, R. Scott Frey, and Eugene Rosa. 2002. "Technology, Risk, and Society." Pp. 329-369 in *Handbook of Environmental Sociology*, edited by Riley Dunlap and William Michelson. Westport, CT: Greenwood Press.

Editors. 2007. Editorial. *The Economist* (9 June):14.

European Commission. 2002. *Directive 2002/96/EC on Waste Electrical and Electronic* Equipment at www.ec.europa.eu/environment/waste/weee/index.

Foster, John Bellamy. 2002a. "The Ecological Tyranny of the Bottom Line: The Environmental and Social Consequences of Economic Reductionism." Pp. 26-43 in *Ecology Against Capitalism*, by John Bellamy Foster. New York: Monthly Review Press.

_____. 2002b. "Let Them Eat Pollution: Capitalism in the World Environment." Pp. 60-68 in *Ecology Against Capitalism*, by John Bellamy Foster. New York: Monthly Review Press.

Foster, John Bellamy, Brett Clark, and Richard York. 2010. *The Ecological Rift: Capitalism's War on the Earth*. New York: Monthly Review Press.

Frey, R. Scott. 1998a. "The Hazardous Waste Stream in the World-System." Pp. 84-103 in *Space and Transport in the World-System*, edited by Paul Ciccantell and Stephen G. Bunker. Westport, CT: Greenwood Press.

_____. 1998b. "The Export of Hazardous Industries to the Peripheral Zones of the World-System." *Journal of Developing Societies* 14:66-81.

_____. 2006a. "The Flow of Hazardous Exports in the World-System." Pp. 133-149 in *Globalization and the Environment*, edited by Andrew Jorgenson and Edward Kick. Leiden, The Netherlands and Boston: Brill Academic Press.

_____. 2006b. "The International Traffic in Asbestos." *Nature, Society, and Thought* 19:173-180.

_____. In press. "The Displacement of Hazardous Products, Production Processes, and Wastes in the World-System." In *Handbook of World-Systems Analysis: Theory and Research*, edited by Salvatore Babones and Christopher Chase-Dunn. New York: Routledge.

Frey, R. Scott, Sabrina McCormick, and Eugene A. Rosa. 2007. "The Sociology of Risk." Pp. 81-87 in *The Handbook of 21st Century Sociology*, Volume II, edited by Clifton D. Bryant and Dennis Peck. Thousand Oaks, CA: Sage.

Geiser, Ken and Joel Tickner. 2006. "International Environmental Agreements and the Information Technology Industry." Pp. 260-272 in *Challenging the Chip: Labor Rights and Environmental Justice in the Global Electronics Industry*, edited by Ted Smith, David A. Sonnenfield, and David Naguib Pellow. Philadelphia, PN: Temple University Press.

Grossman, Elizabeth. 2006. *High Tech Trash: Digital Devices, Hidden Topics, and Human Health*. Washington, D.C.: Island Press.

Grossman, Gene M. and Alan B. Krueger. 1993. "Environmental Impacts of a North America Free Trade Agreement." In *The Mexico-U.S. Free Trade Agreement*, edited by Peter M. Garber. Cambridge, MA: The MIT Press.

_____. 1995. "Economic Growth and the Environment." *The Quarterly Journal of Economics* 110:350-377.

Harvey, David. 2010. *The Enigma of Capital and the Crises of Capitalism*. New York: Oxford University Press.

Hornborg, Alf. 2011. *Global Ecology and Unequal Exchange: Fetishism in a Zero-Sum World*. New York: Routledge.

Hou, Xia, X. L. Peng, X. Xu, L. Zheng, B. Qiu, Z. Qi, B. Zhang, D. Han, and Z. Piao. 2007. "Elevated Blood Levels of Children in Guiyu, an Electronic Waste Recycling Town in China." *Environmental Health Perspectives* 115 (7 July):1113-1117.

Interagency Task Force on Electronics Stewardship. 2011. *National Strategy for Eletronics Stewardship.* Washington, D.C.: Interagency Task Force on Electronics Stewardship.

Logan, Bernard I. 1991. "An Assessment of the Environmental and Economic Implications of Toxic-Waste Disposal in Sub-Saharan Africa." *Journal of World Trade* 25:61-76.

Martinez-Alier, Joan. 2009. "Social Metabolism, Ecological Distribution Conflicts, and Languages of Valuation." *Capitalism, Nature and Socialism* 20:58-87.

Miclat, Merlin. 2011. "Responsible Electronics Recycling Act Introduced in Congress." (24, June) at www.GreenAnswers.com.

Mol, Arthur P. 2001. *Globalization and Environmental Reform: The Ecological Modernization of the Global Economy.* Cambridge, MA: MIT Press.

Moxley, Mitch. 2011. "E-Waste Hits China." IPS (21 July) at www.ipsnews.net/news.

Nnorom, I.C., O. Osibanjo, and M.O.C. Ogwuegbu. 2011. "Global Disposal Strategies for Waste Cathode Tubes." *Resources, Conservation and Recycling* 55:275-290.

Pellow, David Naguib. 2007. *Resisting Global Toxins: Transnational Movements for Environmental Justice.* Cambridge, MA: MIT Press.

Puckett, Jim. 2006. "High Tech's Dirty Little Secret: The Economics and Ethics of the Electronic Waste Trade." Pp. 224-233 in *Challenging the Chip: Labor Rights and Environmental Justice in the Global Electronics Industry,* edited by Ted Smith, David A. Sonnenfeld, and David Naguib Pellow. Philadelphia: Temple University Press.

Rice, James. 2007. "Ecological Unequal Exchange: International Trade and Uneven Utilization of Environmental Space in the World System." *Social Forces* 85:1369-1392.

_____. 2009. "The Transnational Organization of Production and Uneven Environmental Degradation and Change in the World Economy." *Journal of Comparative International Sociology* 50:215-236.

Sepulveda, Alejandra, Mathias Schluep, Fabrice G. Renaud, Martin Streicher, Ruediger Kuehr, Christian Hageluken, and Andreas C. Gerecke. 2010. "A Review of the Environmental Fate and Effects of Hazardous Substances Released from Electrical and Electronic Equipments During Recycling: Examples from China and India." *Environmental Impact Assessment Review* 30:28-41.

Smith, Ted, David A. Sonnenfeld, and David Naguib Pellow, editors. 2007. *Challenging the Chip: Labor Rights and Environmental Justice in the Global Electronics Industry.* Philadelphia: Temple University Press.

Stephenson, John B. 2008. *Electronic Waste: Harmful U.S. Export Flow Virtually Unrestricted Because of Minimal EPA Enforcement and Narrow Regulation.* Testimony Before the Subcommittee on Asia, the Pacific, and the Global Environment, Committee on Foreign Affairs, House of Representatives, September 17, 2008. Available at www.gao.gov.

Summers, Lawrence. 1991. Selections from a World Bank Memo. *The Economist* (8 February):66.

Tsydenova, Oyuna and Magnus Bengtsson. 2011. "Chemical Hazards Associated with Treatment of Waste Electrical and Electronic Equipment." *Waste Management* 31:45-58.

United Nations. 2010. World Development Indicators. Available at http://data.un.org/

United Nations Environment Programme. 2005. *E-Waste, the Hidden Side of IT Equipment's Manufacturing and Use.* New York: United Nations.

_____. 2009. *Recycling – From E-waste to Resources.* New York: United States.

Wallerstein, Immanuel. 2004. *World-Systems Analysis: An Introduction.* Durham, NC: Duke University.

Widmer, R., H. Oswald-Krapf, D. Sinha-Khetriwal, M. Schnellmann, and H. Boni. 2005. "Global Perspectives on E-Waste." *Environmental Impact Assessment Review* 25:436-458.

Williams, Eric, Ramzy Kahhat, Braden Allenby, Edward Kavazanjian, Junbeum Kim, and Ming Yu. 2008. "Environmental, Social, and Economic Implications of Global Reuse and Recycling of Personal Computers." *Environmental Science and Technology* 42:6446-6454.

Yang, Fangxing, Shiwei Jin, Ying Xu, and Yuanan Lu. 2011. "Comparisons of IL-8, ROS and p. 53 Responses in Human Lung Epithelial Cells Exposed to Two Extracts of PM2,5 Collected from an E-Waste Recycling Area, China." *Environmental Research Letters* 6:1-6.

Yu, Jinglei, Eric Williams, Meiting Ju, and Chaofeng Shao. 2010a. "Foreasting Global Generation of Obsolete Personal Computers." *Environmental Science and Technology* 44:3232-3237.

_____. 2010b. "Managing E-Waste in China: Policies, Pilot Projects and Alternative Approaches." *Resources, Conservation and Recycling* 54:991-999

CHAPTER IV

Economics

Economics and Sustainability

William Forbes

The singular focus of economics on profitable margins and rational consumer choice is often seen as the impetus for the broader sustainability movement. Neo-classical economics and corresponding neoliberal policy reinvigorate the "gospel of efficiency" (to use Samuel Hays' term) found in Adam Smith's economies of scale and David Ricardo's comparative advantage and specialization. Milton Friedman's 1970s push towards a pure free market, empowered by the Reagan administration's 1980s deregulation and structural adjustment policies, offset some of the growth in environmental policies.

Thus two decades after the international environmental movement and debates over the need for limits to growth or reliance on "the market" to solve its own problems, the sustainability movement evolved. The Brundtland Report outlined in Our Common Future attempted to have nations reprioritize in the 1990s around a common goal of protecting cultural and environmental options for future generations. Development (neoclassical economic growth based on free trade) was still the underlying theoretical mantra, mitigated by concerns over pollution and disappearing habitats, languages and species. In fact, some major nations expanded their efforts towards free trade in the 1990s, most notably China and India.

Some critics such as former World Bank economist Herman Daly suggested a new paradigm was warranted, based on steady state economics rather than continual growth and its rampant consumption levels. Since the sustainable development movement emerged on a larger scale with the 1992 Rio Conference, the size of the world economy has mushroomed. Princeton economist Paul Krugman won the 2008 Nobel Prize for his economic geography models illustrating the startling simple global effect of economies of scale, lower transportation costs, and specialization. Such factors allowed Toyota to have a reasonable market for their cars in Germany while Mercedes-Benz could be sold in Japan.

The growth of the service sector in developed nations was offset by movement of industry to developing nations like Brazil and China – agglomeration economies mushroomed around urban centers, as did internal migrant workers. The World Bank's World Development Report 2009 focused on economic geography. A key theme was the rapid development history of developed nations, including a sharp increase in disparity of incomes, followed by a much slower evening out (or flattening) of this disparity. Developing nations are now going through almost the exact same process, with equal concern over environmental quality and living conditions in rapidly growing urban areas.

Thus a present look at the human side of sustainability takes a new look at the concerns central to the human condition – does the free market naturally solve enough of its own problems or are Keynesian government interventions necessary? New tracks of research have evolved, however, to help frame and broaden the debates. Studies on human happiness have emerged that challenge the notion of growing income as a good in and of itself. Environmental impacts are showing up on ever larger global scales, such as climate change and species extinctions, with some reports suggesting we are near the threshold or "tipping point" on several issues, moving towards a major, irreversible change.

The news is not all bad. Bangladesh economist Mohammed Yunus won the Nobel Peace Prize for his work helping millions of people off the bottom rung of poverty through microlending. The growth of the global economy has done the same for approximately one billion people, many of them in China and India. Political scientist Elinor Ostrom won the 2009 Nobel Prize in economics for her decades of work portraying the ability of various community members around the globe to work together to successfully manage common property, such as grazing pastures and ocean fisheries. Various examples are emerging of win-win situations between business and environment. Ecological economics has risen to illustrate the local and global value of ecosystem services provided by nature.

This diverse nature of economic value is an important aspect of the human side of sustainability – not simply a rational assessment of consumer choice, but a broad look at values. It also includes a look back at small scale, local economies, with their more intimate relations, as alternatives to the juggernaut of the global economy. This would likely please Adam Smith who, as many note, warned us to address moral richness as well as economic growth in a concept of increasing "wealth" of nations.

THE HUMAN WORLD AND ITS VALUES

Henrik Harjula

Introduction

We humans are like the Norwegian lemming (*Lemmus lemmus*). Under suitable conditions it breeds prolifically and has spectacular migrations, which are sometimes driven by instinct to follow the leader, even to drown in lakes and rivers or scramble down cliffs. We humans tend to do the same in running after material welfare.

In fact, we have ceased to be humans and have been transformed into consumers and numbers on a computer screen. We are mainly focusing on material values, such as cars, computers, and mobile phones. To replace human contacts and relationships, we collect enormous amounts of "stuff" as do hamsters (*Cricetus cricetus),* although these things do not necessarily increase our happiness. We no longer remember how good it feels to meet our relatives and neighbors face-to-face, since we only associate with them through Email, Facebook and Twitter.

Why do we behave like this? The obvious reason is the need to keep the current consumption-based economy growing to keep up our material welfare. As Bill McKibben (2007), in his book *Deep Economy*, aptly remarks: "any faltering of this growth leads quickly to misery: to recession and all its hardships." This model has been - and still is - served by politicians and economists as the only way to material welfare - and even to happiness. True, but let's keep in mind that the foundation for the current economic system was developed in the 18th century and it does not necessarily fit the current state of the world. Then, why is it not converted to meet the current requirements? The apparent

reason is that this system serves those who already are rich and/
or powerful extremely well.

The next sections will elaborate on current human values
and will delineate changes needed to provide foundation for an
equitable and sustainable society.

Current Material Values

The historical context of classical economics was the French
Revolution and industrial development in late 18th century.
Adam Smith's *The Wealth of Nations* (1776) is considered the
beginning of classical economics. Classical economics provided
the foundation for economic growth and capitalism. Capitalism
built on past feudalism and was mainly fueled by the industrial
revolution, which dramatically changed society. Then, a question
came up on how to organize a society around a system in which
every individual sought his or her own material gain. The human
greed embedded in our genes was harnessed from the very
beginning to enhance the benefits of well-off capitalists.

The economic theory was further developed to include
neoclassical economics, welfare economics, micro- and
macroeconomics, and even happiness economics.

Currently, we are very deeply engaged in the system of
procuring material welfare: economic theory assumes that an
individual acts rationally and attempts to maximize utility (a
measure of relative satisfaction) under given side constraints. In
plain English, this means that, according to classical economic
theory, humans need to be as greedy as possible to be able to act
rationally!

Welfare economics, in its current form, has been very
successful in enhancing material well-being, but not for everybody.
As McKibben (2007) explains:

> our economy has been growing, but most of us have
> relatively little to show for it. The median wage in the
> United States is currently the same as it was thirty years

ago. The real income of the bottom 90% of American taxpayers has declined steadily: they earned $27,060 in real dollars in 1979 and $25,646 in 2005. Much the same thing has happened across most of the globe.

This means that only the richest 10% of US citizens have benefitted from economic growth, which is most often measured with Gross Domestic Product (GDP).

Financial liberalization and globalization were strongly advocated as a way to improve the prospects of developing countries for economic growth and poverty reduction. However, there is no evidence that countries without capital controls have grown faster, invested more, or experienced lower inflation (FRBSF Economic Letter, April 8, 2005). Even the poverty reduction has been slow, and still over 1 billion people live on less than $1 a day. Sub-Saharan Africa has even witnessed increase both in the incidence of poverty and in the absolute numbers of poor. Some 300 million people live there on less than $1 per day (UNHDR, 2006). One reason for this could be that the inflow of capital to developing countries - as annual average from 2002-2006 - was some $850 billion, while the outflow was some $1200 billion. Of the annual inflow, global ODA (Official Development Aid) was some $90 billion, but estimated outflow to tax havens was some $620 billion (Eurodad fact sheet). Recent incidents in Tunisia, Egypt, Libya, etc. have given some hints about the real impact of these illicit outflows.

It is not difficult to guess what the situation will be in 2050 when this globe will have 3 billion new people, mainly in developing countries.

In the publication: "Prosperity without Growth", Professor Tim Jackson (2009), Economics Commissioner of the UK Sustainable Development Commission, states that:

> Every society clings to a myth by which it lives. Ours is the myth of economic growth. For the last five

decades the pursuit of growth has been the single most important policy goal across the world. The global economy is almost five times the size it was half a century ago. If it continues to grow at the same rate the economy will be 80 times that size by the year 2100. This growth has delivered its benefits, at best, unequally. A fifth of the world's population earns just 2% of global income. And while the rich got richer, middle-class incomes in Western countries were stagnant in real terms long before the latest recession.

Jackson (2009) elaborates on other effects:

This extraordinary ramping up of global economic activity has no historical precedent. It's totally at odds with our scientific knowledge of the finite resource base and the fragile ecology on which we depend for survival. And it has already been accompanied by the degradation of an estimated 60% of the world's ecosystems...

So, why do we continue supporting so intensively the economic growth which brings little benefits for most of us, if any?

Sustainable Values

The most widely quoted definition of sustainability and sustainable development has been that of the Brundtland Commission of the United Nations on March 20, 1987: *"Sustainable development is development that meets the needs of the present without compromising the ability of future generations to meet their own needs"* (World Commission on Environment and Development 1987). The hard fact is that mankind is currently far away from sustainable development. The present generation can - if lucky - meet its needs, but there will not be much left for future generations. Rapid population growth, emerging scarcity of energy, food, water and other material resources, as well as continuously increasing pollution, will in the foreseeable future severely compromise the current level of well-being. We have to understand that this globe is all that we have, and therefore infinite economic growth in this finite world is simply not possible.

Fortunately, after a long detour, it seems that even economics is returning back to its classical target: *"The greatest happiness for the greatest number of people"* (Bentham 1789). Indeed, it has become clear that the traditional economic indicator - GDP - does not account for the exploitation of natural resources and therefore allows consumption at the cost of future generations. Even more fundamental is the critique that social well-being should not be restricted to economic indicators, but rather to social indicators like family, health, education, social relationships, etc. (Jackson 2009).

Happiness economics is the quantitative study of happiness, positive and negative effect, well-being, quality of life, and life satisfaction and related concepts, typically combining economics with other fields such as psychology and sociology. It typically treats happiness-related measures, rather than wealth, income or profit, as something to be maximized.

Happiness has been a topic of philosophic discussion for thousands of years, but it has recently attracted the attention of behavioral and social scientists. During the past three decades, an explosion of research on happiness has occurred, with a concentration on how to measure it and what relationship it has to national wealth and social policy. Nearly 4,400 articles on this topic were published in the year 2000 alone (*The Independent Review*, Winter 2010).

The *Easterlin Paradox* is the key concept in happiness economics. It is named for economist and USC Professor Richard Easterlin, who discussed the factors contributing to happiness in the 1974 paper: *"Does Economic Growth Improve the Human Lot? Some Empirical Evidence"*. Easterlin found that, within a given country, people with higher incomes are more likely to report being happy. However, in international comparisons, the average reported level of happiness does not vary much with national income per person, at least for countries with income sufficient to meet basic needs. Similarly, although income per person rose steadily in the United States between 1946 and 1970, average reported happiness showed no such long-term trend and declined between 1960 and 1970.

The Easterlin Paradox suggests that there is no link between a society's economic development and its average level of happiness. Richard Layard (2005) further explained that people are concerned about their relative income rather than its absolute level. Layard also argued that "once a country has an annual personal income of $15,000, its level of happiness appears to be independent of the level of personal income.

Stevenson & Wolfers reassessed this paradox, analyzing multiple, rich datasets spanning many decades, in their 2008 paper, *"Economic Growth and Subjective Well-being: Reassessing the Easterlin Paradox"* . Using recent data on a broader array of countries, they established a clear positive link between average levels of subjective well-being and GDP per capita across countries. Stevenson and Wolfers found no evidence of a satiation point beyond which wealthier countries have no further increase in subjective well-being. By examining the relationship between changes in subjective well-being and income over time within countries, they found economic growth associated with rising happiness. However, they noted that the well-being - GDP gradient is about twice as steep for poor countries as for rich countries (Stevenson & Wolfers, 2008).

It is obvious that this discussion will continue, since it is not yet soundly convincing that people earning $1 billion annually would be 1000, 100 or at least 10 times happier than people earning $1 million, as Stevenson & Wolfers' findings tend to indicate.

Currently, general understanding is that GDP should be dropped as the sole indicator for well-being. An emerging consensus seems to support a set of indicators, rather than a single one.

In February 2008, the President of the French Republic, Nicolas Sarkozy, unsatisfied with the present state of statistical information about the economy and society, asked Nobel Prize-winning economists Joseph Stiglitz, Amartya Sen and noted French economist Jean Paul Fitoussi to create a commission, subsequently called *"The Commission on the Measurement of Economic Performance and Social Progress" (CMEPSP)"*. The aim of the Commission was to identify the limits of GDP as a sole indicator of economic performance and social progress, including the problems with its measurement; to consider what additional information might be required for the production of more relevant indicators of social progress; to assess the feasibility of alternative measurement tools; and to discuss how to present the statistical information in an appropriate way. The report was published in late 2009 (Stiglitz Report, 2009). It proposed a number of indicators to cover: 1) Economic performance and material well-being; 2) Quality of life; and 3) Sustainability.

The Franco-German Ministerial Council decided on February 4, 2010 to ask the French Conseil d'Analyse Économique (CAE) and the German Council of Economic Experts (GCEE) to follow-up on the outcome of the Stiglitz Report. This latter report was published in December 2010 (Joint Report, 2010). It evaluated the feasibility of the indicators proposed by the Stiglitz Report and applied those to the German and French data. Happiness as such has not come out in these papers, although it is embedded in the term "well-being". In receiving the Stiglitz Report on 13 September 2009, President Sarkozy and a panel of the world's top economists stated that *"countries need to find ways to measure happiness and well-being alongside raw economic growth and publish the results annually"*.

Simultaneously, The European Commission published a Communication to the Council and the European Parliament: *"GDP and beyond: Measuring progress in a changing world"* [COM(2009) 433 final, 20.8.2009]. The approach taken was similar to the proposals by the Stiglitz Report, and Commission services intended to present a pilot version of an index on environmental pressure in 2010, as methodologies for composite indices and data were already sufficiently mature. The UN Millennium Summit in 2000 and the Istanbul Declaration at the second OECD World Forum on Statistics in 2007 also called for the development of indicators towards measuring how societies are changing by using high quality, reliable statistics to assess progress in a range of areas affecting citizens' quality of life (UN, 2000; OECD, 2007).

A Way Forward

As has been described in previous sections, the current indicator for economic growth and social development - GDP - is no longer sufficient and acceptable. Further, it should not even be used by itself to describe economic growth, as it does not take into account depletion of natural capital, environmental pollution and negative impacts of climate change. Therefore, the so called *"Green GDP"*, *"Genuine Progress Indicator (GPI),"* or another set of comparable measures should urgently be implemented to demonstrate the real economic growth of the future. GDP has steadily grown in the US since 1950. However, when measured by GPI, the US economy has actually stagnated since the mid-1970s as income inequality, environmental degradation, and the failing international position of the US took their toll on real economic progress (Talberth, Cobb et al., 2007).

In this respect, a Chinese example is illustrative. The Green GDP results were published for 2004 in China, demonstrating a loss of $66 billion, equal to 3.05% of the GDP. The calculation included water and air pollution, as well as waste management and pollution accidents. On the other hand, the World Bank estimated that the real GDP reduction in 2004 would have been somewhere between 8-12%, when also including desertification and depletion of natural capital. This would have meant zero or negative GDP growth for 2004. Chinese authorities considered this result too politically damaging and buried the whole idea of the Green GDP (Kirykowicz, 2010).

Consequently, GDP should be replaced by a set of indicators which would reflect the whole content of sustainability: 1) The *real* economic growth; 2) Human well-being/happiness; and 3) Environmental limitations.

Real economic growth could be measured satisfactorily with the Green GDP or GPI. The Green GDP has been proposed to explicitly estimate the contributions of nature to human well-being by subtracting the economic penalties imposed by natural resource depletion and pollution from national accounting. As a result, the Green GDP is meant to advance a more inclusive view of "natural capital" and promote more sustainable management practices (Wu & Wu, 2010). Genuine Progress Indicator (GPI) is a well-being indicator which is based on the Index of Sustainable Economic Development (ISEW) by Herman Daly and John B. Cobb Jr (1989). GPI takes consumption as a basis instead of production, which GDP uses as a basis. It also takes into account factors which reduce well-being, such as uneven income, depletion of natural capital, and environmental pollution and accidents (Lawn, 2003).

Human happiness/well-being seems to emerge as a new paradigm for measuring progress in human society. Recently, UK Prime Minister David Cameron has tasked his advisors to look into happiness and what the British Government could do to promote it. Cameron suggests (The Guardian, 14 November, 2010)

> It's time we admitted that there's more to life than money and it's time we focused not just on GDP but on GWB – general well-being - which can't be measured by money or traded in markets. It's about the beauty of our surroundings, the quality of our culture and, above all, the strength of our relationships. Improving our society's sense of well-being is, I believe, the central political challenge of our times.

Based on calculations by the New Economics Foundation (NEF), Costa Rica is the greenest and happiest country in the world. The Happy Planet Index (HPI) includes a new list that ranks nations by combining measures of their ecological footprint and the happiness of their citizens. The United States features 114th in the table. The top 10 is dominated by countries from Latin America, while African countries fill out the bottom of the table (NEF, 2009).

Several countries, most notably Canada and France, are currently looking at similar initiatives under pressure to put less store in conventional economic measures such as GDP. Development of suitable social indicators is currently under way, including health, education, personal activities, social relationships, political voice and governance (Stiglitz Report, 2009; Joint Report, 2010; COM(2009) 433 final, 20.8.2009; NEF, 2008).

Simply measuring happiness is not enough, however. A happy life includes a secured income, family, job, health, access to cultural events, etc. To facilitate the happy life, the liberalization and globalization of economics should be revisited. Since the current globalized system is unable to maintain employment, a basic salary should be considered for everybody. By this way, the current - often humiliating - social security system, if it exists at all, could be scrapped to a large extent. There is enough affluence in this world to cover the expenses, it is currently accumulating in too few pockets. At the same time, financial markets should be regulated tighter to avoid speculation in stock markets and to close tax havens, whether situated in London or in the Cayman Islands.

It is good to keep in mind that the economic system is man-made and it can be modified as needed, unlike the finite natural system - the planet earth - which provides the only available support for human life and the global economy.

References

Bentham, J. 1789. *An Introduction to the Principles of Morals and Legislation;* Reprint: Kitchener, ON, Canada: Batoche Books, 2000.

Commission of the European Communities. 2009. "Communication from the Commission to the Council and the European Parliament: GDP and beyond - Measuring progress in a changing world", Brussels, 433 final 20.8.2009; http://eur-lex.europa. eu/LexUriServ/LexUriServ.do?uri=COM:2009:0433:FIN:EN:PDF. (accessed April 2011)

Daly, H. and J. B. Cobb, Jr. 1989. *For the Common Good.* Boston, MA: Beacon Press

Easterlin, R. A. 1974. "Does Economic Growth Improve the Human Lot?" In, Paul A. David and Melvin W. Reder, eds., *Nations and Households in Economic Growth: Essays in Honor of Moses Abramovitz.* New York, Academic Press, Inc.

Eurodad fact sheet. http://www.eurodad.org/uploadedFiles/Whats_ New/Reports/factsheet_capitolflight08.pdf.

Federal Reserve Bank of San Francisco. 2005. "Financial liberalization: How well has it worked for developing countries?" FRBSF Economic Letter Number 2005-06, April 8, 2005; http://www.frbsf. org/publications/economics/letter/2005/el2005-06.pdf (accessed April 2011).

French Conseil d'Analyse Économique (CAE) and the German Council of Economic Experts (GCEE). 2010. Joint Report: *Monitoring economic performance, quality of life and sustainability,* December 2010; http://www.sachverstaendigenrat-wirtschaft.de/ fileadmin/dateiablage/Expertisen/2010/ex10_en.pdf (accessed April 2011).

Jackson, T. 2009. *Prosperity without growth? The transition to a sustainable economy.* London, UK: Sustainable Development Commission; http://www.sd-commission.org.uk/publications/ downloads/prosperity_without_growth_report.pdf (accessed April 2011)

Kirykowicz, A.. 2010. "China & Green GDP", *Climatico*. February 3, 2010, http://www.climaticoanalysis.org/post/china-green-gdp/ (accessed April 2011)

Layard, R. 2005. *Happiness: Lessons from a New Science*. New York: Penguin Press.

Lawn, P. A. 2003. A theoretical foundation to support the Index of Sustainable Economic Welfare (ISEW), Genuine Progress Indicator (GPI), and other related indexes. *Ecological Economics 44: 105-118*.

McKibben, B. 2007. *Deep Economy: The Wealth of Communities and the Durable Future*. New York: Times Books;

New Economics Foundation. 2008. *National Accounts of Well-being: bringing real wealth onto the balance sheet*;http://www.neweconomics.org/sites/neweconomics.org/files/National_Accounts_of_Well-being_1.pdf (accessed April 2011)

New Economics Foundation. 2009. *The Happy Planet Index 2.0: Why good lives don't have to cost the Earth*;http://www.happyplanetindex.org/public-data/files/happy-planet-index-2-0.pdf (accessed April 2011)

Organization for Economic Cooperation and Development. 2007. "Istanbul Declaration." The OECD 2nd World Forum, 27-30 June 2007, Istanbul, Turkey; http://www.oecd.org/site/0,3407,en_21571361_31938349_1_1_1_1_1,00.html (accessed April 2011)

Smith, A. 1776. *An Inquiry into the Nature and Causes of the Wealth of Nations*.

Stevenson, B. and J. Wolfers. 2008. *Economic Growth and Subjective Well-Being: Reassessing the Easterlin Paradox*, Brookings Papers on Economic Activity, Spring 2008. http://bpp.wharton.upenn.edu/jwolfers/Papers/EasterlinParadox.pdf (accessed April 2011).

Stiglitz Report. 2009. Stiglitz, J. E., A. Sen and J.-P. Fitoussi: *Report by the Commission on the Measurement of Economic Performance and*

Social Progress, http://www.stiglitz-sen-fitoussi.fr/documents/
rapport_anglais.pdf (accessed April 2011)

Talberth, D. J., C. Cobb, N. Slattery 2007. *The Genuine Progress
Indicator 2006: A Tool for Sustainable Development*. Oakland,
California: Redefining Progress: The Nature of Economics; http://
www.environmental-expert.com/Files%5C24200%5Carticles%5C1
2128%5CGPI202006.pdf (accessed April 2011)

The Guardian. 2010. "David Cameron aims to make happiness the
new GDP, 14 November 2010." http://www.guardian.co.uk/
politics/2010/nov/14/david-cameron-wellbeing-inquiry (accessed
April 2011).

The Independent Review. 2010. http://www.independent.org/
publications/tir/article.asp?a=771 (accessed April 2011).

United Nations. 2000. "Millenium Declaration 55/2, 18 September
2000." http://www.un.org/millennium/ (accessed April 2011).

United Nations. 2006. *Human Development Report 2006; Summary;
Beyond scarcity: Power, poverty and the global water crisis.*
http://hdr.undp.org/en/media/HDR2006_English_Summary.pdf
(accessed April 2011)

World Commission on Environment and Development. 1987. Our
Common Future. Oxford, UK: Oxford University Press.

Wu, J. and T. Wu (2010), "Green GDP". In, *Berkshire Encyclopedia
of Sustainability*, Vol. II, The Business of Sustainability. Great
Barrington, MA: Berkshire Publishing , pp. 248-250. http://leml.
asu.edu/jingle/Web_Pages/Wu_Pubs/PDF_Files/Wu+Wu-2010-
GreenGDP.pdf (accessed April 2011)

The Tragedy of the Commons and Climate Change

Lee Payne

The tragedy of the commons is a fable that expresses the relationship between human nature and the use, or misuse, of "common-pool" environmental resources (Hardin 1968, Bitsell and Bulkeley 2004). One of the examples of the "commons" Garret Hardin uses in his classic paper in *Science* is an area where local sheepherders graze their sheep. There is a limit to the number of sheep that can graze the commons without endangering its sustainability. Human nature is such, though, that each herder will act in their self-interest by maximizing the number of their sheep grazing in the commons. Thus, the commons is overgrazed and depleted of value.

Clack and York (2005) apply this "tragedy" to modern accumulation of carbon dioxide (CO_2) and other greenhouse gasses in the atmosphere. These increased gasses are problematic because they delay escape of long-wave radiation from the Earth's atmosphere and increase global temperatures, much like a car windshield heats a parked car on a summer's day. Prior to the industrial age, there was a relative balance between the release of CO_2 gasses and the re-absorption of CO_2 gasses. Clack and York argue that, "carbon is absorbed and contained in nonliving forms, such as oceans, glaciers, and rocks, which serve as sinks, helping [to] limit the accumulation of CO_2 in the atmosphere" (2005, 403). These "carbon sinks" are the equivalent of the commons that are shared by all nations and act as carbon "scrubs" for the environment.

The industrialization of developed and developing countries has altered this balance. To use Hardin's terminology, self-interest in the pursuit of capital and mass production has depleted the commons (stable atmosphere) to the point of global concern. It can be argued that the "increasing concentration of carbon dioxide … in the atmosphere has likely contributed to the observed 0.6° C increase in global temperatures over the past one hundred years" (Clack and York 2005, 393). Projections by the International Panel on Climate Change (IPCC) predict a 1.5 to 6.0° C increase in global temperatures during the 21st Century (Clack and York 2005, 393). Foster (2002, 21) contends that an increase of 4° C "would create an earth that is warmer than at any time in the last 40 million years."

Clearly, the current overuse of carbon sinks by industrialized countries is not sustainable. The commons are being depleted. As such, it is imperative that standardized criteria for sustainability, including carbon intensity for all goods and international energy efficiencies and emissions standards, be identified and implemented.

The Private Argument

Proponents of "economic modernization" theory argue that, although economic development has created environmental problems, further economic development can solve these problems instead of adding to them (York, Rosa, and Dietz 2003). The assumption is that, "in capitalist economies, business has a strong incentive to invest in research and development that can lead to technological innovations … [while] in controlled economies, no such incentives exist as investors do not necessarily profit from their inventions" (York, Rosa, and Dietz 2003, 284).

In support of "economic modernization" theory, consider the following arguments. An energy resource often linked to economic growth is oil – the assumption being that higher prices slow economic growth. In support of this, Hickman, Huntington, and Sweeney found that, "two years after a 50 percent oil price increase, real output had fallen 2.9 percent, unemployment had increased 1.2 percent, and prices had increased 2.0 percent"

(1987, 22). However, Goldstein, Huang, and Akan (1992, 260) argue that these effects are short lived. They contend that "higher energy prices stimulate greater energy *efficiency*, so that GDP continues to grow while energy consumption remains more level." As evidence, they point to the increase in automobile miles per gallon from the 1970s through today. While some of these improvements have been realized through policies and regulations, many improvements may be linked to this efficient response to prices, a hallmark of "economic modernization" theory.

The Public Argument
On the side of public regulation, proponents argue for the "treadmill of production" theory developed by Schnaiberg. This theory argues that "modern societies, particularly market dominated ones, are driven by a relentless commitment to growth, despite its social and ecological costs" (Clack and York 2005, 394). The treadmill of production theory is closely linked to the "Jevons paradox." Economist William Stanley Jevons pointed out in the 1860s the inherent contradiction of economic modernization, arguing that improvements in efficiency actually increase the use of natural resources under capitalist conditions.

Clack and York (2005) offer empirical evidence in support of the Jevons paradox. They point to increases in carbon efficiency in the United States, the Netherlands, Japan, and Austria from 1975 through 1996. While all four countries realized significant increases in carbon efficiency, they also experienced increases in total CO_2 emissions and CO_2 emissions per capita.

Implicit in the lessons of the tragedy of the commons is the need for environmental protection—be it through public regulation, private initiative, or a combination of the two. To date, little room for compromise can be found between the public regulation and private initiative schools of thought. Because modern production systems are growth dependent, private enterprise is unlikely to accept the "treadmill of production" argument. However, there may be room for compromise or cooperation.

Negative Externalities

Regardless of the approach taken, one of the goals of sustainable development is to reduce the negative externalities associated with human production and human consumption; negative externalities are the byproducts of human production and human consumption and can take the form of air, water, and soil pollution, increased waste, and resource depletion, to name a few. For example, the "American Dream" posits that everyone should strive for a house with a little white picket fence, two cars in the garage, a television in every room, 2.5 children, and a cell phone in every pocket.

It can be argued that each of the items on the American Dream list is driven by economic development and that each create negative externalities. Building homes and fences deplete forests that scrub CO_2 from the atmosphere; driving automobiles depletes fossil fuels and contributes to the increasing levels of CO_2; watching televisions, especially the new and popular plasma variety, adds to pollution through burning of coal that produces most of our electricity; having children increases population and puts further demands on farming, ranching, and fishing industries and creates more waste that must be disposed of; and cell phones create problems with demand for "conflict minerals" and the disposal of rechargeable batteries. In reality almost everything humans engage in on a daily basis, and everything associated with production, has some negative externality associated with it. It is the accumulation of these negative externalities that are destroying the commons.

The Challenge

The challenge to reducing negative externalities in a capitalist system is finding a harmonious balance between public regulations and private initiatives. As pointed out here and in other essays in this chapter, this can be difficult because of a lack of trust on both sides. The public sector assumes the private sector will sacrifice the public good in the pursuit of profits, while the private sector assumes the public sector will regulate to the point that profits will disappear. Freudenburg (2005, 101) addresses several "assumptions" related to economic growth, production, and environmental resources.

> Argument number three is that, whatever their size, the heavily polluting activities are vital to the economy because they involve specific high-value materials or products that are effectively impossible to produce without high levels of accompanying environmental damage. The fourth through sixth possibilities have to do with assumptions/arguments that *more vigorous regulation would be unwise/irrational*, even if those heavily polluting industries are less important economically than generally assumed. Argument four is that the costs of regulation would be so onerous as to provide virtual guarantees that the firms in question would go out of business. Argument five is that, if regulated, the firms would simply move to so-called third-world countries where regulations are less stringent. The sixth and final argument is that, if regulated, the firms in question would merely pass along costs to "consumers," including other businesses, creating ruinous effects for the economy as a whole.

In response to assumption three, Freudenburg (2005) concludes that high levels of pollutants are likely in older industries that utilize outdated, inefficient technologies. Therefore, modernizing these industries and technologies may reduce pollutants. Where assumption four is concerned, Freudenburg (2005) provides empirical evidence that the costs of compliance with limits on sulphur dioxide (SO_2) emissions in the early 1990s were less than a tenth of the projected costs. Addressing assumption five, Freudenburg (2005) found that, in general, regulated industries have not chosen to leave the U.S. and that, of the industries that did leave, 84 percent moved to heavily regulated, developed countries. Finally, Freudenburg (2005) dismisses assumption six with a simple cost/benefit analysis, arguing that consumers would be willing to assume modest cost increases for increased environmental benefits. In addition, he contends that even a doubling of the cost of certain materials would lead to a modest five percent impact for the economy as a whole (Freudenburg 2005).

A Possible Solution

In an effort to promote responsible private initiatives, steps can be taken to recognize and license businesses that promote the social, environmental, and economic well-being of the communities they serve. In addition, attempts to reformulate measures of economic output to include social well-being, environmental degradation, and resource scarcity should be pursued by private entities. One possible solution may be "cap and trade" measures.

Research on the effectiveness of cap and trade produces mixed results (Stavins 1998, Jacoby and Reiner 2001, Kennedy 2002, Pizer 2006, Parry, Walls, and Harrington 2007, and Metcalf 2008). What cap and trade legislation seeks to do is put public caps on negative externalities like pollutants while allowing private enterprise to engage in trading units of pollutants for monetary gain. The concept is fairly simple, with a goal of limiting the total amount of pollutant produced collectively by all firms . Public regulations put a maximum cap on the amount of pollutants and private industries coming in under the cap can then trade or sell their unused units of pollutants to private industries that do not come in under their cap.

For example, the copper smelting industry produces negative externalities in the form of air and water pollutants. The public sector, taking public health and sustainable development into consideration, determines the maximum amount of air and water pollutants that the copper smelting industry can generate. All of the copper smelting plants combined cannot exceed this limit. The individual copper smelting plants have options under cap and trade.

Freudenburg (2005) notes high levels of pollutants are likely in older industries that utilize outdated, inefficient technologies. One option for older, less efficient plants is to reduce their pollutants by modernizing their facilities – modernization theory. If modernizing is too costly, there is another option available. Newer, more efficient plant facilities that do not produce their allotted amount of pollutants can sell their unused units of pollution to the older facilities unable to meet their cap. Cap and trade produces economic incentives to produce fewer pollutants than allowed, while protecting the overall commons by capping pollutants at a sustainable level. Common recognition of carbon dioxide as a pollutant remains a policy obstacle in the US.

Conclusion

The commons are being threatened by the level of human production and consumption. There are finite amounts of fossil fuel resources. Renewable resources are, in many instances, being depleted at a quicker rate than they can be replenished. Externalities associated with carbon dioxide could pose the greatest risk. The public and private sectors are capable of working together and need not be at odds on sustainable development. The study of common-pool resource management is a growing subdiscipline in environmental policy. Elinor Ostrom won the 2009 Nobel Prize in economics for decades of work on communities that sustainably self-manage commons around the world (Ostrom 1990). Is cap and trade the answer to every environmental problem threatening the commons? No, but cap and trade is one possible solution to some of the more pressing environmental problems threatening sustainability.

References

Bitsell, Michele M.; Harriet Bulkeley. "Transnational Networks and Global Environmental Governance: The Cities for Climate Protection Program." *International Studies Quarterly*. Vol. 48, No. 2 (Jun., 2004), pp. 471-493.

Clack, Brett; Richard York. "Carbon Metabolism: Global Capitalism, Climate Change, and Biospheric Rift." *Theory and Society*. Vol. 34, No. 4 (Aug. 2005), pp. 391-428.

Foster, John Bellamy. *Ecology Against Capitalism*, (New York: Monthly Review Press 2002).

Freudenburg, William R. "Privileged Access, Privileged Accounts: Toward a Socially Structured Theory of Resources and Discourses." *Social Forces*. Vol. 84, No. 1 (Spe., 2005), pp. 89-114.

Goldstein, J. S., X. Huang, B. Akan (1997). Energy in the World Economy, 1950-1992. *International Studies Quarterly*. 41 (2): 241-266.

Harding, G. 1968. "The Tragedy of the Commons." *Science,* Vol. 162 no. 3859 pp. 1243-1248.

Hickman, B. G., H. G. Huntington, J. L. Sweeney (1987). *Macroeconomic Impacts of Energy Shocks*. Amsterdam: North Holland Publishing Company.

Kennedy, Peter W. "Optimal Early Action on Greenhouse Gas Emissions." *The Canadian Journal of Economics*, Vol. 35, No. 1 (Feb., 2002), pp. 16-35.

Jacoby, Henry D. and David M. Reiner. "Getting Climate Policy on Track after the Hague." *International Affairs*, Vol. 77, No. 2 (Apr., 2001), pp. 297-312.

Metcalf, Gilbert E. "Using Tax Expenditures to Achieve Energy Policy Goals." *The American Economic Review*, Vo. 98, No. 2 (May 2008), pp. 90-94.

Ostrom, Elinor (1990). *Governing the Commons: The Evolution of Institutions for Collective Action*. New York: Cambridge University Press.

Parry, Ian W. H., Margaret Walls and Winston Harrington. "Automobile Externalities and Policies." *Journal of Economic Literature*, Vol. 45, No. 2 (Jun., 2007), pp. 373-399.

Pizer, William A. "The Evolution of a Global Climate Change Agreement." *The American Economic Review*, Vol. 96, No. 2 (May, 2006), pp. 26-30.

Stavins, Robert N. "What Can We Learn from the Grand Policy Experiment? Lessons from S)2 Allowance Trading." *The Journal of Economic Perspectives*, Vol. 12, No. 2 (Summer, 1998), pp. 69-88.

York, Richard; Eugene A. Rosa; Thomas Dietz. "Footprints on the Earth: The Environmental Consequences of Modernity." *American Sociological Review*. Vol. 68, No. 2 (Apr., 2003), pp. 279-300.

Sustainability: Towards the New American Dream

Cindy L. Pressley

A full hour before the party reached the city they had begun to note the perplexing changes in the atmosphere. It grew darker all the time, and upon the earth the grass seemed to grow less green. Every minute, as the train sped on, the colors of things became dingier; the fields were grown parched and yellow, the landscape hideous and bare. And along with the thickening smoke they began to notice another circumstance, a strange, pungent odor . . . The new emigrants were still tasting it, lost in wonder, when suddenly the car came to a halt, and the door was flung open, and a voice shouted—"Stockyards!"[1]

Upton Sinclair's *The Jungle* (1906) tells the story of Jurgis Rudkus, an immigrant who came to the Chicago stockyards to obtain wealth and prosperity. Unbeknownst to Jurgis, his new environment was filled with environmental horrors that would lead his family down a path of despair. Sinclair's plan, when penning Jurgis' story, was to examine industrial Chicago "but once there he found that the product itself was as poorly regulated as the horrible conditions under which it was produced" (Dickstein, 1981, p. viii). *The Jungle*, a contributing factor in the passage of the 1906 Food and Drugs Act (Dickstein, 1981), retains relevance as it reminds us of the connections between economy and environment. Sinclair showed the public that intervention was

---

1   Sinclair, 1906, pp. 25-26

necessary to sustain the city. This need for intervention continues in the twenty-first century.

Sustainability crosses multiple fields. Paehlke (2005, p. 37) suggests "Sustainability is thus first and foremost about product design, industrial ecology, public policy, and even a radical sociocultural adaptation of the material aspects of the American dream". Paehlke points out a common criticism in that sustainability reflects stagnancy, essentially a lack of progress. Industrialization and urbanization have been landmarks for progress in achieving the American dream. However, externalities occurred in achieving this progress. These externalities include polluted air and water, diminishing natural resources, and a further divide between wealth and poverty.

To lessen the effect of these externalities the concept of the American dream should be adapted, much as Paehlke suggests, such that a landmark of progress includes sustainability. Our world-view has been dominated by economism, a view where economic growth is considered the main indicator of human well-being. This should be altered. Paehlke (2001) notes sustainability has the potential to become a world-view that competes with economism.

It is argued here that government regulation is the appropriate place to start to adapt the American dream to a world-view that focuses on sustainability.

> In its best form, the modern regulatory system can be seen as a kind of post-New Deal republicanism. Its goal is to respect private property and freedom of contract, but also to permit a large range of governmental activity in the interest of economic productivity and protection of the disadvantaged—while simultaneously adhering to the original belief in the governmental process as one of deliberation oriented to the public good rather than as a series of interest-group trade-offs. (Sunstein, 1990, p. 12).

Three elements which help define the modern regulatory system are economic production, protection of the disadvantaged, and orientation towards public goods. These three elements are similar to three indicators of sustainability: "economic growth, social well-being (including social equity) and environmental quality (including resource sustainability)" (Paehlke, 2001, p. 9). The modern regulatory system could be used to further the acceptance of a world-view geared to sustainability. Before providing an illustration of an area where this may be accomplished, it is important to discuss why and how regulation can be used in a capitalist democracy such as the United States.

Regulatory Necessity

Levin (2006) discusses the development of regulation of color additives where the 1906 Food and Drugs Act "empowered the Secretary of Agriculture to ban unsafe use of synthetic dyes known as coal-tar colors, so-called because they were made from bituminous coal and other petroleum products" (Levin, 2006, p. 447). Levin explains how the Food and Drug Administration (FDA) eventually was given control over these areas. Later, in response to a public scandal involving the use of coal-tar colors in eyelash dyes, causing women to go blind, the FDA's jurisdiction was expanded to include cosmetics. Industry, left to itself, was not engaging in vigorous testing to ensure the safety of its products. While it is not true that all industry members take short cuts in the name of increasing the purse, some have and others continue to do so (consider the voluntary recall[2] of products such as peanut butter, eggs and celery in the first decade of the twenty-first century).

Regulation is often passed to ensure that industries cannot escape the strictures of a system where the public, i.e., consumers, maintain basic rights - in that the food, air, water, and energy they consume should not cause them un-assumed harm. Regulation is used to balance the power between producers and consumers.

2 At the time of the recalls the FDA did not have the power to force food recalls.

Consumer protection requires both economic and environmental safety as well as long-term sustainability.

In the last seventy-five years most successful countries gradually came to understand that their own citizens share a common fate, requiring the active role of government to ensure that every citizen has the chance and means (through public education, public health, and basic infrastructure) to participate productively within the society, and to curb society's dangerous encroachments on the physical environment. (Sachs, 2008, pp. 3-4).

While the activist approach is offered here to support government regulation, the regulatory approach is not free of flaws.

Rosenbaum (2008) discusses how one of "the longest running and least resolvable conflicts in environmental policy making is contention over the economic cost and fairness of environmental regulations" (Rosenbaum, 2008, p. 22). Rosenbaum states that as the 1970s was ending, there were numerous political pressures to take into account the economic implications of environmental regulations. While there is a vast literature dealing with the relationship between environmental regulation and economic cost, it is accepted here that environmental regulation in the United States is not overly excessive, as the amount spent by the United States on environmental regulation compares to that of other industrialized countries, even if public opinion often assumes the United States spends more (see Rosenbaum, 2008).

Regulating for Sustainability
Popular media has addressed the food crisis in America by pointing out problems of agribusiness, such as: heavy environmental tolls from the use of large amounts of fossil fuels;

the amount of waste produced by livestock; the amount of chemicals needed to produce feed for livestock and protect crops; antibiotics necessary to keep livestock healthy enough to eat; and the growing obesity epidemic facing the United States (Walsh, 2009). A range of public policy decisions impact agricultural production.   Doering (1992) argues that both farm and non-farm policies impact farming practices in the United States. Traditional farming practices and policies were less focused on the environmental impacts of those practices and policies and more focused on concerns such as rural conditions and incomes, efficiency, "and conserving natural resources as part of the base of agricultural productivity" (Doering, 1992, p. 22). Traditional practices and policies included items like commodity programs and acreage restrictions. Outside factors influenced farming as well, such as the invention and growth of the use of tractors and pesticides, which altered the need to diversify crops and maintain livestock and pasture areas for draft work animals.

Government policies are only one factor that impacts farming and, even in a democratic capitalist system, farming is an area where government has intervened to a great extent for purposes such as stability of food supplies, farmer income, and consumer prices. Current policies and current changes to policies are not likely to have a great impact on changing farming practices in the United States. According to Doering (1992): "The cost and complexity of the command and control approach appears unreasonable given the number of farms and the very specific resource base and management capacity associated with each one" and "The alternative of taxing inputs that support unsustainable practices will vary in effectiveness depending on the value in use of the inputs" (p. 34). Overall, Doering believes that new approaches to policy must be created that will alter farming practices towards becoming more sustainable.

Alternative forms of agriculture are not yet clearly defined or accepted by those who study agro-ecosystems (Vandermeer, 1995). Government intervention to increase study and expansion of alternative forms of agriculture, particularly sustainable agriculture, could be valuable.

> High-productivity farming is often seen as the foe of biodiversity conservation and, indeed, with bad farming practices, farming can be ecologically destructive. At a more basic level, however, high-productivity farming is vital for biodiversity conservation, since the higher the yield per hectare of arable land, the fewer hectares of arable land are needed to provision the population with foodstuffs . . . Yet the twenty-first-century Green Revolution needs to be environmentally friendly and ecologically savvy from the start. This would mean adopting the lessons of the new agroecology, which combines high-productivity agriculture with sustainable land management. (Sachs, 2008, p. 149)

Focusing on agricultural production could provide a way to expand public interest in sustainability by focusing on a pressing human problem, America's food crisis. By re-examining traditional farm subsidy programs, such that funding is diverted from the now common large agribusiness corporate farm toward small/medium family farms that use innovative organic sustainable agricultural practices, government could simultaneously promote a segment of the local economy that is a traditional part of American life while promoting new approaches to sustainable agriculture.

Government regulation need not stop with production. By providing regulatory programs and incentives to producers that provide for the consumption of organic sustainable agriculture by those in the low income strata of society (for example creating sustainable consumption options under the popular Women, Infants and Children or WIC program), government could stave off some critics of sustainability who contend that:

> sustainable development á la WCED [World Commission on Environment and Development] promotes normal economic growth as the remedy for environmental degradation. Thus, the idea can contain no ecological or moral content . . . An idea of sustainability in which ecological health takes precedence over economic development must be anchored in ecological principles and social justice. (Clark, 1995, p. 236)

It is this last concept of social justice that government regulation can be especially useful in expanding environmental sustainability. Government regulation can focus on making available sustainable agricultural products to those who are often left out of the sustainable consumption process such as the poor, who often do not have access to or are unable to afford food produced using organic sustainable farming practices.

Conclusion

Government regulation should be used to promote sustainable practices among multiple strata of society including those with little political and economic power that are sometimes overlooked in larger discussions of economic and environmental policy. Pure free market systems are problematic in that they do not allow intervention for the purpose of ensuring competition and protecting consumers who do not have the knowledge or financial ability to shop elsewhere. Allowing for regulatory change in the production and consumption of food may be the most appropriate way in which to begin the shift to a new American dream.

Government regulation may be a useful mechanism to use to begin altering our economically based world-view to one that focuses on sustainability. However, paradigmatic revolution where sustainability becomes a goal equal to that of economic development is not going to happen overnight. The creation of regulation can help to push for social change, but other changes in society must occur as well. If Jurgis' story were told today, what would you want his story to say?

References

Clark, J.G. (1995). Economic development vs. sustainable societies: Reflections on the players in a crucial contest. *Annual Review of Ecology and Systematics, 26*, 225-248.

Dickstein, M. (1981). Introduction. In Upton Sinclair, *The Jungle*, v-xviii. NY, NY: Bantam Books.

Doering, O. (1992). Federal policies as incentives or disincentives to ecologically sustainable agricultural systems. In R.K. Olson (Ed.), *Integrating Sustainable Agriculture, Ecology, and Environmental Policy*, pp. 21-36. Binghamton, NY: The Haworth Press.

Levin, R.M. (2006). The story of the Abbott Labs trilogy: the seeds of the ripeness doctrine. In Peter L. Strauss (Ed.), *Administrative Law Stories*, pp. 399-428. NY, NY: Foundation Press.

Paehlke, R. (2001). Environmental politics, sustainability and social science. *Environmental politics*, 10(4), 1-22.

Paehlke, R. (2005). Sustainability as a bridging concept. *Conservation Biology*, 19(1), 36-38.

Rosenbaum, W.A. (2008). *Environmental Politics and Policy*. 7th ed. Washington, D.C.: CQ Press.

Sachs, J.D. (2008). *Common Wealth: Economics for a Crowded Planet*. NY, NY: Penguin Books.

Sinclair, U. (1981). *The Jungle*. NY, NY: Bantam Books. (Originally published in 1906).

Sunstein, C.R. (1990). *After the Rights Revolution: Reconceiving the Regulatory State*. Cambridge, Massachusetts: Harvard University Press.

Vandermeer, J. (1995). The ecological basis of alternative agriculture. *Annual Review of Ecology and Systematics, 26,* 201-224.

Walsh, B. (August 31, 2009). America's food crisis and how we fix it. *Time*, 30-37.

Sustainability from a Market Perspective

Ray Darville

Introduction

"It's the economy, stupid." This is one of the most remembered quotes from President Bill Clinton given during and after his presidential campaign to emphasize what is important to America and to the American people. His claim is a pragmatic one that gets at the core of where each American lives and works. Moreover, his claim also sets out a core historical value of the place of the economy in American society. Without a strong, vibrant, changing economy, the United States and its people are in grave peril. Thus, all other issues confronting American society must be considered and analyzed in connection with the economy. One salient issue is sustainability, which must be successfully dealt in the best interests of the long-term health of society as a whole and the individuals comprising society.

This essay lay outs the claim that sustainability will not occur unless the economic dimension is addressed properly. This means that both government and business must address sustainability in coordinated, effective ways. We know that a government-regulation approach with little or no consideration for or input from business is doomed to fail miserably. Conversely, by working together government and business can generate a sustainable world such that the environment, communities, families and the economy can thrive.

Market Efficiency

The above campaign slogan resonates with discussions surrounding sustainability. One of the driving forces behind using market mechanisms to create a more livable world is the value of efficiency (VanDeVeer and Pierce, 1994). It is business, because of the profit motive, that must constantly confront efficiency and adapt its practices to be more efficient; government, by its nature and structure, does not have the same motivation or need. It is through market efficiency that profits are generated; these profits are then used to grow the business through additional capital. These profits also provide capital for return on investment to investors. In general, the more efficient a business is, the greater the profits. And, government with its oversight and regulations often hurts efficiency and reduces profits.

The Driving Force of Profits

One of the challenges of all businesses is the need to maximize profits. Each firm, in order to maximize its profits, must produce its goods and services more cheaply than other competing firms. With profits, firms are able to pay their employees' wages, salaries, and benefits, but are also able to pay their cost of operation expenses and also importantly are able to re-pay their investors. Moreover, without profits, companies are not able to reinvest in their own enterprises. Without profits, employees will lose their jobs. Without profits, communities will suffer higher unemployment rates. Without profits, investors will take away their financial support. Richard Douthwaite (1992: 8) asserts, "It is not just that firms like growth because it makes them more profitable; they positively need it if they are to survive." In other words, without profits, sustainability is not a value of companies or individuals. Without profits sustainability perhaps is a good idea, but nonetheless is only an idea.

Decision Making

Another factor in using market mechanism to create a sustainable world is who participates in decisions. Business and industry leaders are well suited because of their knowledge, training, and experience. Government managers are simply managers and not true experts in their fields. In other words, government managers often do not have the substantive understanding to make informed, effective decisions regarding environmental issues. Businesses hire highly trained experts because they must enact practices that are efficient and ones that meet environmental standards. On the other hand, government agencies may have experts in some instances, but these individuals are not experts in how science affects business.

The Command-and-Control Approach is Flawed.

The Command-and-Control approach is one that focuses on "preventing environmental problems by specifying how a company will manage a pollution-generating process" (Stuart, 2010). This approach was popular particularly during the early stages of the current environmental social movement of the 1960s and 1970s. The approach largely is an engineering approach to solving specific environmental problems (point source pollution, for example). As scholars began to recognize and study non-point sources of pollution, they have realized that this approach is not effective. The more current, more effective approach is to have a market-based, or performance-based, approach.

This approach seemingly requires government agencies to specify not only the goals, but also the methods or mechanisms by which businesses must meet these goals. Furthermore, government agencies usually provide complicated, detailed prescriptions that often are impractical or cost-prohibitive to follow. Government managers often do not have the scientific training to decide what technologies or processes are in the best interest of both the environment and businesses. An example comes from regulations required to adhere to the 1977 Surface Mining Control and Reclamation Act (Rosenbaum, 2008). To deal with surface pollution, companies were required to move all runoff through one or more sedimentation ponds. Business argued that other approaches were more effective and cost efficient such as straw dikes and vegetative cover, which could produce the same outcomes, at remarkably lower cost. In one case involving a subsidiary of General Electric the sedimentation pond cost $335,000 to build while a reasonable alternative cost only 10%

as much. In another situation, the National Research Council, an arm of the National Academy of Sciences, recommended a much less expensive technology that was equally effective (Rosenbaum, 2008). These two cases illustrate the need for government to not prescribe the methodology, but rather provide consultation and guidance to businesses as they develop cost effective and environmentally-effective ways to create a cleaner, more sustainable world. All business owners and managers understand that increased costs associated with environmental protection and sustainability are passed on to consumers. While government officials may not be concerned about costs, all businesses and consumers are concerned.

Another failure of the command and control approach is that the public is unable to comprehend not only the regulations, and their nuisances, but also their technical specifications. For the average adult, this information is impossible to understand. Thus, government agencies often suffer from poor public relations. Citizens believe that government agencies are acting arbitrarily. Thus, many individuals see government agencies as overbearing and unsympathetic to businesses. One would have to believe that average adults have a less difficult experience understanding market forces, the need to cut costs, and the need for businesses to operate in a profitable environment.

Cost-Benefit Analysis

Cost/Benefit Analysis (CBA) also plays a role in the interplay between government agencies and businesses. Some individuals embrace cost-and-control approaches because the outcomes are clear and measurable (Environmental Literary Council, 2010). However, while this may be the situation, the issues are many here. First, it is known that specific outcomes produced by government agencies require specific measurement procedures and analysis; these measurements and the subsequent data analysis are costly not only to government, but also to businesses. Companies may spend thousands or millions of dollars from their budgets annually to meet overly specific criteria when those expenditures could be used to further develop the technology needed to better address the problem.

Economic incentives (Environmental Literary Council, 2010) have several advantages, which are ignored in a command-and-control approach. Incentives are the key to business remaining an active partner in solving the sustainability problems; in contrast, the command-and-control approach means that the businesses become passive recipients of government regulation. By drawing businesses into a market approach, they are better positioned to solve problems more effectively and efficiently. Businesses are able (because they have the incentive) to create efficient solutions. Moreover, because government agencies are not involved as heavily, they are less required to spend time, labor, and money in the data collection and analysis part of environmental protection.

One example, in particular, stands out as illustrative of the success of cap-and-trade compared to command-and-control mechanisms (Agricultural Carbon Market Working Group, 2010). The Environmental Protection Agency (EPA) in 1990 developed a program to reduce SO_2 emissions through a cap-and-trade approach. In the years since the program began, ambient concentrations of SO_2 were reduced by 40% in the Northeast and Mid-Atlantic areas of the United States. The cost associated with the reduction was minimized because the regulated entities were able to trade pollution allowances. Those participating in this approach were able to reduce pollution at a greater rate than the law requiring the program required. In fact, Robert Stavins, a faculty member in the John F. Kennedy School of Government, has written extensively on market-based approaches. He estimated in one economic analysis that implementing a cap-and-trade program rather command-and-control saves about $1 billion annually in dealing with SO_2 emissions (Stavins, 1998).

Tragedy of the Commons

The tragedy of the commons presents a challenge to markets and market forces. The tragedy focuses on the use of or misuse of environmental resources. In the original story, there is a common area used by sheep herders to graze their sheep. Obviously, the sheep need to graze, but if overgrazing occurs, the commons can be destroyed and ultimately with this destruction will come the ruination of the sheep and the sheepherders' livelihood. The real tragedy of the commons is that these commodities are not held privately, but rather the commons represents a "held by all" concept. And, furthermore, given human nature and what science knows about joint owner (joint ownership is no ownership), the real tragedy is that the tragedy of the commons could be avoided through the application of property rights creating private property and individual concern for the resource. It is the market in the tragedy of the commons that is not allowed to work as it should. The most important mistake is not over-grazing of the sheep (use of resources), but rather the most important mistake is the non-use of the market.

Conclusion and Recommendations

The key to sustainability is finding and maintaining the correct balance between government involvement (regulation and enforcement) in sustainability and free enterprise's ability to be innovative. In essence, the goal is to "align private incentives and society's environmental interests (Sachs, 2008). In fact, Sachs offers four policies that could be used to encourage this alignment. How could this be accomplished?

First, in agreement with Sachs, there should be a tax on environmental harm; obviously, free enterprise would not support this approach because of increased cost basis for producing goods and services.

Second, there should be an expansion of the use of permits for pollution. Permits can be traded and businesses understand cost and benefits involved because the permits are quantified phenomena. This approach has been successful as mentioned previously.

Third, industry performance standards should be put into place, which gives sustainability targets for business. This could include a more local focus such as a zoning approach. In essence, the idea is that not all solutions work best for all localities and all businesses. By zoning solutions, the solutions will be more efficient.

Fourth, another solution is to change the way we do business and charge for the use of natural resources. An example is water usage. Generally, the more water used monthly, the less money is charged per gallon of water. This may act as an incentive to use more water. What if the direction was reversed? What if companies paid less money per gallon if they use less water and more money per gallon once their water usage crosses a specific threshold? This approach could be used not only for water, but also for other limited natural resources such as for electricity, gas, refuse usage, and even gasoline.

Fifth, if sustainability is to become a greater reality, then more integrated government-business relationships must be developed. What we have now is government agencies on one side and business on the other side of a table. They see each other as oppositional, not in collegial relationships. By creating more effective councils, they work together instead of against one another. Government might also give tax breaks for companies that meet pre-determined sustainability targets. Again, this would provide incentives, not simply punishment to companies. This might also work at the state and federal level. The federal government in conjunction with the states could provide targets for each state. If a state (including the businesses in that state) meets the sustainability target, the federal government could issue additional money for use by the state government for environmental work.

References

Agricultural Carbon Market Working Group. 2010. http://www. agcarbonmarkets.com/documents/TCG%20White%20Paper_ CCA%20vs%20CAT_Final.pdf

Costanza, Robert, John Cumberland, Herman Daly, Robert Goodland, Richard Norgarrd, Nancy Goulubiewski, and Cutler Cleveland. "An Introduction to Ecological Economics: Chapter 4". In: *Encyclopedia of Earth.* Eds. Cutler J. Cleveland (Washington, D.C.: Environmental Information Coalition, National Council for Science and the Environment). [First published in the Encyclopedia of Earth September 18, 2008; Last revised Date September 18, 2008; Retrieved October 29, 2010 http://www.eoearth.org/article/An_Introduction_to_Ecological_Economics:_Chapter_4

Douthwaite, Richard. 1992. *The Growth Illusion: How Economic Growth Has Enriched the Few, Impoverished the Many, and Endangered the Planet.* Devon, UK: Green Books.

Environmental Literacy Council. 2010. "Regulatory Policy vs Economic Incentives." http://www.enviroliteracy.org/article.php/1329.html. Accessed October 29, 2010.

Rosenbaum, W.A. (2008). *Environmental Politics and Policy*, 7th edition. Washington, D.C.: CQ Press.

Sachs, Jeffrey. 2008. *Common Wealth: Economics for a Crowed Planet.* London: Penguin Books.

Stavins, Robert. 1998. What Can We Learn from the Grand Policy Experiment? Lessons from SO_2 Allowance Trading." *The Journal of Economic Perspectives*, Vol. 12, No. 3, pp. 69-88.

Stuart, R. (2010). Command and Control Regulation. In: *Encyclopedia of Earth.* Eds. Cutler J. Cleveland. Washington, D.C.: Environmental Information Coalition, National Council for Science and the Environment.

VanDeVeer, Donald and Christine Pierce. 1994. *The Environmental Ethics and Policy Book: Philosophy, Ecology, and Economics.* Wadsworth: Belmont, CA.

Sense of Place and the "Triple" Bottom Line

Dan Shilling

It's nearly impossible today to attend a conference about economic development, city planning, travel and tourism, land management, or cultural and recreational amenities and not encounter a panel or keynote presentation on "sense of place." That simple phrase, powerful but vague, has become a buzzword for community development across numerous sectors: economic, environmental, and social. Unfortunately, the more popular the concept, the more likely it will be misused. If economic development, in particular, becomes the sole arbiter of place, which should also embrace a healthy mix of natural and cultural environments, opportunities for authenticity and enhanced quality of life, and thus sustainability, are at risk.

After reviewing several past and current voices that helped shape today's conversation about place and economics, this essay suggests that, above all, *revealing* a community's existing character, with the assistance of a diverse and engaged public, is key to developing a robust, enduring sense of place.

Mass-Produced Communities

Critics occasionally argue that a great deal of today's economy is stuck in the Industrial Age – a Fordist model, in the sense Henry Ford pioneered an assembly-line approach to commerce that revolutionized business in particular and society more broadly. In this view, scale counts – size and number. A company that moves more products from one fiscal quarter to the next is successful, regardless of environmental or social impacts.

One result of adapting Ford's assembly-line strategy to the built environment is a "Geography of Nowhere," as James Kunstler

(1993) famously labeled it. Today's sprawling, undistinguishable, and uninspiring residential neighborhoods, complains the author, are reachable only by ever-widening highways, and impart no sense of identity. Similarly, islands of bland commercial buildings usually provide poor jobs, while their economies are designed to perpetuate the growth machine. Overall, this development devours 160 acres a day nationally, and, central to our discussion, the typical metropolitan blob paves over a region's distinctive character with a goofy homogeneity that engulfs cultural, built, and natural landscapes.

A built economy of scale can increase returns for stockholders, but the dismal and distant malls planted at nearly every intersection's cloverleaf accelerate the decay of *real* main streets, while zoning has eliminated the public commons – the places people meet as *citizens*, not consumers. Notice the names developers bestow upon their new commercial pods: "Towne Centre," always with an "e" on "town" and "center" spelled the British way. "We're very urbane, cultured, think Paris in the '20s." But, as the courts have ruled, they're anything *but* a public square.

Earlier Voices

After a short stint at the Albuquerque Chamber of Commerce in 1918-19, renowned conservationist Aldo Leopold (1991, p. 100) lamented the local boosters' attempts to bury his city's distinctive cultural, environmental, and built assets beneath a juggernaut called Bigness: "Can anyone deny that the vast fund of time, brains, and money now devoted to making our city big would actually make it better if diverted to betterment instead of bigness?" Leopold's theme – better, not bigger – would prove central to later analyses of place.

"A rootless, aimless, profoundly disharmonized environment has replaced the indigenous one," observed Leopold's friend Benton MacKaye (1928, p. 71), in his prescient survey of "green" city design. If people know MacKaye today, they probably remember him as father of the Appalachian Trail. Trained as a forester, the scrappy MacKaye was also a member of the Regional Planning Association of America, which included Lewis Mumford and other influential voices. Similar to Leopold, who urged caretakers of land to "throw your weight around" in the political arena, MacKaye (1928, p. 118) encouraged planners to *act* on their bonds to place:

> Here is a dormant but vital and specific conflict in men's minds: it is the subconscious effort to preserve and to develop the inherent human values of a country (on the part of all the members of a society) against that other subconscious effort to develop the mundane values of an exotic mechanized iron civilization (on the part of the proprietors of that civilization)...Here is the *most* immediate function of the regional planner: it is for him to "take sides" in this coming conflict, and to fight, with the sharp weapons of visualization, for the intrinsic human values of his country and his world.

MacKaye's colleague Lewis Mumford emphasized a "humanized" approach to city planning that he hoped might reorient social values in the early 20th century. Here Mumford echoes Leopold, who valued conservation as a tool for changing values, his primary mission. Words such as "love" and "respect" pepper the prose here, which also introduces an ethical framework and touches on the role of culture. If planners are to value their place, and citizens are to love it, Mumford (1946) encouraged them to "understand what love meant to Socrates and Saint Francis, to Dante and Shakespeare...." That's not something one hears from many planning departments.

In *Design with Nature*, landscape architect Ian McHarg, another colleague of Mumford's, heeded Leopold's call to reform values, not only our tools. His book's very title anticipates Benyus

(1997) and other practitioners of "biomimicry" – the practice of copying natural organisms in order to design tools, systems, medicines, and technologies. McHarg (1969, p. 151) also stressed the view, shared by Leopold, MacKaye, and Mumford, that places constitute a web, a built and social ecology:

> Such is the method – a simple sequential examination of the place in order to understand it. This understanding reveals the place as an interacting system, a storehouse and a value system. From this information it is possible to prescribe potential land uses – not as single activities, but as associations of these.

Further, McHarg's (1969, p. 23) sketches of a "humane city" illustrate how a place's design shapes and mirrors social relations: "There is a widening certainty that the Gross National Product does not measure health or happiness, dignity, compassion, beauty or delight, and that these are, if not all inalienable rights, at least most worthy aspirations."

Sociologist Ray Oldenburg (1989, p. 285) also wrote about the changing shape of communities and its damaging effect on our national character:

> The individual's present relationship to the collective is as empty as it is equitable: community does nothing for them and they do nothing for community. And we continue to shape the environment as if to preserve that perilous arrangement. Segregation, isolation, compartmentalization, and sterilization seem to be the guiding principles of urban growth and urban renewal.

In our rush to *grow* economies, rather than *develop* places, cities have prospered primarily as disconnected business hubs – ignoring public space, what Oldenburg calls "great good places." How many people living in a suburban cul-de-sac can walk to a local tavern? Most can't because zoning regulations, written to advance the expediency and simplicity Ford sought, have eliminated diversity, a key concept for the health of ecosystems and an equally vital part of built designs. Urbanist Jane Jacobs (1961, p. 14) agrees: "the need of cities for a most intricate and close-grained diversity of uses that give each other constant mutual support, both economically and socially."

These commentators suggest the journey to the intersection of place and coin provides both promise and caution. Among the significant promises, Jacobs, Leopold, Mumford, MacKaye, McHarg, and Oldenburg say livable urban design is good for the soul. More recent observers, such as economist Richard Florida, believe a robust sense of place is good for the pocketbook. I'd go further – it's good for democracy. However, one caution repeatedly asserts itself: if regions focus too much on Fordist schemes to advance economic benefits, "the tail *can* wag the dog."

Revealing Sense of Place

Richard Florida (2002, 2005) suggests cities should enhance their sense of place to attract the "Creative Class," because this demographic segment earns more, spends more, and stimulates a healthy economic climate. It's not difficult to figure out why large cities like Phoenix or smaller burgs like Boise and Spokane provide incentives to develop the ingredients that contribute to vibrant place-based economies: educational facilities, cultural centers, offices for white-collar professionals, strong park systems, healthcare amenities, and cutting-edge technology projects like Phoenix's T-Gen research park.

Florida trumpets cities crowded with historic structures as opposed to downtown malls (Savannah), places with a healthy local business climate (Missoula), that are committed to education and culture (Boston), that privilege pedestrians over cars (Portland), and serve as headquarters for knowledge-based industries, not just more call centers (Austin) – in short, settings that represent everything the Geography of Nowhere is not.

Similar to Jane Jacobs and other urbanists mentioned here, as well as today's smart growth advocates, Florida (2005, p. 45) sees places as interconnected webs: "[S]uccessful places are built up as complex, multifaceted ecosystems that, like those occurring in the natural world, defy simplistic linear thinking." Just as ecologists consider diversity key to the health of natural ecosystems, so is diversity central to healthy human networks, including built environments. Thus "place" is not just *more* stuff, but the appropriateness *of* and the connections *between* natural and built ingredients.

A common blunder is that communities feel they need "more, more, more" to create a sense of place. They build sports stadiums, malls, theme parks, hotels, conference centers, parking structures, and miles of thoroughfares to connect them. Investing a portion of those dollars in enhancing *what's already there* – for instance, historic districts and *real* parks (not the manufactured kind) – would go a long way toward creating an authentic product. Look at what many towns have done with First Friday art walks, farmers markets, and other community projects, which cost cities a fraction of a new stadium.

Fortunately, doing the right thing is often easier and less costly than the alternative. Benton MacKaye (1928, p. 208) observed over eighty years ago that place rarely needs to be purpose-built. Writing to fellow planners, he said their job "is not to 'plan,' but to *reveal* – to seek the innate design of forces." Abandoning this "innate design," too many of today's new malls, stadiums, or "attractions" never return on their investment because the thinking is backward and the elements are "*out* of place."

McHarg (1969, p. 175) likewise suggests a community's "excellence often results from the preservation...and enhancement, rather than obliteration of this genius of the site." Among other things, McHarg's advice means abandoning the copycat mentality that infects planning. "If the aquarium worked in Baltimore, build one in Denver," even though that Rocky Mountain city's heritage has little to do with marine life. Adopting MacKaye's paradigm – to not just build, but to *reveal* – helps create an *appropriate* and *distinctive* product, not another out-of-place "attraction." Successful place-making is often just a matter of getting out of the way, MacKaye believed, and allowing a community's authentic self to emerge naturally. He, Leopold, and others encouraged place-making that hinges on words some planners habitually erase from their dictionary: *submission* and *restraint*. "Only in the act of submission," historian Wallace Stegner (1992, p. 206) writes, "is the sense of place realized and a sustainable relationship between people and earth established."

In some scenarios, though development reports are sprinkled with place-based lingo, the focus remains on growth, not *developing what's there to serve residents*. The true place-based theme is quality, not quantity; holistic, not linear; "better recipes, not just more cooking," says Paul Romer (2008). Organic design is biomimetic in that it studies nature's designs in order to create resilient human communities.

Allowing a sense of place to emerge organically is what Aldo Leopold called "thinking like a mountain." The mountain *knows*. Submit to and learn from that knowledge. To do so, Leopold suggested "the first rule of intelligent tinkering is to keep all the 'cogs and wheels'." We can translate his dictum to "town thinking": Allow what's already there to improve within the margins of the community's history and heritage; rather than bend nature to human demands, the built environment should blend in naturally and culturally, urged architect Frank Lloyd Wright and landscape designer Frederick Law Olmsted.

Translate the organic code to place-making: It's the difference between "development," done in concert with a community's natural and cultural heritage, and blunt "growth," whose calculus often has little concern for heritage. Leopold (1933, p. 422) called it a "third way," which "denies kitchens or factories need be ugly, or farms lifeless, in order to be efficient." Today's "radical center" draws directly from this view.

Organic development is the difference between tearing down an old gas station to throw up another Burger King, and working with the community to turn the aging relic into a restaurant or playground. It's the difference between converting an old home into an elegant B&B and demolishing it for a boxy Motel 6. It's the difference between scraping a hillside for another Big Mart and partnering with land trusts to buy and preserve the open space as a cultural legacy *and* economic asset. It's the difference between allowing a stream to meander through town on its own terms and cementing and straightening it, so as to "improve upon nature" and build in the floodplain.

The organic approach not only enhances community character, it's often more cost-effective, and not only because of lower infrastructure outlays. Daily and Ellison (2002) write that when Napa, California, returned a regimented, cemented river to its natural course, business boomed, real estate appreciated, and visitors returned.

To plan organically, then, create a "place committee," develop a "place matrix" of sorts, and apply its standards and indicators to every one of your conversations:

- **Diversity**: a vigorous mix of design, scale, and function.
- **Balance**: vitality and harmony, physically and aesthetically.
- **Connectivity:** accord among resources as well as pleasurable passage between them.
- **Association**: local appreciation, regional consideration.
- **Differentiation**: a story that distinguishes your community.
- **Adaptability**: long-term vision that accounts for change.
- **Appropriateness**: within the margins of your natural and cultural heritage.
- **Yield**: sustainable economic networks that circulate profits locally.
- **and Town Thinking**: Is this what the town would do?

Sure, these concepts are as vague as "beauty" and you'll argue endlessly over what they mean. The good news is there are many architects, planners, urbanists, consultants, and scholars who do this work, who *can* quantify and design according to the standards in your matrix; who *are* applying the principles of holistic thinking to community development; who *do* understand and build upon the relationship between environments and economics. The many and diverse organizations that make up the cultural sector should work together to engage and encourage their vision.

"Greenwashing" Sense of Place

Think back to your last stay at a major motel chain. Chances are a sprightly green and blue notice in the bathroom urged you to use towels more than one day: "Waste less water so we can help save the planet." Sounds nice, but critics note the principal goal of these practices is often to lower the motel's costs and improve their reputation, *not* save the planet. At the same time, other activities the motel engages in may be contrary to ecotourism's founding manifestos: do no harm to the land, empower residents, and promote local business. A franchise motel, while washing fewer linens, could undermine all three of those standards.

The *misrepresentation* of ecological correctness for financial gain, called "greenwashing," is unfortunately also evident in other place-based tourism scenarios, such as cultural heritage tourism: the selling of people, sometimes referred to as "human zoos" – exploitation of culture in its crudest terms. "Get a picture of that Amish boy, George!" The hospitality industry knows people who travel to experience sense of place – history, culture, traditions – stay longer and spend more, so they're an attractive target market. That's where submission to local stories comes into play because, just as counterfeit ecotourism doesn't reflect the label, communities can exploit their cultural product – perpetuating stereotypes, marketing myth over reality, whitewashing history, and sometimes just getting it wrong.

Greenwashing regrettably occurs in town planning, too. The New Urbanism movement, at its *root*, is about preserving heritage, reuse and infill, privileging local business, mixed-use design, and, importantly, getting rid of the car. Yet we see marketers use phrases like "New Urbanism" and "green design" as developers build the same vanilla, car-dependent pods, usually named for the thing they displaced. In Quailwood Village outside Prescott, Arizona, both the quail and woods are notably absent, and it's not much of a village. Developers know consumers are thirsty for community, a sense of place, and unspoiled nature, so they speak the dialect. Their "Main Streets" feature coffee shops and other bohemian elements, but the product rarely lives up to the propaganda. Sound ideas, in other words, can be hijacked by forces that don't, or choose not to, invest in them.

My concern is that a similar reworking of meaning is happening to the idea of place, unless we develop holistic and inclusive approaches to the topic. I'm suggesting that communities flip the frame and move away from project-by-project, piecemeal planning that values place solely as an economic driver, and begin with an integrated conversation: integrated as both product *and* process. From the product perspective, a community's story is acted out on at least three place-constituted stages: cultural, natural, and built – people, land, town. Consequently, the groups engaged in place-making – parks, museums, galleries, preservationists – need to get out of their silos and work together. Individually, none of them has much money or clout, but together their voice resonates.

The natural environment, for example, can't be divorced from the cultural. Most national and state parks are not just rocks, rivers, and trees. People lived there. It's a social and cultural ecosystem; it's what we call the story of a place. And if we define, enhance, and sustain it in its most complete and faithful sense, it *will* create this thing called sense of place, because it will be diverse, appropriate, and specific to your history – a distinctive product.

In attempting to uncover a sense of place, distinction is key. Carving out a market niche is what successful companies do, and for towns, where is differentiation more pronounced and more embedded than in their cultural, natural, and historic compositions? It's ironic that while cities are in "sales" – trying to find a market niche – and planners think they're creating a distinctive identity, they often employ a "place in a kit" scheme that the town up the road used: sidewalks full of wooden benches and antique light poles – an approach that leads to fake "boutique towns." Even worse, some villages dress up in an Alpine theme, trying to create an identity for travelers that never existed in the first place. A museum director in one such town told me they're "more historic than they ever were."

More than "stuff," sense of place is about *meaning* and connecting people to that meaning. Place is an *experience*. Think of Nike: they don't sell a product, you often don't see a shoe in their ads; instead, they market an experience. Cities can do the same, with the cultural sector's help, through a narrative that doesn't present place as a commodity, but through a humanistic, integrated approach to place, in all its complexities and ambiguities.

Poetry and Politics

Place-making happens within at least two spheres, what I've called the "Poetry and Politics of Place" (Shilling, 2007). By "poetry of place" I mean a region's defining characteristics, its story, design, and feel. For people hoping to preserve, enhance, and celebrate their community's unique story, these should be heady times, as the chorus of economists who say a healthy place and a robust bottom line are inexorably linked grows louder.

Captains of the economy advise towns to "culturalize" their product, because people are increasingly attracted to unique and historic settings. It's extremely helpful that cultural, educational, environmental, and preservation advocates no longer have to *convince* governments and their economic development agencies that, yes, place is important. But it's also clear, if you watch them in action, that some champions of place-based development haven't the foggiest notion of how to identify, preserve, and develop place – and then "use" it responsibly.

In the mid 1990s, I co-directed a two-year statewide project in Arizona on the nature of community – why some towns have a sense of place and others don't. The one thing we discovered was that *the more people know the history of a place, the more likely they are to be good stewards of that place.* Again, this speaks to the vital role history and heritage play in place-making: not only is history one of the principal ingredients of place, and one of the tools communities use to unearth stories, but knowing local history motivates participants to be better stewards of their place. Citizens and elected officials are less likely to tear down the old house on Elm Street if they know what happened there.

The development industry hasn't donned its sense-of-place attire because it's suddenly grown interested in history, culture, and the environment, but because research shows that regions with the healthiest sense of place enjoy more robust economies. That's fine as far as it goes, but if that's *all* it is, place becomes a mere tool for economic growth, which means the tail *can* wag the dog, and communities ultimately risk compromising the very things that stimulate place.

Here's the question: Does place exist to serve the economy – in other words, is the city's purpose to create jobs – or do jobs follow because the place is healthy? For most communities, I think you know the answer, and I'm urging us to flip the frame.

Place is not just about economic development. Place resides and flourishes in a "triple bottom line" approach, where the economy, society, and environment work together for the health of all three (Elkington 1998, Savitz 2006). Business entrepreneur Paul Hawken (1993, p. 81) says this holistic approach situates the economy as a means, not an end; the market "creates, increases, nourishes and enhances" regional culture and enriches quality of life across the board, including economic health. In effect, communities can *use* the economy to serve place, rather than the other way around. Instead of commercializing culture, culturalize commerce. Planners should redefine their methods using values-based strategies that do not answer solely to the economic bottom line, but also to social and environmental bottom lines: the "triple bottom line."

But to do so, local leaders and practitioners, in partnership with the general public, must step forward and *own* the triple-bottom-line process, which means rewiring what success looks like, embracing another set of values, and partnering with a different cast of characters – redefining, in fact, what constitutes your sense-of-place team. Just the same, these new soldiers in the place brigade – cultural organizations, preservation agencies, and land-use groups – should walk through the door that has been nudged open for them by today's creative economists and join the conversation – and *not* in a token capacity, since they, not the chamber of commerce, are the ones who truly embody place.

Just as hospitals today have ethicists or philosophers on staff because the tough moral questions doctors face are more than technical, so too should we extend humanistic inquiry to place-making ventures because the questions are framed by culture as much as mechanics. As economist Florida (2002, p. 17) writes, "The deep and enduring changes of our age are not technological but social and cultural."

If this work is to go anywhere, it has to have meaning, not end up as another report on the shelf. When communities ask where to begin, I advise them to assemble a place committee, get all of the players in the room, adopt an integrated approach to place-making, pull in some consultants, give the public responsibility and authority, and begin with tough questions: "What do we mean by place? What are its ingredients? What do we value? How do we define and present it? And, further, whose voice isn't here?" Here's how an appropriate plan might develop:

Immediately: Rethink the purpose and meaning of economic development
- Create "Place" Committee, set standards and benchmarks
- Frame place-making as community development
- Leverage the "Triple Bottom Line"

Next Steps: Engage the public
- Forums, surveys, heritage trainings
- Reports, media, officials, "leaders"
- Own the Creative Class discussion
- What is your story? Your identity?
- Beyond single attractions: diversity, context

Future: Invest in place-making conceptually and financially
- Build capacity, conceptualize, monitor (accredit, label, awards program)
- Dedicated funding (determine: advocacy, funding stream, decision makers)
- Purchase, planning, preservation, renovation, interpretation, education, evaluation

These are not topics, questions, or strategies most economic development agencies or chambers of commerce invite, and for the most part we shouldn't expect them to. They speak the language of cost-benefit, return-on-investment, best practices, branding, and marketing strategies. Interpreting a region's story is not their business. But it *is* the business of museums, parks, and preservation agencies, together with the general public.

We need a broader conversation, including the economists and planners – the "experts," if you will – *and* the people working to enhance place. Added to that, the general public represents the third leg in democracy's fabled three-legged stool. Residents can help the other two sectors uncover the slippery "common ground" they often talk about, the so-called "win-win." Many acknowledge that the public isn't involved; they're trapped in their own self-styled enclaves, "bowling alone," according to the sociological label. This challenge returns us to the "politics of place," which *demands* community involvement, so we have to be creative in our approaches to engagement. After all, places are not just economic nuclei; they are people's homes – stories, families, livelihoods, neighborhoods.

To address these challenges, communities can learn from decades of research on civic engagement and apply it to the place dialog. They can also benefit from projects like the Forest Stewardship Council, self-directed citizens working with the public sector, land-use agencies, environmentalists, and Big Timber to ensure the sustainability of both lumber industry profits and community resources. Countless other engagement models exist that towns can and should apply to the conversation about place.

Sense of place is not just a pleasant phrase; it demands that the caretakers of community get political, get active. As Aldo Leopold advised, throw your weight around and remember, it's going to be a long haul. The wonderful writer about our places, Scott Russell Sanders (1993, p. xvi), reminds us, "The work of belonging to a place is never finished." Place is a trajectory, a process, communities evolve. How that evolution happens is the subject of place-making.

The cultural sector has a window of opportunity, created by new trends in economic and community development, new ways of thinking about place and the things people care about. Everything is moving in the right direction; the horse has left the barn and cultural leaders need to saddle up and help steer. It's our responsibility to engage these encouraging voices and demand a seat at the table. Or set our own table.

Sociologist Robert Bellah (1995) and his coauthors in *Habits of the Heart* suggest there is a "social ecology," a network of cultural reciprocities that distinguishes communities, a network from which the development sector has too often stood apart. New partners and perspectives are needed. The most opportunistic links to quality economic growth strategies are multi-layered, cyclical rather than linear, and comparative rather than reductionist, not unlike systems in nature. Considering community development as part of a complex, interrelated whole, where economic reciprocity is evaluated within a values-based bubble, is the first step toward reimagining a community's potential. The cultural sector should be at the forefront of that reimagination. In other words, the *dog* should wag the tail.

References:

Bellah, R. N.; Madsen, R.; Sullivan, W. M.; Swidler, A. Tipton, S. M. 1985. *Habits of the Heart: Individualism and Commitment in American Life.* Berkeley: University of California Press.

Benyus, J. M. 1997. *Biomimicry: Innovation Inspired by Nature.* New York: HarperCollins.

Daily, G. C., K. Ellison. 2002. *The New Economy of Nature: The Quest To Make Conservation Profitable.* Washington, D.C.: Island Press.

Elkington, J. C. 1998. *Cannibals with Forks: The Triple Bottom Line of 21st Century Business.* Philadelphia: New Society. Florida, R.

Florida,Richard. 2005. *The Flight of the Creative Class: The New Global Competition for Talent.* New York: HarperCollins.

_____. 2002. *The Rise of the Creative Class and How It's Transforming Work, Leisure, Community and Everyday Life.* New York: Basic Books.

Hawken, P. 1993. *The Ecology of Commerce: A Declaration of Sustainability.* New York: Harper Business.

Jacobs, J. 1961. *The Death and Life of Great American Cities.* New York: Random House.

Kunstler, J. H. 1993. *The Geography of Nowhere: The Rise and Decline of America's Man-Made Landscapes.* New York: Simon & Schuster.

Leopold, A. 1991. "A Criticism of the Booster Spirit" in Susan L. Flader and J. Baird Callicott, eds. *The River of the Mother of God and Other Essays by Aldo Leopold.* Madison: University of Wisconsin Press.

_____. 1933. *Game Management.* New York: Charles Scribner's Sons.

MacKaye, B. 1928. *The New Exploration: A Philosophy of Regional Planning.* Urbana-Champaign, IL: University of Chicago Press.

McHarg, I. L. 1969. *Design with Nature.* Garden City, NY: Doubleday & Company.

Mumford, L. 1946. *Values for Survival: Essays, Addresses, and Letters on Politics and Education.* New York: Harcourt Brace.

Oldenburg, R. 1989. *The Great Good Place: Cafes, Coffee Shops, Community Centers, Beauty Parlors, General Stores, Bars, Hangouts, and How They Get You Through the Day.* New York: Paragon House.

Romer, P. 2008. "Economic Growth" in *The Concise Encyclopedia of Economics.* Library of Economics and Liberty. http://www.econlib.org/library/Enc/EconomicGrowth.html (8-24-11).

Sanders, S. R. 1993. *Staying Put: Making a Home in a Restless World.* Boston: Beacon Press.

Savitz, A. 2006. *The Triple Bottom Line.* San Francisco: John Wiley & Sons.

Shilling, D. 2007. *Civic Tourism: The Poetry and Politics of Place.* Prescott, AZ: Sharlot Hall Museum Press. Parts of this essay originally appeared in this book.

Stegner, W. 1992. "The Sense of Place" in *Where the Bluebird Sings to the Lemonade Springs: Living and Writing in the West.* New York: Penguin.

WHY WOULD I LIVE THERE?

Tom Mote

Much to the amusement of his guests, Mark Twain used to say: "Everyone wants to talk about the weather, but no one ever does anything about it."

I have to confess a similar sentiment when it comes to the topics of community development and sustainability. Perhaps it's not as obvious to others that our culture is sliding in some disturbing ways, enabled by technology, entertainment, and a narcissistic cultural message bent on acquiring more. We are numbed to school shootings, homicides, and assaults against people. Recently, when a troubled child in our neighborhood kidnapped our dog and tied him to a tree in the woods, the police were not surprised - they knew immediately who had done it.

In the world we want to live in, how do we practically help shape communities to become sustainable, living, organic "places for people"? After all, if no one wants to live there, what kind of a community did we create?

Some of the answers to these questions might surprise us. First, the way a community is designed not only seals its commercial fate, but that same design will determine whether it will have any long-term viability as a place people want to live. And it doesn't take a crystal ball to determine which ones will be successful—one needs only to look at the design intent and execution, both clearly evident throughout a development, to know whether it is capable of sustaining a population.

Second, we must recognize that cultural issues are addressed in individual choices, things we have the ability to change, affect, and lead. When you and I fail to participate in constructive dialogue about critical issues, our society begins to die. Every choice we make in isolation of others is a choice repudiating a basic fact—that none of us can or want to live on this planet by ourselves. So, different results require us to make different choices, likely based on different criteria.

Third, the method of governance we establish, allow, and perpetuate has everything to do with our confidence in the social capital networks in our communities, and in our ability to actually create places that are habitable by human populations. If we elect people based on qualifications, passions, and service orientation to the betterment of the citizenry, we have a far different result than when we have trouble finding enough people to run for office, and begin asking people to run so we can keep quorum minimums during voting. Our citizenry will only receive the type of governance that we require.

This essay approaches sustainability, and more specifically, sustainable communities, from a triple bottom-line perspective. There are numerous non-governmental organizations that advocate for environmental activism, yet have no sustainable business model. Further, many businesses have very little passion for addressing environmental needs. In a culture where words are thrown carelessly across cultural battle lines, a community needs all three legs of a very important stool in order to be successful:

- Ecological sustainability – addressing the critical environmental concerns of any place, including health, natural resource usage, habitat, water and land use, and conservation of heritage areas

- Financial sustainability – addressing the need for a society to derive value from the work of others, to create and sell goods and services, and to enable a lifestyle where jobs can be created and careers built; and

- Social sustainability – dealing with the ability of an area to attract people to live, play, work, dine, and labor together based on the natural beauty or the inherent qualities of that place.

These three elements can and must accompany any efforts that community leaders undertake to invent or reinvent themselves if they are to be successful. These elements are not in conflict—they are, in fact, in harmony, and when we assume they are in conflict, and over-emphasize one of them at the expense of the others, we do so at our own peril. Examples of success and failure can be seen every day across America.

Where to Begin

Most people begin the conversation on sustainable communities with an environmental discussion. At the risk of being misunderstood, I believe sustainability begins with people and their choices. A reflection of our values can be seen in our ability to create jobs and to preserve natural resources, but people interacting with others is what makes a place a real Place.

And in our culture today, we are killing off the future of our economy each week, driving jobs out of our cities, and creating pressure for people who once lived happily in rural areas to move into urbanized areas, adding to congestion, traffic, health problems, and lifestyle challenges. This is evidenced by the declining population in rural counties in every state in the US, and by the rising pressure on cities to provide an ever-expanding network of services across an ever-widening infrastructure. This is the sustainability problem that most people like to talk about, but it started before the demand for more roads/cars/toll lanes/ use of farmland, and if we want to get this right, we have to study small town America.

In a sense, small towns are the microcosm of where our culture came from. The heartbeat of America in 1776 was small business owners passing down their legacies from generation to generation, ideally improving the ideas and practices - making the farm, the store, the shop, the practice more efficient and more productive. New entrants to the job market made enough to set themselves up as entrepreneurs, and continued this process. This is no different from today—the true creation of wealth in America is in the ability to own your own business and to benefit from the efforts and risks, and learn from the failures.

Over the past several decades, however, small towns have had to compete with big cities for labor. Kids that grow up in small towns went off to big cities to attend college (we told them they were second class citizens if they had to work with their hands for a living), and then they never came back. The valedictorians graduated and left their hometowns, and the dropouts stayed. Small towns historically have done a poor job of appealing to employers, individuals, colleges, and other capital networks to create "centers of attraction," creating a downward spiral financially.

Instead of seeing these trends and working together, small town leaders focused on their own survival, lacked the vision to aggregate and work with other communities to make their appeal more broadly, and lacked the sophistication to get their message in front of the right market.

What they had as their greatest asset was not truly realized— until recently. Small town leaders are again beginning to realize that they have a secret weapon that no big city has. They have the ability to affect real change in governance quickly, to create the economic environment that attracts capital and entrepreneurs, and to put in place systems that sustain growth based on natural resources nearby. Further, some small town leaders have grasped the fact that they have not been the answer, but may have been the problem, and have established the framework for effective leadership that enables their citizens to trust in, to invest in, and to visualize a different future for their town.

This solution, actually, includes both financial and social sustainability (it's very hard to separate these two elements of a sustainable lifestyle). For example, when sociologists refer to active social capital networks in communities, we often think of libraries, museums, schools, places of worship, charity organizations, eateries, and the like. Yet all of these require money—capital— in order to enjoy. If there is no way to earn money nearby, or if a city is actively engaging in practices that drive businesses away--excessive taxation, arbitrary gamesmanship with capital development, onerous permitting and city staff behavior—capital will leave, either because of the prospect of losing money, or because capital sources recognize failed governance structures, regardless of the symptoms.

In every community that struggles across the United States, every single one of them would benefit from engaging in an "entrepreneurship campaign"—specifically, preparing their cities for new small businesses to move there, set up shops and jobs there, and live, work, eat, and play there. This happened in Fairfield, Iowa in the late 1990s, and it is now happening all over the state of Texas, thanks in large part to active community development efforts sponsored on a state-wide level, and focused on Entrepreneur Ready Communities (www.tcre.org).

Because social capital always precedes private capital, community development happens before economic development makes any sense. This is the biggest challenge in today's small towns—helping city leaders recognize that when we get this wrong, no amount of capital investment in economic development or job growth will affect real and lasting change. Since public action sparks private market reaction, it is critical that city leaders "get it." Many do not, but an increasingly large number of ordinary citizens are running for office in small towns across America to demonstrate what leadership looks like in changing the future of their cities.

USDA studies now show that more and more Baby Boomer generation citizens are choosing to move back to small towns because of the lifestyle benefits of leaving the big cities; they are choosing towns that have done their homework and fixed their city governance. The urgency of your local governance "getting it" has never been more urgent.

Broken Designs, Broken Communities

There are a lot of jokes about real estate developers, and

you can't throw an iPhone through your local video store without hitting a half dozen movies that trash real estate development, realtors, and other related professionals as bigoted, greedy, self-serving, narcissistic villains. In our home, it has become a little bit of a game as we watch kid's movies, and see the "noble savage" character that comes into conflict with the "dirty developer", and how the savage wins because he loves the earth more than the developer. The thinking, apparently, is - if you love clichés, then the more clichés you can pack into a children's movie, the funnier it is. At least it makes the kids laugh.

Contrary to popular thought, 80% of the American population lives in single family homes in non-urban core areas. This means, 4 out of 5 of us have lawns, trees, and driveways. Yet all of us that have those amenities got them from someone who took some substantial risks to invest in land, entitle it and improve it, and market it for construction of homes. Most of these wildcatters go bankrupt.

The fact of the matter is that real estate development is a dangerous business. Think about the home you live in now—at some point, the site was not a "homesite," and the materials used to construct the home were extracted, processed, and installed to create the architectural systems that hold your home up. If someone had not done that, you wouldn't have a house. But the test of whether you will ever get the value out of that home that you put into it is when you go to sell the home—and then, when it's too late, you will hear the market's perception of "your house," for better or for worse.

If your home had to be torn down fifteen years after it was built, would you call that sustainable? Of course not, even if it was half the cost of other homes in the neighborhood. No one buys a home that way, intentionally. Yet across communities in the United States today, structural failure rates on homes built in the past decade are astronomically high, primarily because the way the home was built symbolized the level of care that went into the entire development process—it was fast and cheap.

Building scientists have demonstrated it costs no more to build a home properly—one that is energy efficient and will stand for up to 100 years--than it does to slap a home together, assuming the builder is watching and monitoring the construction properly. Why do we as a culture accept fast, cheap products that are bad for us and our families?

What happened all those years ago, when the earthmovers were doing the site work, will come into play as you examine the future of your home investment. In fact, the design work done by earnest and well-meaning professionals 50 or 100 years ago, while the land plan was still a concept, is affecting you today. Unlike technology, good land use and planning don't change over time—these principles remain the same. What makes Monticello such a fascinating study is that 150 years before air conditioning was invented, Thomas Jefferson used physics—thermal massing, berms, heat induction, and natural ventilation—to create systems that keep Monticello cool in the summer, warm in the winter, have fresh air regardless of outside climates, and all of the natural sunlight a person could want. He didn't need electricity to make it happen.

When someone tells you that design is not that important, run. You can tell a broken community the minute you drive past the front monument sign and see long rows of identical homes, similar colors, few trees, cramped streets, lots of cars, garage doors, roofs, and driveways. Surely someone foresaw that the end result of these design choices would be the residential "train wrecks" we see around us today.

Show me a place where people want to look at, touch, and interact with architecture, and I will show you a sustainable community. Point out a place where people know they will accidentally bump into people they know when they get their coffee, and I will show you a place where people want to be. And there is nothing a city can do to induce traffic in a free economy-- nothing can create this if the design is wrong.

Misalignment

Here is the biggest challenge of creating sustainable communities. Because decisions are made in layers, and the layers are not reversible or fixable, any mistake made on the front end of a community will be magnified a thousand fold throughout. Developers are typically motivated to sell lots to builders or buyers at the highest possible price - more lots, more money. The faster the sale, the lower the carrying costs. Many of them fall into pure commodity thinking- putting lots in two to three programmed sizes, in front of a predictable set of homebuilders. The builders have regional or national buying programs, mass design shops, and proven construction systems with very specific detailed cost programs. They have to do this to hit price points and be effective. That leaves the homebuyer, who virtually has no choices (other than cosmetic ones) about how the home faces on the site, how it uses the land, uses the water, leaves the foliage, or affects the watershed. Buyers, in fact, have almost no choices in sustainability at all—except to get out their checkbooks and ante up if they want an energy efficient home.

What is so perverse about this is that manufacturers who make sustainable materials cannot get builders to specify these materials. Builders are not aligned to change specifications or adopt new methods, not aligned to reinvent designs, and not aligned to use sustainable materials that may cost more initially. Few homebuyers are going to ask questions about the site work (though this is changing), since they don't understand the costs of doing the site work, nor the differences between standing curb vs. ribbon curb, open flow vs. culvert, bridge types, easement types, entitlements, road segments and crowning hits, and design speed vs. turn radius discussions. Most homebuyers are looking for a home, and when they get to the builder, the only choices they have left are the colors and the cost per square foot of the home, eerily similar to the way they choose their cuts of meat at the supermarket, only on a slightly larger scale.

Until buyers recognize a different product with different results, they will continue to be skeptical of homebuilders that want to charge major upgrade fees for sustainability packages. This is the only hope for truly energy efficient housing to become a mainstream staple—for consumers to arm themselves with information about construction material, and to demand from the building industry a different type of home that has a lower energy footprint than those we have been building for the past fifty years. Homebuyers also need to inquire about construction methods, recycling and reuse of scrap lumber, use of toxic materials, and climate systems. Instead of focusing on solar panels, buyers ought to be asking about Home Energy Rating System (HERS), energy footprints, and advanced framing.

Builders around the United States have heard this call, and seen the results of survey after survey of the home-buying public requesting energy efficient homes. Some of them are responding, some resisting, and others have just changed their marketing.

Everything from the road section widths, the way homes load, whether the garages are the dominant or secondary features, to how power lines and transformers are treated— everything affects how a neighborhood or a larger community is viewed. All of these design elements have financial ramifications, but since no one wants to live in a blighted neighborhood, the responsibility for preventing this rests on the American public to start making better choices, and requiring the industries (where we spend massive amounts of capital) to listen to what we want.

All of these benefits start with a focus on people first instead of dollars. Ironically, the only real profitable communities are those that are started this way, because they are the only ones possessing the intrinsic value to drive their own pricing independent of other markets. Getting the design right means scaling architecture in such a way that people enjoy it, want to look at it, interact with it, and appreciate it. Getting the plan right means pedestrians have ways to get places without having to share space with cars, where sites don't have to be clearcut or mass graded in order to create home sites. Making the right choices means getting developers, builders, and buyers on the same page regarding the minimal requirements for sustainable designs in the community, and negotiating volume pricing with manufacturers, who then have the incentive to retool production facilities to build more sustainable products. When economics and values are aligned between developers, builders, manufacturers, and homebuyers, then we will have truly sustainable communities.

Fixing City Hall

There is another disturbing trend in American culture today. What we have come to refer to as "economic development," in many cases, is neither economic nor does it help develop the city. When small towns induce large box retailers to come into their city, they not only drive out small business owners, they send profits and asset values to a corporate office in another city. When the retailer decides sales are not adequate, the city's investment makes it easier for them to shutter their store—having less initial investment in it- leaving vacant storefronts, box stores, retail pads, and all kinds of related problems all over the United States.

While there is nothing inherently wrong with big box retail stores, retail sales tax will not help small towns ride out a recession. Because 90% of all new jobs will come from business already in the community, cities who fail to practice responsible business retention and expansion methods, and instead, use economic development funds to induce outside parties to compete with local investors, are leaving a legacy of devastation for future generations to clean up. It makes no sense to replace business owners and entrepreneurs with low-paying retail jobs, many of which require the employees to use public assistance. No wonder our Main Streets in "Small Town America" are empty. Maybe we should have spent the $5 million fixing the water, sewer and sidewalk in front of the general store, or building a parking garage that could generate income to cure the parking problem on Main Street, instead of selling the future of our towns in exchange for seeing our pictures in the paper.

Whether or not these activities are politically motivated, this practice is neither socially nor financially sustainable, and wrecks small town economies for decades. None of us wants to see our tax dollars doing this, and this cannot be our standard for economic development. Surely we are smarter than that.

Thriving economic communities, on the other hand, are places where private capital networks want to locate, since local leaders have already created capital-friendly environments. Government leaders have streamlined permitting processes, opened their doors to transparent governance practices, and economic development professionals have a targeted yet diverse strategy for creating links in the economic chain of their communities. New businesses have incubation areas, thriving creative talent pools, an educated workforce, and access to capital. None of this happens if communities are not ready to make critical long-term choices focused on the well being of the people that live there.

Broken Windows

A question often arises when discussing communities that are desperately broken. Vacant lots, high crime rates, hostile business environments, vagrancy, vandalism, and dilapidated and blighted structures make significant statements about the communities that tolerate them. Whether or not a community has the foresight to see these things coming is one issue—whether the community has the leadership or courage to address them when it happens is another matter entirely. What is to be done?

Yet the timing, extent of degradation, lack of resources, or overall psychology of a Place has more to do with the causes than the solutions. You can pour billions of tax dollars into certain areas, and they will never be fixed because of the human behavior that brought the conditions about in the first place. The chaos, property loss, and indignity inflicted on citizens in forcing them to endure such conditions is offensive—yet this happens in every urban area and in many rural areas.

Personal choices have less to do with economic status, and more to do with personal pride. When communities lack pride, they lack the basic will power to change their situation and to make better choices. Residents adopt the attitude of "What's the Use?" - versus having a dream to improve things by working together. This is not a warm and fuzzy conversation where people decide to work together—it takes city and community leaders opening an arsenal of weapons in a focused burst on the problems at hand. Policing, condemnation of dilapidated buildings, public private partnerships with developers to oversee improvements and manage infrastructure, and use of economic development funds to reinvent areas.

None of this happens without effective leadership and governance. None of this happens until someone decides they won't take it anymore. Eventually, these areas turn into boiling points of civil strife, and people begin acting out. Some take to the streets, some organize protests, some set fires, loot, and destroy homes and businesses. This is not honorable behavior—but it is the result of a society without respect.

Whether it involves a home owners association, city council, or utility board, leaders who fail to lead cause pain and suffering for everyone within their influence. You can replace broken windows all day, but as long as no one cares about the message sent when people keep breaking the windows, you will never actually address the problem.

What is required is a new generation of *community leaders*, agents of change that understand the financial aspects of redevelopment and who can encourage and support investment in specific, targeted activities. This conversation only happens when citizens realize they have choices.

When someone catches a glimpse of a different future—not a future that could be, but a future that MUST be, and personalizes that calling by activating others to follow, real change becomes possible.

Sometimes the only thing that needs to happen to affect change is to pass the microphone to someone who actually has something to say.

What Works

After presenting these ideas, people often approach me and ask, "What would you recommend we do to start?" Over the years, I have seen some really good, brilliantly simple ideas. Most of them are not mine.

- As you're out mowing your lawn this weekend, edge, trim and mow your neighbor's yard. 80% of the work is getting out the mower and cleaning up, so how much more work would it be? Naïve? Perhaps, but I lived in a community where the neighbors on both sides of me reveled in "beating" the other guy, and whoever got started did all three smaller yards before the others got home. I have never enjoyed my time in a home more—the lawn was a symbol of the investment we made in each other.

- Adopt a weekend a month where, instead of spending the day mowing and watering, hire the neighborhood kid that does lawns to do the work, and show him how you need it done. Then take the time and do a Habitat for Humanity project instead.

- During the next city council meeting, conspire to bring a large group of people to the meeting for no reason other than to say thank you to your public servants for their gift of time and energy, and if you feel appropriate, offer some citation from a local volunteer organization.

- Coordinate with the local Boy Scout troop to do a pancake breakfast or pasta dinner at the local firehouse. This used to be a staple in one of my former neighborhoods—a massive neighborhood outpouring, and I have never seen grown men get so "teared up" as when young boys presented them plaques honoring their service and sacrifice, and stating they were watching them as role models.

- Take an elderly person to the park, get to know them, and walk their dog.

- Sponsor a blood drive for the local hospital.

- Adopt a military unit fighting overseas, and pour out a dose of home for them by shipping food, handmade notes of appreciation from kids, especially if a spouse or child is left at home. If there is a family with a member deployed overseas, look after the family, help them out, and adopt them as an outreach project.

- Thank our sailors, Marines, airmen, and soldiers when you see them at the airport. Buy some prepaid phone cards and hand them out when you see them.

- Leave a neighbor a batch of muffins—just because you made a batch for your own kids.

- Organize a community garage sale/food drive/fund raiser for a local charity.

- Organize an Adopt-A-Teacher program with the local PTA. Tell teachers and parents that you do care, you do notice, and it does matter what they do.

Conclusion

Real change in our culture will require more than blogging, hand-wringing, or tweeting. In point of fact, while we have seen revolutions started in Middle Eastern countries using social networking during the past year, it is absurd to think that technology is our answer—we already have the best technology.

Politics isn't the answer—we already have politics with no clear answers emerging.

As Americans, we have the luxury of turning our heads while our culture loses the ability to grow things, build things, and repair things. We can tell our kids they should all work in offices. We can eat whatever food we want, be as large as we want, drive whatever cars we want. We can pretend we don't hear about school shootings, homicides every night, and witness the ongoing erosion of civil liberties on virtually every level of our society. We can pretend it doesn't affect us to never speak to our neighbors, to build $30,000 home media rooms so we don't have to interact with others at the local cinema, and to tune only to cable news and talk shows that cater to our particular ideology. We can pretend that the increasing shrillness of debate from our elected officials is not an indicator of the overall lack of respect our culture shows for people. We can do this.

We have those rights, for a while. Unlike teeth, however, problems do not simply go away when we ignore them. In a culture where people are afraid to confront others and to have awkward, challenging conversations, there is little hope. This is not what made our country great, and it certainly is not what men and women have been fighting and dying for these past two centuries. We owe more to our children and grandchildren, and until we get it through our heads that it's not about my way, or your way, or my candidate vs. your candidate, we can never share a common future.

What we are seeing today is the radical subversion of a free society, a system in which citizens abdicate their responsibility to protect the interests of future generations, and engage in reckless, destructive, and permanent structural damage. This type of negligence would get us all sued if we behaved this way at work, but it is killing American society as surely as any outside threat could ever do. If we plan on bringing it back, we had best start making some different choices in an economy that values people, and not just stuff.

In a world that revolves around people, choices are made based on scale, experience, interaction, touch, and personal value, not on cost. Cost is a concept that takes into account the human spirit, experience, and personal values. How much does it cost to disrespect someone down the street by throwing trash in their yard? It's free, isn't it? Multiply that by 300 million decisions to do that just once a day, then twice, and then throw trash on the road. This visual starts to illustrate the breakdown of society, a culture where people don't observe red lights, lanes, stop signs, school crossings, or personal property rights. A culture that fails to focus on people is doomed to fail, because it will consume itself to death. That is not an America where I want to live. Throwing trash in someone's yard is not free simply because it didn't cost me anything. It costs me everything.

Real communities are tangibly different from those that never made this turn. When a community is broken, you don't have to go through a complex analysis to sort out whether it's functional or not—just ask the guy working the counter at the gas station on the outskirts of town, or the waitress at a local restaurant, or a clerk at the grocery store. Everyone that lives in a broken town knows it's broken—someone will come along and fix it, right?

Sustainable communities are places where people feel unique value; they have critical social networks where others want to invest in them and in their lives; they have economic viability due to jobs and employment opportunities and housing that meets their financial needs; and they can contribute to the wellbeing of future generations by engaging in smart decisions about use of land, transportation, carbon emissions, energy consumption, reuse of building materials, and respect for natural resources.

Sustainable communities are places where people have structures to debate controversial topics respectfully, to support local business owners and entrepreneurs, to have visibility into their local government, and to exert leadership over critical parts of their lives. This is not a naïve or nostalgic notion—such communities exist all around our country in various forms. What is so remarkable is that every community could look like this, if we made the correct choices.

Communities that possess this triple bottom line of social, environmental, and economic sustainability have organic value— they have the ability to perpetuate, renovate, and reinvent themselves because they have engaged people groups to invest together in a place, not in things.

These "places for people" exist everywhere, and are waiting for someone to come along and pick up the microphone.

CHAPTER V

Conclusion

Toward A Livable Community

Brian Murphy, Jerry Williams, Tom Mote, Eric Davis,
William Forbes

The previous essays have, in one way or another, all wrestled with the social dimensions of sustainability suggesting that a sustainable future is not possible if solutions are limited to the domain of science and engineering. It is true that new technologies will be necessary, and that better use of energy and natural resources will be a large part of a sustainable future. However, sustainability requires quite dramatic social change. As we have seen, social change is never easy, and generally requires consideration of scientifically less tangible factors, examples of which are a sense of place and history, faith, economics, and a reconsideration of the ethics of moderation. To date, these human factors have not been squarely addressed in the sustainability debate and therefore often stand in the way of change. The task ahead will require that we find a way to incorporate the human dimension into plans for a sustainable future.

In this concluding chapter, we offer a model of sustainable community development that includes concern for the often neglected human dimension. Specifically, we attempt to show how we get from *here* (the state of communities today) to *there* (a sustainable world). It is important to note that we do not propose national or global solutions. Certainly, there is a role for national and global attention to these matters, but our focus will be at the level of the local community. We contend that human beings live, raise families, and make decisions about the future using their immediate circumstances as the test for truth. As a result, a sustainable future will be found primarily through the transformation of local communities. This transformation, as we will now see, is all the more important given the current state of local communities in the United States.

The Current Situation

Major cities in the United States are already taking steps to address the demands being imposed by sustainable development. Governmental offices charged with sustainability are proliferating quickly in metropolitan areas. Small and rural towns, however, lack the planning capability and resources to conduct such complex analysis on their own. It is for this reason that attention will focus upon these communities in an effort to translate the principles discussed throughout the book into real-life.

According to the federal government, 17 percent of the nation's population and almost 80 percent of its land are classified as non-metropolitan (United States Department of Agriculture, September 30, 2009). Significantly, the people who reside outside urban areas differ from the nation at-large in several important ways, including the following:

- **Age**—an older population due to the migration of young adults coupled with an influx of those over age 50, culminating in a median age that is four years older than in metro areas (Kirschner, Berry and Glasgow, 2009);
- **Income**—a lower income, with median household income only 78.7 percent of metro areas (United States Department of Agriculture, September 8, 2010);
- **Employment**—higher unemployment, with rural unemployment in 2009 at 9.8 percent compared to 8.7 percent in urban areas (McBride and Kemper, 2009);
- **Poverty**—higher poverty rate, with the non-metro rate exceeding "the metro rate every year since poverty was first officially measured in the 1960s" (United States Department of Agriculture, July 2004:1).

This demographic nightmare has produced a decades long

hemorrhaging of people with skills and education. A recent study confirms that the exodus of the young from rural regions is continuing and even accelerating (United States Department of Agriculture, September 2010). The result is that the nation is segregating by education, with 29.9 percent of urban adults holding a B.A degree compared to only 16.8 percent in rural areas (Gallardo and Bishop, October 18, 2010). Put simply, non-metropolitan America is stuck in a demographic pattern that is leading to further and deeper decline because there is little social capital available to reverse the negative trends.

Rural occupations, once dominated by farming and mining, are shifting to low wage manufacturing to compensate. Yet this avenue of job creation is proving unsuccessful in an era of globalization where U.S. salaries cannot compete against the wages paid in places like China and India. Rural America is losing in its ability to deliver a livable income. While low skill manufacturing is largely a dead end for stimulating economic revival, most rural regions have little alternative except to continue promoting cheap labor as a way to lure investment into their communities.

As communities become poorer, land in rural areas has dropped in value causing an erosion of property taxes as the primary source of local government revenue. Quality of life, in turn, suffers as schools, hospitals, and other public services become more difficult to finance at meaningful levels. The solution adopted almost uniformly across the nation is switching to sales taxes to fill the fiscal vacuum. Consider the case of rural Arkansas. "In 2007 property tax revenue accounted for approximately 27 percent of local revenue generated by county governments, declining from 31 percent in 1999. In contrast the sales tax generated approximately 26 percent of local county government revenue in 1999 and increased to 29 percent by 2007" (Farmer and Miller, 2011: 40).

With property tax rates declining, economic developers were often forced by city councils to change their focus from attracting primary employers--those companies producing or providing a product to state and national markets—to a focus on attracting retailers and their accompanying sales taxes. While this strategy is myopic, it became the "new game" in economic development for many cities and counties. The goal was to attract as many big box retail outlets that a city could encourage developers to build. In a booming market, economic developers could take credit for the new stores and restaurants as well as the retail sales tax they generated. Citizens were more excited about a new retailer or restaurant than about a new industry hidden in an office or industrial area of town. But the downturn in the economy quickly showed the fallacy of the retail-focused strategy. Big boxes follow two things, income and rooftops. Retailers do not come and sales taxes do not flow without the quality of life and the jobs that attract people to fill the houses and spend their discretionary income.

Dependence on retail has led to a worsening of the quality of life rather than to its improvement. One study discovered that counties with Wal-Mart stores experienced greater increases in family poverty rates. The authors speculate a likely explanation is that "Wal-Mart stores destroy civic capacity in the communities in which they locate by driving out local entrepreneurs and community leaders (Goetz and Swaminathan, 2004:2)." Store owners who once had a middle-class existence cannot compete and they end up selling their businesses and finding jobs that pay subsistence wages.

Another consequence of "big box" retail is that these stores require large square footage to accommodate their extensive inventories. This need for space compels the stores to be situated at the periphery of the community rather than in downtown locations. Town centers, as a result, are suffering from deterioration and outright collapse. The soul of the community, its uniqueness, soon vanishes because a built environment is essential to identity (Low, 2000). Too often, high school sports remain as the sole unifying ingredient since there is no other civic life in which to become engaged.

In much of rural America, the sad conclusion is that livable communities have largely ceased to function. It is our contention that they can rebound by improving quality of life through sustainable development.

The New Economics of Sustainable Development

For many people, small town America evokes the image of Mayberry, R.F.D.—a place where people want to live. Mayberry epitomizes a community with a sense of place and comfortable quality of life. In practical terms, the community itself is the attraction. The same principle applies in striving to bring about a regional turnaround: economic development must follow community development. After all, private capital is lured by social capital and social capital is lured by quality of life. This circle is a continuing loop. Yet no cookie-cutter model exists since each community has its own distinct cultural values and heritage. These differences must be respected in any planning process for the outcome to have legitimacy.

In the continuing circle of private capital following social capital following quality of life, cities have different ideas on where to start in the circle. Some direct their efforts to quality of life, which typically translates into parks and schools. Other communities put all their eggs in the basket of attracting new primary employers in the hope that, by exporting product out, quality of life will follow as the money from job creation enters the region. Finally, some communities target their efforts on developing a trained and educated workforce as a means of attracting new industry that will, in turn, provide the tax base for better parks and schools. As experience has demonstrated, none of these three strategies is successful independently. The answer to a sustainable community is that all three pieces—quality of life, economic incentives, and social development—must be pursued equally and at the same time.

Successful and sustainable communities have leaders that understand that there are no quick fixes. Economic development must be a long-term, consistent effort requiring a far-reaching vision and patient implementation of a plan. Changing the quality of life in a community means changing its culture and that takes time.

For small communities, stopping the hemorrhaging of young people leaving town means that new, decent paying jobs are available. But recruitment of new industry is an expensive and competitive game that is beyond the reach of most rural communities. Entrepreneurship is the key to success because it grows new jobs at home. This approach involves a concerted effort to teach, encourage, and assist local citizens in starting new companies. It looks for new technology niches and technology transfer. Nothing can happen, however, without leadership in the community. Economic development follows community development.

Today, the term "quality of life" is becoming synonymous with sustainable development because both are based on keeping three goals in balance:

- Economic prosperity
- Social well-being
- Environmental stewardship

This so-called triple bottom-line, where each goal is in harmony with the other two, defines what constitutes a sustainable community as well as a superior quality of life at the same time. Put another way, sustainability benefits people, planet, and profit (Savitz and Weber, 2006). It makes a community a livable place.

The Planning Process

In this section we propose concrete steps toward a sustainable/livable community. In addition to less tangible human concerns, this plan is based upon two economic principles. First, livable communities attract long-term, stable economic growth and are less impacted by national economic downturns. Second, a livable community maximizes economic multiplier effects because money entering the community tends to be exchanged before exiting. As a result, continued economic growth and an improved quality of life are possible. Based upon these principles, our plan has two phases: a community resource inventory and a community engagement plan about how to make use of results from the community inventory by engaging community members and leaders in a public dialogue.

Community Resource Inventory

The community resource inventory is designed to engage communities in a dialogue designed to determine current community assets and to identify the direction the public wants to move. Ideally, the community resource inventory should include the following activities:

- An analysis of social indicators (e.g., demographic data);

- Examination of the community's social infrastructure (e.g., the level and types of civic engagement);

- Through the use of surveys a determination of the community's identity, priorities and its attitudes about quality of life

- The implementation of focus group discussions with opinion leaders

- The evaluation of natural amenities to determine their contribution to civic life;

- A review of the status, levels, and condition of public services (e.g., housing, health care, education).

Community Engagement

The second step of the project will be to develop a plan about how communities can improve their livability and overall quality of life. As pointed out earlier by Belanger, community engagement is a means to take advantage of and build social capital in a community. Along these lines, it is necessary to present the results of the community resource inventory to the community and its leaders seeking community input and therefore vesting. Public meetings, websites, media campaigns, and other means should be utilized. To the extent possible, results should be presented visually with maps, drawing, tables, etc. Comparative data should also be made available. That is, detailed information about comparable communities that have taken steps toward sustainability. Doing so can help to demonstrate the feasibility of the plan.

The Final Plan

Once data from the community resource inventory and the community engagement phases have been collected, the next step is to articulate the final plan. A successful plan will combine the data and feedback from the community with economic considerations and insights from the human dimensions which have been the subject of the present book. These insights include:

1) Economic development always follows human development. For this reason, particular attention should be paid to aspects of community life that are often not considered in economic development plans, features such as natural amenities, social activities, community life, and access to recreational opportunities.

2) Sustainable development must not only consider the immediate economic benefits of a development plan (attracting a new industry, etc.) but also the impact such decisions have upon livability. Economic development that sacrifices livability for immediate economic gain runs the risk of "winning the battle and losing the war."

3) As pointed out earlier by Frye and Williams and Williams, attention to education must be part of a plan for sustainability. This is true in respect to educating the community about

sustainability, but also in terms of reorienting local schools to provide a focus upon the needs of the community not in simply producing "college bound" students for jobs outside the community. Curricula that find room for the study of entrepreneurship, technical training, education in the trades, and for career training in local niche industries are examples of ways in which local schools can be reframed for the benefit of sustainable community development.

4) The economic calculus of a community should be broadened to include noneconomic variables. For example, as suggested by Harjula, the final development plan should include an earnest consideration of human happiness and wellbeing. Similarly, Garvin argues that we should "expand our conception of sustainability."

5) A sustainable community development plan must pay particular attention to the specificities of each community. These specificities include the uniqueness of place (Forbes), History (Barringer) and religious belief (Williams and Lemon).

6) A sustainability plan must also include a clear conception of how the community sees itself. In other words, what is the identity or life of the community? A plan inconsistent with this vision is doomed from the start. Ethical considerations are naturally part of this identity. As Dixon suggests, this identity should consider "sustainability's golden rule." To do so increases the possibility that community identity will at least consider moderation as an ethical principle (Salsberry). While an uncommon sentiment in modern societies such as our own, moderation does indeed have a place in any plan about sustainable development.

7) Similar to a consideration of happiness, the essay by Lauter argues that a sustainability plan should not discount aesthetics. While scientific and economic variables are

crucially important, a plan must appeal to human aesthetic sensibilities. Only a cynical understanding of human existence relies solely upon an "engineering perspective." As Christopher Marlowe so famously implies, it was Helen's beauty that launched a thousand ships not the plans of kings, or politicians, or even engineers.

A Few Concluding Thoughts

We should pause for a moment to consider that, in contrast to the major thesis of this book (that a sustainable future requires consideration of the human dimension), it may indeed be the case that humanness itself interferes with progress toward a sustainable future. In the introductory chapter and in the chapters devoted to cultural change, we considered that culture is quite conservative and, as such, is resistant to change. Even in the face of evidence that our current way of life is unsustainable, we mostly continue about our daily life in an unexceptional fashion. In Albert Camus' novel *The Plague*, a community faced with a pestilence (the plague) went about life as usual in much the same face we confront the sustainability problem today. Camus writes

> In this respect our townsfolk were like everybody else, wrapped up in themselves; in other words they were humanists: they disbelieved in pestilences.

> A pestilence isn't a thing made to man's measure; therefore we tell ourselves that pestilence is a mere bogy of the mind, a bad dream that will pass away. But it doesn't pass away and, from one bad dream to another, it is men who pass away, and the humanists first of all, because they haven't taken their precautions.

> Our townsfolk were not more to blame than others; they forgot to be modest, that was all, and thought that everything was still possible for them; which presupposed that pestilences were impossible. They went on doing business, arranged for journeys, and formed views. How should they have given thought to anything like plague, which rules out any future, cancels journeys, silences the exchange of views. They fancied themselves free, and no one will ever be free so long as there were pestilences.

By arguing for the importance of the human dimension, we should not lose sight that sustainability is not "made to man's measure." While humans may be the only creature on the planet to worry about sustainability, the cold truth is that nature has limits, limits by which humans, their societies, cares, and concerns are most certainly constrained.

References

Farmer, F. and Miller, W. (2011) *Rural Profile of Arkansas 2011*, University of Arkansas Cooperative Extension Service Printing Services.

Gallardo, R. and Bishop, B (October 18, 2010) "The B.A. Divide," *Daily Yonder: Keep It Rural*, http://www.dailyyonder.com/ba-divide/2010/10/17/2995.

Goetz, S. and Swaminathan, H. (2004), "Wal-mart and County-wide Poverty," http://cecd.aers.psu.edu/pubs/povertyresearchwm.pdf

Kirschner, A., Berry, H. and Glasgow, N. (January 2009), "The Changing Demographic Profile of Rural Areas," *Rural New York Minute*, Community and Rural Development Institute, Issue Number 25.

Low, S. (2000) *On the Plaza: The Politics of Public Space and Culture*, Austin: University of Texas Press.

McBride, T. and Kemper, L. (June 2009) "Impact of the Recession on Rural America: Rising Unemployment Leading to More Uninsured in 2009,"*Rural Policy Brief*, RUPI Center for Rural Health Policy Analysis, University of Michigan, Brief No. 2009-6.

Savitz, A.W. and Weber, K. (2006) *The Triple Bottom Line: How Today's Best-Run Companies Are Achieving Economic, Social and Environmental Success—and How You Can Too*, San Francisco: Jossey-Bass.

United States Department of Agriculture (September 2010) *Rural America at a Glance: 2010 Edition*, Economic Research Service, Economic Information Bulletin Number 68.

United States Department of Agriculture (September 8, 2010) "Rural Income, Poverty, and Welfare: Income and Nonfarm Earnings," Economic Research Service, http://www.ers.usda.gov/Briefing/IncomePovertyWelfare/RuralIncome.htm.

United States Department of Agriculture (September 30, 2009) "Rural Population and Migration," Economic Research Service, http://www.ers.usda.gov/Briefing/Population/.

United States Department of Agriculture (July 2004) "Rural Poverty at a Glance," Economic Research Service, Rural Development Research Report Number 100.

Appendix A
Policy Recommendations for a Sustainable Future
Stephen F. Austin State University
Center for a Livable World Workshop
Austin, Texas
June 1-3, 2010

Overview

While the topic of sustainability has captured headlines on a global basis, little progress is being made to address the situation because ideology has overtaken reasoned discussion. Positions are now staked at the polar extremes, locked in the circular debate whether environmental disaster can be averted without sacrificing economic growth. The result is that movement has become stalled in achieving a consensus direction on how to proceed.

A workshop conducted in the state capitol building of Texas sought to break through the ideological impasse by bringing all interests to the table. Sponsored by the Center for a Livable World at Stephen F. Austin State University, representatives from corporations, non-governmental organizations, public policy agencies, and academia met in closed door sessions for 1 ½ days to develop a set of recommendations to which all participants could subscribe. It is now clear a roadmap does exist that can drive the discussion of sustainability in a direction that bridges differences.

Sustainability is difficult to talk about, in part, due to the absence of a standard definition. To provide a common frame of reference, we agreed to adopt a meaning developed at a United Nations conference in which sustainability is understood as the effort to "meet present needs without compromising the ability of future generations to meet their needs." The goal of sustainability, in other words, is to ensure the world remains livable now and forever.

While it is easy to conclude the world should get no worse, what has been lacking is a shared vision on how to produce this outcome. The workshop managed to formulate a wide-ranging set of practical recommendations to guide the effort. The participants, however, want to emphasize two points. First, the workshop was successful despite ideological conflicts because dialogue was kept civil. It is important to recognize that differences do not necessarily impede progress. Second, resource supply and use patterns, especially as they impact population, require a more inclusive social conversation to identify a path that cuts across value divisions. Some policy solutions will demand more time to make headway.

Recommendations

1. The Role of Education

A public commitment to sustainability requires a shift in culture that cannot be accomplished by relying on the government alone. While a change in habits can be imposed by law, sustainability ultimately depends upon the cooperation of almost every individual in adopting new patterns of behavior. Personal responsibility is, at bottom, the key to preserving a livable world and education is the best vehicle to bring about this cultural shift. A public literate about sustainability will be better equipped to make informed decisions and follow through with or without legal threats.

The following recommendations outline the minimal steps that should be taken:

- Integrate concepts related to community well-being, localism, sustainability, internet use, and civic responsibility into the educational curriculum at all levels;

- Encourage more opportunities for students to obtain practical experience related to sustainability out-side of the classroom (such as service learning, internships, and science fairs);

- Emphasize the importance of vocational/technical education about sustainable occupations as well as the role of sustainability in all occupations;

- Provide continuing education opportunities for adults focusing on sustainability (such as organic gardening, energy efficient home conversion, and transportation alternatives);

- Incorporate licensure or certification on sustainability for professional degree programs (such as MBAs) and through continuing education units;

- Provide consumers with enough information to make informed buying decisions that promote sustainability;

- Require transparency in product labeling and product ingredient information so that consumers can be informed about sustainability metrics, including life cycle, impacts, resource consumption, and intensity (e.g., gallons of water per widget produced, kilowatt-hours consumed per square foot).

2. Consistent Standards

Sustainability is a global concern that cannot be resolved by nations acting in isolation. Resources are not distributed uniformly enough around the globe to tolerate neglect of sustainability as a public policy priority much longer. An international dialogue is necessary to ensure that countries apply compatible regulatory standards where possible. Otherwise, products and services that degrade the environment will always find access to the market-place. The public must be made aware that economic growth and sustainability are not entirely mutually exclusive. These responsibilities belong to all levels of government: national, regional, and local. Any weak link will be exploited to the detriment of all.

The following recommendations outline the minimal steps that should be taken:

- Standardize criteria for sustainably produced consumables from field to table, including carbon intensity for all goods and post-consumer recycled content for all manufactured goods;

- Encourage trade groups and associations to develop standards and measures on sustainability specific to their industry;

- Promote a zero-waste production goal through policy, incentives, and regulation;

- Create international energy efficiency and emissions standards for global transportation systems;

- Recognize and license businesses that promote the social, environmental, and economic well-being of the communities they serve;

- Reform tax codes to include consideration of non-economic sustainability impacts;

- Conduct comprehensive cost-benefit and lifecycle analyses that include non-economic sustainability factors in contracts, projects, programs, and policies;

- Reformulate measures of economic output to include

social well-being, environmental degradation, and resource scarcity.

3. Community Planning

Sustainability is about quality of life. Since communities are the places where daily life is experienced, the development of sustainable practices must begin here. Communities must be brought into engagement to agree upon measures that have widespread support. Sustainability is more likely to succeed if people have a personal investment in the policies that shape their lives. Engagement is especially important because communities differ in terms of values, needs, resources, and economic diversity. No template exists; each community must define its own formula on how to achieve a livable existence.

The following recommendations outline the minimal steps that should be taken:

- Identify and eliminate economic disincentives to sustainability that apply equally to the government and the private sector;

- Increase the use of renewable resources and the recovery of precious materials while discouraging non-compostable/non-recyclable waste;

- Complete an updatable and accurate inventory of environmental services provided by common natural features (e.g., trees, soils, wetlands) to document their social, environmental, and economic benefits;

- Implement uniform building codes consistent with responsible consumption and sustainability;

- Engage community stakeholders in identifying and addressing local issues related to well-being and sustainability as part of the master-planning process;

- Provide access to technical assistance to develop, implement, monitor, and evaluate sustainability initiatives;

- Facilitate local sustainable projects such as: development of green infrastructure/subdivisions, community gardens/farmers' markets, and the use of resources and land in multi-objective ways;

- Use sustainable development as an explicit economic development tool;

- Design and conduct energy efficiency retrofit programs for low-income households.

Conclusion

Movement toward sustainable public policies should not be further delayed by political infighting. We have demonstrated that consensus can be accomplished through reasoned discussion. We strongly urge policymakers to reflect upon the proposed recommendations. They will not solve all problems but they constitute a social strategy that has no ideological bias. The excuse for inaction has been removed.

Workshop Participants

John Blount, Director, Architecture & Engineering Division, Harris County

Libby Cheney, Head of Safety, Environment & Sustainable Development,
     Shell Oil

Jennifer Clymer, Environmental Program Coordinator, Austin Climate Protection
     Plan

Caleb Crow, President, Little Foot Consulting

Alex Garvin, President and CEO, AGA Public Realm Strategists

Gary Hampton, Dean of Applied Technology, Austin Community College

Henrik Harjula, Principal Administrator, Environment, Health and Safety Division
     (OECD)

Lauren Heine, Science Director and Partner, Clean Production Action

Marilyn Johnson, Director, Environmental Initiatives & Sustainability, IHS

Jill Jordan, Assistant City Manager, City of Dallas

Jonathan Kleinman, Program Director, CLEAResult Consulting

Richard MacLean, Executive Director, The Center for Environmental Innovation

Tim Mohin, Director, Corporate Responsibility, Advanced Micro Devices

Thomas Mote, Senior Project Manager, Hines Interests

Ed Quevedo, Senior Counsel, Paladin Law Group ® LLP

Robin Schneider, Executive Director, Texas Campaign for the Environment

Russel Smith, Executive Director, Texas Renewable Energy Industries Association

Laura Spanjian, Sustainability Director, City of Houston

Mark Vickery, Executive Director, Texas Commission on Environmental Quality

Mark Wysong, Vice President of Environment, IHS

CONTRIBUTORS

OUTSIDE CONTRIBUTORS

Eric Davis is Director of Real Estate & Economic Development Consulting Services at Adams Engineering, based in Dallas and Tyler, Texas.

R. Scott Frey is Professor of Sociology and Co-Director of the Center for the Study of Social Justice at the University of Tennessee.

Alex Garvin is President and CEO of AGA Public Realm Strategists, Inc., a planning and design firm in New York City.

Henrik Harjula is former Principal Administrator for the Environment, Health, and Safety Division, Environment Directorate, Organization for Economic Cooperation and Development (OECD), based in Paris, France.

Ken Lauter is an award winning poet. He has also worked as a mayor's aid in St. Louis, Missouri and as an environmental activist.

Maya Lemon is a sociology student at Hendrix College in Conway, Arkansas.

Tom Mote is Vice President of Operations for the Hines Corporation.

Dan Shilling is a humanities and sustainability researcher at Arizona State University and former Executive Director of the Arizona Humanities Council.

Herman Wright is Executive Director of the Long Black Line Organization, focusing on the history, preservation, and restoration of African-American Rosenwald schools and associated buildings.

CONTRIBUTORS FROM STEPHEN F. AUSTIN STATE UNIVERSITY

Kathleen Belanger is Associate Professor of Social Work. Her research emphasis includes rural sustainable community development and faith and sustainability.

Wilma Cordova is Assistant Professor of Social Work with an emphasis in Hispanic communities.

Ray Darville is Professor of Sociology with an emphasis in human dimensions of natural resources.

Ben Dixon is Assistant Professor of Philosophy. His emphasis area is environmental philosophy.

William Forbes is Associate Professor of Geography and Director of the Center for a Livable World.

Jerry Frye is Professor of Communication Studies. His interest is in persuasion and cultural variables involving sustainability.

Brian Murphy is Dean of the College of Liberal and Applied Arts. His academic background is in political science, European studies, and transatlantic policy on sustainability.

Lee Payne is Assistant Professor of Political Science. His research emphasis includes American Politics.

Cindy Pressley is Assistant Professor of Public Administration. Her research emphasis includes environmental law and environmental policy.

Jeffery Roth is Assistant Professor of Geography. He specializes in environmental and historical geography.

Kelly Salsbery is Assistant Professor of Philosophy. His research emphasis includes applied ethics.

Jerry Williams is Chair of the Department of Social and Cultural Analysis. His academic emphasis area is environmental sociology.

Michelle Williams, Ed.D, is Assistant Professor and Director of the Middle Level Grades (4-8) Online Completer Program in the Department of Elementary Education.

CPSIA information can be obtained at www.ICGtesting.com
Printed in the USA
LVOW072138120712

289847LV00002B/4/P